Editor
Rachelle L. Levitt

CITIES REBORN

 **the Urban Land Institute**

ABOUT ULI

ULI–the Urban Land Institute is an independent, nonprofit research and educational organization incorporated in 1936 to improve the quality and standards of land use and development.

The Institute is committed to conducting practical research in the various fields of real estate knowledge; identifying and interpreting land use trends in relation to changing economic, social, and civic needs; and disseminating pertinent information leading to the orderly and more efficient use and development of land.

ULI receives its financial support from membership dues, sales of publications, meeting registrations, and contributions for research and panel services.

ULI PROJECT STAFF

J. Thomas Black — Staff Vice President, Research
Frank H. Spink, Jr. — Director of Publications
Rachelle L. Levitt — Director of Education and Project Manager

Nancy H. Stewart — Editor
Cynthia R. Collins — Word Processing
Robert L. Helms — Staff Vice President, Operations
Regina Agricola Grieb — Production Manager
M. Elizabeth Van Buskirk — Art Director
Helene E. Youstra — Artist
Kim Rusch — Artist

Recommended bibliographic listing:

Rachelle L. Levitt, ed., *Cities Reborn*, Washington, D.C.: Urban Land Institute, 1987.

ULI Catalog Number C32
Library of Congress Catalog Number 87-50398
International Standard Book Number 0-87420-667-7

Cover photo for Pittsburgh by Clyde Hare.

AUTHORS

THE PROCESS

Rachelle L. Levitt is director of education at the Urban Land Institute and specializes in various aspects of public/private partnerships.

BOSTON

Jeffrey P. Brown is an economic analyst with the Boston Redevelopment Authority and prior to that was an economic analyst for the Massachusetts Energy Facilities Siting Council. Brown specializes in monitoring employment and business activity in Boston.

LOUISVILLE

George H. Yater was managing editor and is currently a contributing editor of *Louisville* magazine, published monthly by the Louisville Chamber of Commerce. He has also served as director of news services for the Kentucky Department of Public Information.

PITTSBURGH

Bessie C. Economou has a private consulting practice in city planning in Pittsburgh. She was formerly the executive vice president of the National Housing Conference, a national public interest lobbying organization based in Washington, D.C., and prior to that, held positions in the New York State Urban Development Corporation and New York City's Housing and Development Administration.

ST. LOUIS

Richard C. Ward is principal and **Robert M. Lewis** is an associate with Team Four Research, a planning and development consulting firm in St. Louis. **S. Jerome Pratter** is a partner with The Stolar Partnership, a St. Louis law firm.

REVIEW COMMITTEE

Boston—Donald E. Megathlin, Jr., principal, Economic Research Associates, Cambridge, Massachusetts

Louisville—Gordon B. Davidson, partner, Wyatt, Tarrant & Combs, Louisville, Kentucky

Pittsburgh—Joel P. Aaronson, partner, Reed Smith Shaw & McClay, Pittsburgh, Pennsylvania

St. Louis—E. Terrence Jones, professor of political science, University of St. Louis–Missouri, St. Louis, Missouri

CONTENTS

ACKNOWLEDGMENTS

BOSTON

Lois Levit Basilio, an outside research assistant to the Boston Redevelopment Authority, helped to complete the final drafts of the project case studies. In particular, she skillfully researched redevelopment at the Charlestown Navy Yard. The following staff members of the Boston Redevelopment Authority contributed invaluable comments, insights, and data for this report: Ralph Memolo, Pamela Wessling, James English, Paul McCann, Alex Ganz, and Milton Abelson. The word processing of Mary Shelton, Arielle Warren, and Roberta Downey was excellent, and the charts prepared by Greg Perkins and Stephen Kunze added much to the report.

Paul Yelder, Paul Horn, and Jim McParland of the Economic Development Industrial Corporation provided useful comments and facts on Crosstown Industrial Park. Theresa Carten and Paul Davis of Immobiliare New England furnished a wealth of information on the Charlestown Navy Yard projects. Thanks are also due Rachelle Levitt, director of education of the Urban Land Institute, for her review of the manuscript, comments, and editing.

LOUISVILLE

Contributors of data and other information on Louisville include Louisville Central Area, Inc., the Louisville Chamber of Commerce, and individuals associated with the various projects.

Public agencies providing data include city and county finance departments, the Louisville and Jefferson County Office for Economic Development, the Landmarks Commission, the Parking Authority of River City, and the United States Census Bureau.

PITTSBURGH

Paul Brophy, former executive director of the Pittsburgh Urban Redevelopment Authority, recruited the author, Bessie Economou, for this undertaking and gave generously of his time and counsel. Moreover, he extended the invaluable services of Linda Campbell, executive secretary of the Pittsburgh Urban Redevelopment Authority, who efficiently and patiently organized and produced the typed notes/outlines and drafts involved in a project of this scope. Special thanks are due to Dixon R. Brown, administrative assistant to H. J. Heinz II, for making available the office space and facilities in which the work for this project was conducted. Robert B. Pease, executive director of the Allegheny Conference on Community Development, shared both the resources of his office and his more than 33 years of experience in the reshaping of this city—10 years of which were as executive director of the Pittsburgh Urban Redevelopment Authority.

Numerous others from the private and nonprofit sectors and from the Department of City Planning, the Urban Redevelopment Authority, the Pittsburgh Area Transit (PAT), and the office of the mayor enriched this report with their knowledge and experience.

ST. LOUIS

Thanks are due the members of the report's technical advisory committee: Dennis Coleman, community development officer, Mercantile Bank; Barbara Geisman, executive director, St. Louis Community Development Agency; Fred Perabo, director of community affairs, Ralston Purina Company; and John Roach, vice president, Pantheon Corporation.

Appreciation is also due the people who contributed information for this report through written materials and interviews. Special acknowledgment is made of the following sponsoring organizations, which provided funding for the preparation of the report: Ralston Purina Company; Pantheon Corporation; Mark Conner Builder and Developer, Inc.; McClellan, Giinther & Associates; *St. Louis Post-Dispatch*; Downtown St. Louis, Inc.; Mercantile Bank; W.A. Thomas & Associates; Cordage Mill Associates; Lindell Development Corporation; Home Builders Association of Metropolitan St. Louis; and the city of St. Louis.

FOREWORD

Cities Reborn evolved from the notion that the redevelopment stories of the nation's moderate-sized cities had not adequately been told and that many lessons can be learned from their experiences. Four cities, representing successful downtown and inner-city redevelopment experiences, were selected—Boston, Massachusetts; Louisville, Kentucky; Pittsburgh, Pennsylvania; and St. Louis, Missouri. We then went about the task of finding authors to write on each of these cities. Funding for development of the chapters came from each city's business community and/or city government.

The opinions expressed in *Cities Reborn* are those of the authors and therefore reflect whatever backgrounds and viewpoints they brought with them. Nonetheless, each chapter presents a comprehensive and informative examination of the redevelopment process and strategies used by each city.

To offer a balance of viewpoints, we asked a knowledgeable individual from each city to review the chapter on that city and to write a commentary on its future prospects. As no two cities are alike, the redevelopment approach used by these cities cannot necessarily be applied to other cities. But, their experiences provide valuable lessons for cities undergoing redevelopment and offer some solace to those facing the difficulties inherent in the process.

Rachelle L. Levitt
Editor

CITIES
REBORN

THE PROCESS

THE PUBLIC/PRIVATE DEVELOPMENT PROCESS

Fountains near St. Louis Union Station enhance the downtown.

Each decade since the 1940s has seen public policies aimed toward urban revitalization. The 1980s, however, appear to be a watershed decade as city after city turns its attention to rebuilding declining downtowns and inner-residential neighborhoods. In particular, the private sector has increasingly recognized the high-quality development potential of downtown areas, and the public sector has seen the potential for retaining and increasing jobs and the economic base of the city.

By examining the development process and strategy of four cities—Pittsburgh, Pennsylvania; St. Louis, Missouri; Boston, Massachusetts; and Louisville, Kentucky—this book illustrates the turnaround. Each city, faced with severe economic troubles, used the distinctive elements of its community to reverse the decline. Each city found its downtown abandoned, having lost major retail and offices to the suburbs. Inner-residential neighborhoods were in a state of decay, and the central business districts lost their reason for existence. Yet, through the combined efforts of the public and private sectors, these cities are becoming new centers for commerce, tourism, and shopping. Building upon the natural assets of the city and their neighborhoods, they are becoming stable and desirable communities in which to live. The case cities were selected because they are representative of the problems of many older, moderate-sized cities in the United States and have demonstrated successful redevelopment programs, though each has further problems to deal with.

These cities also point up the tension that exists between the downtown and neighborhoods regarding the expenditure of public resources. Although the vitality of a city is linked to the health of its downtown, continual pressure is exerted to attend to the needs of inner-city neighborhoods. Downtowns generate a significant portion of the jobs and taxes for a city and are essential to a city's reputation and social atmosphere. Therefore, revitalization strategies understandably have focused strongly on the downtown. But for revitalization ultimately to succeed, a balance must be reached between development in the downtown and development in the neighborhoods. The St. Louis experience provides a good illustration of this balance.

In each of the four cities, the importance of political support for overall revitalization and for individual projects cannot be overestimated. As described in the following chapters, such political support can well decide the fate of a project—and of the city itself.

The public/private relationships formed within four cities to implement revitalization provide invaluable lessons to those cities and developers embarking on redevelopment projects. Bridging the gap left by dwindling federal funds, local public and private sectors teamed up to invest their own resources in revitalizing their cities. By doing so, each sector benefited.

FOUR CITIES AS PROTOTYPICAL EXAMPLES

The case studies reflect the changing philosophies behind the efforts to rebuild cities. St. Louis illustrates how public programs can be designed to stimulate private investment in a distressed economy. Its residential and commercial buildings had suffered the ravages of classic urban abandonment, but were not destroyed. Thus, there was a sizable inventory of buildings, which resulted in large Community Development Block Grant allotments. St. Louis exhibited the problems endemic to cities that used urban renewal to clear blighted properties without having specific projects tied to the cleared areas, leaving large parcels of land undeveloped for long periods of time. The city's experience also vividly illustrates the tension that exists between the revitalization of neighborhoods and the downtown economy; the city fully recognized that redevelopment must reach the neighborhoods as well as the downtown so that benefits are balanced between the two. The authors of the St. Louis chapter contend that the first step toward successful redevelopment is to encourage individuals and groups with the vision to see the advantages of a revitalized city. It is they who will maintain the momentum and enthusiasm to implement strategies and make them work.

Pittsburgh's experience shows how the business community can marshal its forces to bring about

The city of St. Louis, through indirect involvement, has created a positive business climate that has generated dramatic revitalization in the downtown and older neighborhoods.

Through the concerted efforts of the public and private sectors Pittsburgh has brought new vitality to its downtown and has begun to diversify its economy.

Clyde Hare

development. In this case, the corporate base was key to revitalizing Pittsburgh's downtown. Pittsburgh also provides a dramatic example of the coordinated and mutually reinforcing efforts of the public and private sectors. To its credit, Pittsburgh avoided the problem of wholesale urban renewal clearance that had haunted St. Louis and many other American cities. Its revitalization efforts focused on both the neighborhoods of the city and on the downtown, on good design and amenities to serve the public, on improved transportation facilities, and on aggressive marketing of the city's assets. While carrying out this program, the city successfully transformed its economic base from one that had depended on heavy industrial uses to one that is diversified, with a growing number of uses oriented to high technology. Whether that trend will continue still remains to be seen.

In Louisville, the strengths of the public and private sectors together overcame significant negative market forces, showing once again the importance of such joint efforts. As explained in the Louisville chapter, the effectiveness of that joint public/private effort was made possible by the support and participation of the corporate executives in the city. Because of the city's relatively small size the business community could work together in a tightly knit effort to deal with any problems which, again, because of the city's size, were not overwhelming. Described also are the problems Louisville encountered with the urban renewal phase—and how these problems were overcome. Yet to be solved are long-term disputes between the city and county governments that have caused political and economic problems for Louisville, a situation also experienced by the city of St. Louis.

Boston provides an example of the effective use of federal funds to initiate revitalization. The amount of federal funds expended on urban renewal projects in Boston in the 1960s was enormous. Other federal grants, such as Economic Development Administration grants, were vital to industrial development. Boston's development process has shown that public investment can stimulate substantial private investment for the economic development of the city. The expenditures and the planning efforts of the city of Boston and the commonwealth of Massachusetts were vital to the development of the downtown and neighboring areas.

Revitalization, however, has stopped short of Boston's neighborhoods. Although the city has long recognized the need for substantial investment in the neighborhoods, it lacks the federal funds once available for such projects. It has therefore tried to steer private investment to the neighborhoods and to require private developers to contribute toward public needs and amenities. This effort has culminated in the controversial linkage program established by the city to connect financially new development to low- and moderate-income housing in neighborhoods. Tackling this sensitive area has become paramount to the city's development activity. Under Boston's linkage program, any new commercial or institutional development of more than 100,000 square feet requiring zoning relief is charged an exaction fee of $5 a square foot to provide low-income housing in the neighborhoods and $1 a square foot for job training. Developers in the downtown pay the fee to the Neighborhood Trust in seven equal annual installments; those outside the downtown pay in 12 installments.[1]

THE DEVELOPMENT PROCESS

Most development in the United States has occurred through a conventional development process, by which the public and the private sectors performed independent functions and therefore tend to remain at arm's length. Any mix of function was seen as a conflict of interest on the part of the local government. The public sector was expected to perform a regulatory and broad planning function, while the private developer originated projects based on market information and formulated a specific plan for the project independent of any public involvement. Even during the implementation of the project, the interaction between the developer and the local government was minimal and for fairly routine procedures such as building inspections. Consequently, the public sector did not have to assume any risks or costs that were typically borne by the private sector.[2]

In most cases, a project is still initiated by a private developer and only peripherally does it involve the public sector in the inner workings. Such projects are defined as conventional. Market forces drive

[2] Robert E. Witherspoon, *Codevelopment: City Rebuilding by Business and Government* (Washington, D.C.: ULI–the Urban Land Institute, 1982.), p. 5.

the development and outside market forces are fairly minimal.

Over the last 30 years, however, as illustrated by the four case studies in this book, joint public/private development has become a growing trend, particularly in projects that would otherwise not have occurred. Such intervention in the market has been used successfully to stimulate urban revitalization in downtowns and in inner-city neighborhoods. A number of cities are well known for their codevelopment efforts—Baltimore, Maryland; San Antonio, Texas; Milwaukee, Wisconsin; Philadelphia, Pennsylvania; Indianapolis, Indiana; and others. Each city has developed its own method to harness private investment to stimulate revitalization of that city's economy. The individual characteristics and history of each city determine which methods are most appropriate. Concurrently, various forms of governmental structures were developed to

The city of Boston experienced a surge of development from the 1970s through the 1980s that reshaped its once low-scale skyline.

[1] Douglas R. Porter et al., *Downtown Linkages* (Washington, D.C.: ULI–the Urban Land Institute, 1985.), p. 53.

Don West

handle the public/private development process. As the public sector has become more involved in deal making, concerns have been raised about the objectivity of the public sector in regulating development. Such concerns, however, have not slowed the trend toward codevelopment. Experience has indicated that early joint efforts between the public and private sectors paves the way to conventionally financed projects, stimulating the desired growth in the city.

FEDERAL INTERVENTION

The first federal grant program that endeavored to revitalize the urban areas of the United States was the urban renewal program, adopted as part of the 1949 Housing Act. The experience in Pennsylvania, as described in the chapter on Pittsburgh, as well as the earlier public housing programs, provided the basis of the urban renewal program. The philosophy behind the program depended on slum clearance as a means for commercial and industrial redevelopment. The idea, which seems naive in retrospect, was to revitalize the declining areas of American cities through large-scale land acquisition and clearance. The act specified that local agencies were to assemble, clear, and prepare sites for sale or lease for uses specified in a redevelopment plan. Federal capital grants would pay two-thirds of any losses by local agencies on such projects. The other one-third could be contributed in the form of local "grants-in-aid," that is, land donations, installation of public improvements, and other contributions. The use of the public power of eminent domain was based on the premise that the clearance of a slum averted a crisis.[3]

Under conventional urban renewal, the public sector concentrated on planning and land assembly and the private sector on project-related activities. With hindsight the development industry has learned that land clearance alone does not provide the stimulus for economic development. The relocation of residents was a troublesome byproduct. There are successful examples of urban renewal, such as those described in the Pittsburgh chapter. Nonetheless, experience has shown that many projects were not designed to meet market conditions and other projects were so delayed that market conditions had changed (see the chapter on St. Louis). Although urban renewal resulted in numerous vacant lots throughout the downtowns of America, it taught many lessons that were applied in the years that lay ahead.

As the urban renewal program matured, emphasis was increasingly placed on rehabilitation of structures or very selected clearance of a site, rather than on total clearance. In the 1960s, federal efforts toward urban revitalization took a different tack. Assistance became neighborhood-oriented, which permitted smaller-scale activities. The amount of aid that flowed from the federal to the local level increased. Among the grant-in-aid programs was the model cities program, a demonstration effort designed to illustrate how neighborhoods could be revitalized. The program was to encompass the economic and social problems facing the neighborhoods as well as physical revitalization. It stressed local planning, citizen involvement, and coordination of all federal grant programs.[4] The funds available from the federal government to the demonstration neighborhoods were, however, inadequate to have any major impact on communities and, support for the program waned during the Nixon administration. During this period, such programs as Section 236

of the Housing Act made available substantial funds for low- and moderate-income housing.

In the 1970s a significant move was made toward decentralizing federal categorical grant programs—the major programs being model cities, urban renewal neighborhood development, and housing rehabilitation. The "new federalism" changed the roles of the local and federal governments, instituting the Community Development Block Grant program (CDBG), in which the Housing and Community Development Act of 1974 assembled a variety of programs into one grant (the CDBG) allotted to cities needing it. The cities could then decide how to use the funds locally. The theory underlying the decentralization of federal programs was that a federal official could not effectively design a local program. Although federal guidelines for the use of the funds were established, this dramatic change in public policy provided local governments considerably more latitude in the use of federal funds— for example, in the choice and location of projects and in the organizational arrangements with which to administer the program.[5] Local governments were given the responsibility to develop strategies for the redevelopment of distressed areas, removing some of the "grantsmanship" that had been key to receiving federal funds in the past. The CDBG funds were allocated to cities based on a formula that included such factors as poverty, population, and overcrowding.

The public policy pendulum swung again toward the end of the 1970s when the Carter administration came into power. As described above, under the conventional approach to urban renewal, cities acquired and cleared sites for private redevelopment, without the promise of private investment. Public development agencies often overestimated the potential for private redevelopment. As a result, existing businesses were displaced,

[3] Ashley A. Foard and Hilbert Fefferman, "Federal Urban Renewal Legislation," *Urban Renewal: The Record and the Controversy* (Cambridge, Massachusetts: MIT Press, 1966).

[4] M. Carter McFarland, *Federal Government and Urban Problems* (Boulder, Colorado: Westview Press, 1978), p. 84.

[5] Ibid., p. 71.

neighborhoods and commercial areas disrupted, and scarce public dollars spent without achieving the hoped-for redevelopment. In response to the problems of traditional urban renewal, an approach was designed that, in effect, tied public investment to private investment. The concept of such public/private partnerships became the basis for the Urban Development Action Grant (UDAG) program, initiated in 1976 and administered by the U.S. Department of Housing and Urban Development. Urban Development Action Grants enabled local governments to work closely with the developer to design a project. Cities could use UDAGs to entice developers to invest in areas that they would not otherwise have been disposed toward. Part of an arsenal of tools designed to stimulate economic development, UDAG funds are available to many of the developments in distressed cities of the country.

A number of the projects described in the forthcoming chapters used UDAG funds. Regardless of the outcome of the budget processes at the federal level, the UDAG program has had a profound effect on the way in which the public and private sectors do business. Although not directly attributable to UDAGs, a new environment has been created. New kinds of partnerships have formed among all institutions involved in real estate. It is not uncommon to see universities, corporations, railroads, hospitals, foundations, and others taking an active interest in real estate development. Furthermore, all proceeds from UDAG loans go to the cities, where they become a revolving fund for CDBG-related activities, thus prolonging and extending the use of the funds.

The Urban Development Action Grant program is administered as a competitive categorical grant program. A project is selected on the basis of need, on the number of jobs it will create, on the ratio of UDAG funds to the amount of private sector investment in the project, and on the feasibility of the project. Projects in cities suffering the greatest degree of economic distress are given priority. Developers may use UDAGs for secondary financing; or to finance infrastructure, parking structures, and other elements of a project that could act as the catalyst to make a project feasible.

In 1981, the Economic Recovery Tax Act authorized a 25 percent investment tax credit (ITC) for rehabilitation expenditures on certified historic properties, a 20 percent credit for nonresidential structures at least 40 years old, and a 15 percent credit for nonresidential structures at least 30 years old. (The investment tax credit provision replaced the 1976 Tax Reform Act that allowed a five-year accelerated depreciation and a 10 percent ITC for rehabilitation expenses on industrial/commercial buildings for investment in certified historic properties.) The ITC stimulated a significant amount of successful rehabilitation activity in older cities, as shown by several of the case studies in this book. To be designated a historic structure by the Department of the Interior a building must either be listed in the National Register of Historic Places or be located in a Registered Historic District and certified by the Department of Interior as of historic significance to the district. A Registered Historic District is one listed in the National Register of Historic Places or one designated by a state or local government under a statute certified by the Department of Interior, in which case the Department of Interior must also certify the district.[6]

The Tax Reform Act of 1986 changed the rehabilitation tax credit once again, allowing a 20 percent credit for historic properties and a 10 percent credit for structure built before 1936. With the benefits reduced, the number of buildings eligible for the rehabilitation tax credit was also reduced.

[6] Albert A. Walsh, *Real Estate Investment After the Tax Acts of 1981 and 1982* (Washington, D.C.: ULI–the Urban Land Institute, 1983), p. 13.

LOCAL INTERVENTION

UDAGs are one of several tools that have been developed over the last 10 years to assist the public sector in forming what is commonly known as public/private partnerships or codevelopment. Many of the local actions involved efforts to improve the development environment by providing infrastructure, tax abatements, tax-exempt financing, enterprise zones, second mortgages, equity sharing, land writedowns, and land leases. Such intervention has significantly altered the conventional development process and introduced the public sector as a viable actor in the development process. The key to successful public intervention in the development process lies in the city's ability to capitalize on its resources and use of incentives to make a desirable real estate project feasible for both public and private participants. Some entrepreneurial local governments have—through their own initiative and their willingness to take risks—become joint venture partners with private developers on some projects. The four cities examined provide examples of various techniques that can be used to cast the city in a more entrepreneurial role.

Large-scale urban projects require enormous front-end costs. One developer involved in public/private ventures has established the following questions to use as criteria for determining the preliminary feasibility of such projects.[7]
• Is the proposed site ready for development? Has it been acquired by the city or under the control of the city or its agencies? Is it zoned or otherwise prepared so that it will require only a relatively short permitting process?
• Are the city planners or their agencies sophisticated in their

[7] William F. Caldwell, Caldwell American Investments, Inc., Troy, Michigan, recommended these criteria in a speech delivered at the World Congress on Land Policy, London, England, July 1986.

knowledge of the permitting process? Have they conducted preliminary market and feasibility studies to back up their land use proposal for the site? Is the proposed use compatible with the initial analysis of the market for this project?

- What is the political climate at the city, county, and state levels? Are these governments committed to the redevelopment of their cities? Will this particular site be a pioneering effort or will it enhance other planned development already underway or in place? Is the city realistic about the required infrastructure for the site? What other types of deals has the city made to promote development in its downtown? To make its downtown locations competitive with suburban sites, does the city fully understand the need to bridge the gap left by an economic shortfall?

- Is the business community committed to the redevelopment of its city? Who are the business leaders, and what is their history of participation? Is there an agency or a quasi-public corporation in place to bridge and coordinate the political/business activities? Is it funded? Are the business leaders knowledgeable about the land use industry? Are the city's financial institutions participants in this power structure? Will they invest in their own downtown?

- What is the estimated time it will take to move the proposed project from preliminary feasibility studies to a successful construction start? (A rule of thumb is whether the project can be financed in three years' time or less).

- Does the mayor have courage? The mayor will have to make some hard political and business decisions to initiate and encourage development in his or her downtown.

The cities described in this book have met many of these criteria. Thus, one can understand why their efforts in attracting developers and companies have been successful. The previous track records and the dedication of the public and private sectors were essential to the successful efforts of these cities.

TRENDS

As the commercial revitalization of the American city continues, the challenge will lie in balancing the affluence of the downtowns with the low- and middle-income neighborhoods. In addition, the mix of uses, including in-town residential use, must be maintained. Although market forces may cause a downturn in the trend toward revitalization, and the movement toward city living may slacken (particularly as young urban professional couples have children and move to the suburbs), thoughtful planning for the overall and balanced redevelopment of America's cities will ultimately bring success.

The changes in the structures of real estate transactions are significant and possibly here to stay for a time. An increase in the number of nontraditional development partnerships is likely to continue. Fully documented here are the development experiences of four cities that have taken major steps toward economic recovery and physical revitalization. The story is by no means complete, but much progress has been made.

BOSTON

BOSTON
A COMMENTARY

Greater Boston is one of the most dynamic real estate markets in the country. Despite a shakeout in high-technology industries, other sectors of the region's economic base remain vibrant. Several economic indicators testify to Greater Boston's strength in the real estate market. For example, the overall office area vacancy rate of 13 percent, while increasing, is well below the national average of 18.3 percent. Although overbuilding has occurred in Greater Boston, particularly in the suburbs, absorption is strong at 7.1 million square feet. Clearly, the healthy real estate market of the last seven years has resulted in overbuilding with accompanying problems of inadequate infrastructure and overburdened transportation systems.

Boston has one of the healthiest office markets in the country due to a major expansion and diversification of its economic base, plus a highly controlled development environment. Approximately 1.3 million square feet of office space was absorbed in 1985 and 1.7 million square feet in 1986, and the vacancy rate continues to drop. Lease rates per square foot typically run in the low $30s for existing Class A space and in the high $30s to low $40s for new space. In the next few years, the pace of development will accelerate. Approximately 4 million square feet of office space is scheduled for delivery this year.

Christopher Columbus Park with the Boston skyline in the distance.

Ashwani Vasishth and Shakeel Hossain

The brisk economic growth in Boston has been matched by a growth in population for the first time in 50 years. The city's population stands at approximately 620,000, with a corresponding and sustained growth in employment. Construction activity exceeded $1 billion for the first time. Cultural and entertainment activity—including the performing arts, museums, colleges and universities, and hospitals—represents a strong aspect of the city's economic vitality. Tourism-related development has also increased. More than 4,500 hotel rooms will be added to the hotel stock by the end of the decade, representing almost 40 percent of the total number of hotel rooms in the city.

During the first six months of 1986, office leasing activity in both Boston and the suburbs continued at a vigorous pace. While the overall Boston vacancy rate for offices was 8.2 percent, the downtown vacancy rate, also moving steadily downward, was 5.1 percent, with the suburbs hovering at 20 percent. Downtown and the suburbs both maintained high levels of absorption at 1.4 and 1.2 million square feet respectively.

Construction and development remain healthy, particularly in the Back Bay and the financial district. As an indication of its economic strength, the city, through the Boston Redevelopment Authority (BRA), is presently reviewing 30 projects that would involve major new and rehabilitated space in the city. Some of the more notable projects are the Prudential Center expansion, North Station/Boston Garden, and the Fan Pier project. Major projects under construction include International Place, 75 State Street, Rowes Wharf, 150 Federal Street, New England Life, and Heritage on the Garden.

In addition to the better known areas like Back Bay, the waterfront, and the financial district, peripheral markets like North Station, the leather district, Fort Point Channel, and Charlestown are vibrant and viable markets. Even in these peripheral markets, the office vacancy rate dropped below 13 percent with rents between $18 to $20 a square foot.

Although its real estate market is the envy of many U.S. cities, Boston is not without problems that must be dealt with to maintain a competitive edge. Basically, six issues need to be addressed:

- *The serious shortage of affordable housing and the lack of strong residential neighborhoods to meet growing employment and population trends.* A real need exists for housing (both new and rehabilitated) for low-income families earning under $17,000 and for moderate-income families earning between $17,000 and $28,000. To meet this urgent demand, various new housing initiatives—such as the Housing Opportunities Partnership—that are available through the state government or the Massachusetts Housing Finance Agency should be used more frequently.

- *The fact that no housing has yet been built in connection with the city's linkage program, which has set aside $25 million for housing and related programs.* Several legal hurdles must be overcome to implement the linkage-enabling legislation.
- *Unemployment in certain groups.* Although Boston enjoys a low unemployment rate overall, certain segments of the population— teenagers, for example—have relatively high unemployment rates. It is important to stress job training and to relate academic training to the job skills needed in the 1980s. In 1985, Boston had the lowest unemployment rate (3.2 percent) of the 33 largest metropolitan areas.
- *Homelessness.* Boston is estimated to have 5,000 homeless persons. Although the plight of the homeless is not unique to this city, the unfortunate fact is that not everyone has benefited from the city's economic vitality.

Festivities in Boston Harbor on Harborpark Day.

Don West

Performances are popular events at Faneuil Hall.

- *Boston's stringent and demanding regulatory environment.* The recent Interim Planning Overlay District Report (IPOD) places new and strict height limitations on development along the waterfront and in downtown, While the concept of the IPOD may be laudable, few districts have been designated for new development. In fact, only 3 percent of the downtown area is designated for growth. These new zoning regulations will limit the height of new buildings to 300 feet for at least the next two years until the final zoning rules are formulated.
- *Failure to accommodate more quickly important transportation needs.* The depression of the Central Artery and provision of a third harbor crossing have long been considered very important to transportation. As of this date, final approval of these two major public projects is not assured, although it appears probable that the improvements will be undertaken.

In summary, the Boston area real estate market has witnessed unprecedented growth over the last seven years. All indications are that growth will remain strong but at somewhat reduced levels from those achieved in the last seven years. The Boston market still has long-term vitality, and is regarded favorably by lenders, who are frequently willing to take more risks there than in other parts of the country.

Donald E. Megathlin, Jr., is a principal with Economic Research Associates, Cambridge, Massachusetts.

INTRODUCTION

B oston presents a prime example of a city in which public investment and planning spurred private investment in the downtown area. From the mid-1970s through 1985, the city experienced a surge of development that reshaped its topography and infused its downtown area with economic vitality. Economic growth and investor confidence also created an opportunity for Boston to negotiate and secure resources from private development that could be used to lessen the disparity in economic opportunity between downtown and the neighborhoods of Boston.

Before 1960, Boston slumbered through three decades that were marked by erosion of the city's economic base, a population exodus that began in the 1950s, and a shrinking stock of well-worn housing. The public began to stir in the 1950s with the "New Boston" movement, but not until the 1960s did it become fully aroused and begin to take bold action. Key public investments in infrastructure, aggressive planning, and a pioneering private investment conceived in the 1950s by the Prudential Insurance Company launched the downtown into a period of intensive new construction and rehabilitation.

After the national recession of 1974–1975, Boston experienced 10 years of substantial employment growth that was interrupted only by the national recessions in 1980 and 1982. By 1984, the long population decline had ended, with most neighborhoods having gained residents since 1980. Also, in 1984, construction had reached a record level and Boston faced a surplus of development proposals. At that point, the city grasped the opportunity to influence the location and magnitude of development in order to lessen the disparity of income between downtown and the neighborhoods.

An aerial view of Boston's Back Bay, a traditional residential area experiencing commercial development.

HISTORICAL PERSPECTIVE

BOSTON IN 1960

By several key measures, the Great Depression lasted 30 years in Boston. An index of earned income in Boston workplaces, measured in constant dollars, shows that from 1929 to 1959, real earned income increased only 26 percent, or less than 1 percent per year over the period. (See Figure 2-1.) Only the government sector, bolstered by public works projects, showed significant growth. Earned income dropped in wholesale and retail trade, stayed the same in construction, and grew slightly in the finance and service sectors. At the national level, on the other hand, real earned income had more than doubled, with only transportation and public utilities experiencing a less-than-twofold increase. (See Figure 2-2.) In fact,

FIGURE 2-1
INDEX OF EARNED INCOME IN CONSTANT DOLLARS BY SECTOR IN SUFFOLK COUNTY: SELECTED YEARS 1929–1984[1]

Sector	1929	1940	1950	1959	1967	1975	1980	1984
Total Nonfarm	1.00	0.95	1.12	1.26	1.65	1.71	1.89	2.14
Construction	1.00	0.65	0.99	0.97	1.38	1.36	0.81	0.98
Manufacturing	1.00	0.74	1.12	1.24	1.25	0.96	1.04	1.01
Transportation and Public Utilities	1.00	0.86	0.99	1.21	1.43	1.71	1.96	2.09
Wholesale and Retail Trade	1.00	1.05	1.02	0.83	1.10	0.87	0.78	0.88
Finance, Insurance, and Real Estate	1.00	0.97	1.07	1.58	2.25	2.35	2.75	3.64
Services	1.00	0.87	1.05	1.41	2.35	3.25	4.03	4.89
Government and Government-Related Enterprise	1.00	1.66	1.97	2.66	3.36	3.70	4.45	4.25

[1] 1929 = 1.00.
Source: Regional Economics Information System, Bureau of Economic Analysis, U.S. Department of Commerce, 1986.

FIGURE 2-2
INDEX OF EARNED INCOME IN CONSTANT DOLLARS BY SECTOR IN THE UNITED STATES: SELECTED YEARS 1929–1984[1]

Sector	1929	1940	1950	1959	1967	1975	1980	1984
Total Nonfarm	1.00	1.11	1.78	2.49	3.45	4.13	4.99	5.28
Construction	1.00	1.09	1.96	2.73	3.60	3.73	4.56	4.32
Manufacturing	1.00	1.09	1.96	2.73	3.60	3.73	4.56	3.40
Transportation and Public Utilities	1.00	0.95	1.41	1.78	2.23	2.79	3.49	3.40
Wholesale and Retail Trade	1.00	1.15	1.74	2.21	2.83	3.41	3.98	5.01
Finance, Insurance, and Real Estate	1.00	0.87	1.26	2.07	2.90	3.41	4.73	5.75
Services	1.00	1.04	1.49	2.31	3.62	4.77	6.15	7.48
Government and Government-Related Enterprise	1.00	1.91	2.65	4.31	6.86	9.28	9.87	10.36

[1] 1929 = 1.00.
Source: Regional Economics Information System, Bureau of Economic Analysis, U.S. Department of Commerce, 1986.

Boston had not enjoyed a period of sustained prosperity since before the 1890s.[1]

During the 1930s, textile manufacturers in and around Boston faced a slump in demand that severely reduced production and led to numerous plant departures. Manufacturing in the city did not reach 1929 production levels until the late 1940s. World War II heightened the demand for armaments and related manufacturing in Boston by 52 percent from 1940 to 1950. Construction picked up at the same pace, and growth spread to the service-producing sectors.

Boston joined in the national economic expansion in the 1950s as employment in services, finance, insurance, real estate, and, in particular, government grew appreciably. The city lagged behind national and regional growth rates throughout the decade, however. More notable was the rapid growth in earned income in suburban

cities and towns in the Boston area. Manufacturing activity took hold, expanded, and often relocated in the suburbs, due primarily to new and improved highways and to abundant, relatively cheap land outside the city. Concurrent shifts in population swelled the suburban labor force available for manufacturing establishments, created new opportunities for suburban retail trade, and required more local public services.

The paucity of construction in Boston was the most striking characteristic of the city from 1930 to 1960. (See Figure 2-3.) The 26-story Hancock Tower (1947) and the 10-story New England Mutual Life Insurance Company (1939) were the only major additions to Boston's office stock during that period.[2]

The 3.2 million square feet of private office space constructed

from 1931 to 1960 amounted to only 40 percent of the office construction that occurred in the 1920s.[3] Boston had a low-rise downtown skyline in 1960; only the old Hancock Tower (rising 495 feet) and the 1915 U.S. Custom House (rising 496 feet with 32 stories) exceeded 300 feet in height.

The number of retail trade establishments in the central business district of Boston decreased by 15 percent from 1948 to 1958.[4] No major construction occurred in that sector.

Downtown Boston's hotel stock shrank from 11,568 rooms in 1930 to 6,630 rooms in 1960, a 43 percent loss.[5] The additional rooms in a few new hotels, the largest of which was the 333-room Bradford Hotel (built in the 1930s) on Tremont Street, were more than offset by the disappearance of more than 20 hotels from the market during that period.[6]

Public investment from 1930 to 1960 was also at a historically low level. Boston's net funded debt indicated the lack of capital spending during those years: in 1956, the net funded debt was less than half that of 1930.[7] Federal funds made an impact on Boston, however. The construction of public housing added over 11,000 units to the city's housing stock during the 1940s and 1950s. The newly created Boston Redevelopment Authority used urban renewal funds to carry out a "wholesale demolition of the West End" in 1958.[8] This infamous project displaced people, disrupted

[1] "The Livable City," *The Boston Globe*, November 11, 1984, p. 4.

[2] Walter Muir Whitehill, *Boston: A Topographical. History*, 2d ed. (Cambridge, Massachusetts: Belknap Press, 1979), pp. 189–90.

FIGURE 2-3
BOSTON'S OFFICE MARKET BY DECADE OF CONSTRUCTION: 1800–1985
(In Square Feet)

Decade of Construction	Private Office Space[1]	Public Office Space
1800–1820	173,000	50,000
1800–1840	185,000	0
1840–1860	100,000	20,000
1860–1880	430,000	0
1880s	496,000	0
1890s	3,360,000	140,000
1900s	2,850,000	0
1910s	3,170,000	773,003
1920s	8,330,000	125,539
1930s	1,300,000	1,107,491
1940s	1,460,000	0
1950s	448,000	0
1960s	3,593,000	1,856,055
1970s	11,327,000	2,212,500
1980–1985	5,654,700	1,430,000
Total	42,876,700	7,714,558

[1] Includes square feet of classes A, B, and C office space in operation at the end of 1985.
Source: Research Department, Boston Redevelopment Authority, 1986.

[3] Michael Matrullo, Research Department, Boston Redevelopment Authority, "The Office Industry Survey," 1979, p. 38.

[4] U.S. Bureau of the Census, Census of Retail Trade, 1948–1982.

[5] Jason E. Kelly and Sara E. Wermiel, Research Department, Boston Redevelopment Authority, "Hotel and Convention Center Demand and Supply in Boston," 1979, p. H-14.

[6] Whitehill, op. cit., p. 186.

[7] Anthony Artuso, Research Department, Boston Redevelopment Authority, "Boston's Infrastructure," 1984, p. 201.

[8] Whitehill, op. cit., p. 201.

FIGURE 2-4
POPULATION AND LABOR FORCE CHARACTERISTICS: 1930–1980

	1930	1940	1950	1960	1970	1980
Population (Thousands)	781	771	801	697	641	563
Nonwhite (Percent)	2.6	3.1	5.3	9.8	18.2	30.0
Under 20 Years Old (Percent)	33.2	29.8	28.9	32.1	33.3	26.9
20 to 64 Years Old (Percent)	61.3	62.2	61.4	55.7	53.9	60.5
Over 65 Years Old (Percent)	5.5	8.0	9.7	12.3	12.8	12.7
Foreign Born (Percent)	–	–	–	15.8	13.1	–
Median Age	–	–	32.6	32.9	28.1	28.9
Households (Thousands)	–	212	219	224	218	218
Persons per Household	–	3.36	3.37	2.93	2.77	2.4
Civilian Labor Force[1]						
Male Participation (Percent)	84.4	77.2	75.2	75.9	72.0	68.1
Female Participation (Percent)	35.2	34.0	35.3	42.7	47.8	52.7
Occupations of Employed (Percent)						
Professional, Technical, Managerial	–	18.1	18.2	18.8	22.5	30.2
Clerical and Sales	–	27.2	28.0	29.6	32.6	30.2
Crafts	–	12.8	13.6	12.4	10.2	7.7
Production Workers	–	18.8	19.8	20.0	13.8	9.7
Service, Including Household	–	17.9	14.6	14.6	16.8	18.4
Laborers, Including Farm	–	5.3	5.8	4.6	4.2	3.8

[1] Ages 14 and older during 1930–1960 period and ages 16 and older during 1970–1980 period.
Source: U.S. Bureau of the Census, 1930–1980.

neighborhoods, and destroyed buildings to create a vast vacant area just northwest of the central business district. Eventually, the apartment towers of Charles River Park and related structures occupied much of the space, but the city clearly had to find less destructive ways to spend urban renewal money in the 1960s.

Demographic data complete the profile of a sleeping city. Boston's population fell slightly in the 1930s, then rebounded after World War II to reach a peak of 801,000 in 1950. (See Figure 2-4.) The rapid growth of Boston's suburbs in the 1950s coincided with a 13 percent drop in population in Boston—a downward trend that would continue until the early 1980s. The racial makeup of Boston changed notably during this period: the percentage of nonwhite persons grew from 2.6 percent in 1930 to 9.8 percent in 1960. Consistent with national trends, the size of households began to decrease in the 1950s and continued to diminish into the 1980s.

The composition of Boston's labor force changed along with the city's dynamic economy. In 1960, working residents were employed mostly in production and sales jobs: as shown in Figure 2-4, crafts and production workers accounted for 32 percent of all workers, while sales and clerical jobs accounted for 30 percent. Professional, technical, and managerial positions accounted for 19 percent of the jobs in 1960, a distribution that had changed only slightly since 1940. By 1980, however, the proportion of workers classified as crafts and production workers diminished by almost one-half, as the professional, technical, and managerial occupations absorbed 30 percent of all working residents.

Only in the 1950s did local public policymakers begin to play a positive role in Boston's revival. In effect, the city's political leadership had been at odds with its wealthy private sector since the early part of the century. The political clout of Irish immigrants and

their offspring was epitomized by James Michael Curley, who was elected mayor for four terms between 1914 and 1949. Curley was a colorful, combative, Democratic Irish-American politician who defended the rank and file and the "neighborhoods" against the so-called Republican Yankees (the Boston Brahmins), who controlled most of the wealth and private investment in Boston. Because of their disgust with Mayor Curley's patronage and populist policies, private investors curtailed their investments in Boston. Meanwhile, the mayor pursued a pay-as-you-go spending policy that delayed or shelved capital projects in the public sector.[9]

The 1949 mayoral election became a turning point for investment in Boston. The city's Yankees supported a movement, dubbed "New Boston," that backed John

---

[9] *The Boston Globe*, op. cit., p. 8.

B. Hynes against James Michael Curley. Although Hynes was also an Irish Catholic, he became the New Boston candidate and won the election. From that time, downtown and its problems of physical blight, economic erosion, and population decline ascended on the political agenda. The neighborhoods would not again reach priority status until the 1980s. Although the New Boston movement had only modest intentions and results in the 1950s, it set the stage for bolder public initiatives in the 1960s. Indeed, the timing was fortuitous; years of neglect had made Boston ripe for investment just when the national economy began a decade of robust growth. A remark made in 1957 by the great urban historian Lewis Mumford was blunt, but true: "Boston's backwardness is its principal asset."

BOSTON IN THE 1980s

In 1985, Boston had a thriving downtown that was supported by a transformed urban economy. Fresh from a record year of construction activity in 1984 and hale with the first growth in population since the 1940s, the city and its downtown exhibited a vitality that would have been barely imaginable in 1960.

By a variety of measures, Boston's downtown had achieved a high degree of economic health. The city experienced a sustained recovery after the recessions of the early 1970s. As shown in Figure 2-5, employment grew by 82,500 jobs, or 16 percent, from 1976 to 1985, with the downtown area accounting for more than half of the additional jobs. Growth from 1976 to 1985 approached the average growth rates in New England of 27 percent and in the nation of 23 percent.

Comparative unemployment rates also indicated a strong economic performance in Boston. In the 1970s, Boston and its metropolitan area typically had higher unemployment rates than the nation. After 1979, average annual unem-

ployment rates in Boston and the metropolitan area fell and remained below national rates. (See Figure 2-6.) In fact, the Boston metropolitan area's unemployment rate of 3.2 percent in December 1985 was the lowest of the 33 largest metropolitan areas. The city's average rate for 1985 was 4.6 percent, the lowest level since the 1960s.

Construction activity surged to a peak in 1984 as projects involving new construction, rehabilitation, and conversion were completed, exceeding $1.1 billion in construction costs. (See Figure 2-7.)[10] The 1970s and early 1980s brought a dramatic increase in office and hotel development, as illustrated in Figures 2-8 through 2-11. Development has been intensive since

---

[10] John Avault, Mark Johnson, and Jane VanBuren, Research Department, Boston Redevelopment Authority, "Boston Development," September 1985.

FIGURE 2-5
EMPLOYMENT BY INDUSTRY, CITY OF BOSTON: 1976–1985[1]

Industry	Thousands of Employees							Change 1976–1985	
	1976[2]	1980	1981	1982	1983	1984	1985	Number	Percent
Agriculture/Mining	1.0	0.9	1.0	1.1	1.2	1.3	1.3	0.3	23.2%
Construction	14.7	11.4	11.7	11.9	12.0	12.8	13.7	−1.0	−6.9
Manufacturing	53.8	52.3	51.1	50.0	47.4	47.3	42.5	−11.3	−20.9
Transportation/Public Utilities	34.8	37.5	37.9	36.7	36.9	39.1	36.6	1.8	5.2
Wholesale Trade	31.2	28.5	28.4	26.3	27.2	28.9	25.8	−5.4	−17.4
Retail Trade	57.9	58.6	58.4	57.8	59.6	63.1	63.7	5.8	9.9
Finance/Insurance/Real Estate	64.7	72.9	75.3	78.5	79.5	81.7	85.1	20.4	31.6
Services	168.4	201.5	203.2	206.3	213.2	220.1	225.9	57.5	34.2
Hotel	4.9	6.4	6.8	7.6	8.6	9.3	10.2	5.3	108.9
Medical	56.6	64.1	63.7	64.3	64.9	65.9	65.9	9.3	16.2
Educational	23.5	25.8	25.9	25.9	27.3	27.4	27.7	4.2	17.9
Cultural	5.1	6.1	5.6	5.7	6.1	6.1	6.3	1.2	24.0
Social/Nonprofit	18.2	19.6	19.7	19.5	19.9	20.8	20.5	2.3	12.7
Business	30.4	37.7	37.9	38.2	40.6	43.7	47.2	16.8	55.3
Professional	22.4	31.6	33.5	34.9	35.3	35.7	36.3	13.9	62.2
Personal and Repair	7.3	10.2	10.1	10.2	10.5	11.2	11.8	4.5	62.6
Government	84.8	97.2	94.7	89.4	92.1	94.2	99.2	14.4	17.0
Total Employment	511.3	560.8	561.7	558.0	569.1	588.5	593.8	82.5	16.1%

[1] Proprietors are included in the employment by private industry types.
[2] Figures for 1976 are estimates based on the 1980 ratio of Boston to Suffolk County data from the Department of Employment Security economic data base for Suffolk County.
Sources: Massachusetts Division of Employment Security; U.S. Department of Commerce, Bureau of Economic Analysis; and County Business Patterns, Massachusetts.

1981, with no letup in sight. In fact, the city began to turn away some developers as concerns increased about overbuilding in parts of the downtown.

The population decline that began in Boston shortly after 1950 ended in the early 1980s. Migration patterns reversed the trend and pushed the population up to almost 620,000 in 1985, representing an increase of around 57,000, or 10 percent, from the 1980 count made by the U.S. Bureau of the Census.[11]

[11] The latest (July 1984) census from the U.S. Bureau of the Census reported a population of 570,719; the Massachusetts State Census reported a population of 620,000 in 1985. These figures differ due to the different statistical methods used.

FIGURE 2-6
UNEMPLOYMENT RATES: SELECTED YEARS 1970–1985

Year	Boston City	Boston Metro Area	Massa- chusetts	New England	United States
1970	4.9%	4.0%	4.6%	4.9%	4.9%
1975	12.8	10.5	11.2	10.3	8.5
1977	9.5	7.8	8.1	7.6	7.0
1979	6.5	5.2	5.5	5.4	5.8
1980	6.1	5.0	5.6	5.9	7.1
1981	7.0	5.7	6.3	6.3	7.6
1982	9.1	6.7	7.9	7.8	9.7
1983	7.8	5.8	6.9	6.8	9.6
1984	5.5	4.1	4.8	4.9	7.1
1985	4.6	3.4	3.9	4.4	7.2

Sources: U.S. Bureau of Labor Statistics; and Massachusetts Division of Employment Security, 1986.

FIGURE 2-7
COST OF CONSTRUCTION, REHABILITATION, AND CONVERSIONS IN BOSTON
ACTUAL AND PROJECTED: 1975–1989
(In Millions of 1984 Dollars)

Year	Office	Retail	Medical	Educational	Recreation and Cultural	Parking and Transportation	Industrial	Hotel	Exhibition	Residential	Totals
1975	$601.8	$12.1	$6.2	–	$2.5	–	$3.6	$62.0	–	$77.4	$765.5
1976	152.0	10.1	117.7	$3.4	9.6	$1.7	1.5	–	–	111.9	407.9
1977	103.7	18.3	0.0	119.6	–	–	–	–	–	99.3	341.0
1978	14.3	78.8	66.8	8.9	21.2	–	9.5	–	–	78.8	278.3
1979	23.8	4.8	0.0	21.9	12.2	–	7.2	11.1	–	62.5	143.4
1980	18.8	5.1	87.6	15.4	7.5	–	6.8	–	–	57.1	198.5
1981	171.2	9.1	453.4	14.3	19.4	3.4	42.1	36.5	–	113.6	863.0
1982	111.0	15.7	78.1	0.5	8.7	8.1	30.8	102.0	–	78.7	433.7
1983	57.1	16.5	75.2	28.6	18.8	56.0	71.5	126.8	$14.7	140.1	605.4
1984	611.7	113.2	70.0	25.5	29.6	57.1	46.2	141.1	2.5	60.5	1,157.4
1985	258.9	29.1	40.2	4.6	25.1	104.7	84.4	123.5	–	154.4	824.9
1986	200.8	21.3	2.0	6.6	5.6	86.9	7.0	–	38.4	214.0	582.5
1987	498.2	31.5	136.5	–	8.8	46.6	–	25.5	–	136.9	884.0
1988	190.4	6.5	–	–	–	19.0	33.2	29.2	100.0	18.7	397.0
1989	224.7	12.0	–	–	17.0	–	–	–	–	172.3	425.9
Totals	$3,238.5	$384.1	$1,133.6	$249.3	$186.1	$383.5	$343.6	$657.7	$155.6	$1,576.2	$8,308.3

Source: Research Department, Boston Redevelopment Authority, 1986.

FIGURE 2-8
BOSTON'S PRIVATE OFFICE SPACE, 1985:[1]
SQUARE FOOTAGE BY ORIGINAL DECADE OF COMPLETION

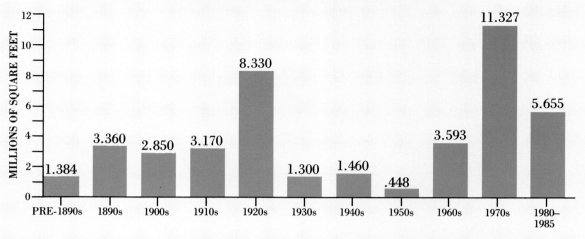

[1]Includes all privately built class A, B, and C office space; in 1985, this totaled 42.9 million square feet.

FIGURE 2-9
BOSTON'S OFFICE CONSTRUCTION
ANNUAL PRIVATE OFFICE SPACE COMPLETIONS: 1960–1985[1]

Year	Millions of Square Feet	Year	Millions of Square Feet
1960	.142	1973	1.131
1961	0	1974	.190
1962	0	1975	5.213
1963	0	1976	.348
1964	0	1977	1.023
1965	1.000	1978	0
1966	1.166	1979	0
1967	.235	1980	.008
1968	.800	1981	.990
1969	.250	1982	0
1970	.900	1983	.324
1971	2.382	1984	3.600
1972	.140	1985	.733

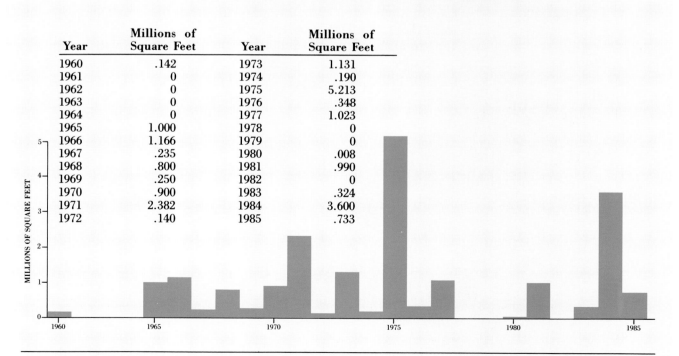

[1]Totaled 20,374,700 square feet in 26 years. Rehabilitations are excluded.

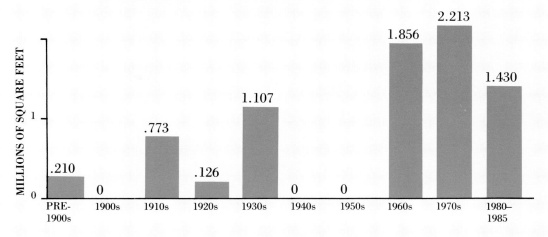

FIGURE 2-10
BOSTON'S PUBLICLY BUILT AND OPERATED OFFICE SPACE, 1985:[1]
SQUARE FOOTAGE BY ORIGINAL DECADE OF COMPLETION

[1]Totaled 7.7 million square feet in 1985.

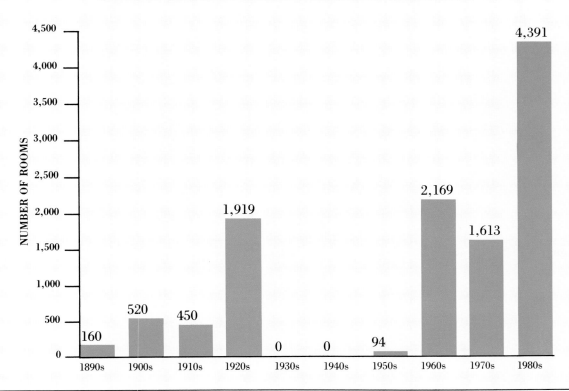

FIGURE 2-11
BOSTON'S HOTELS, 1985:[1]
STOCK OF ROOMS BY ORIGINAL DECADE OF COMPLETION

[1]Totaled 28 hotels with 11,316 rooms at year end 1985. Does not include neighborhood motels, executive (long-term) suites, tourist homes, hostels, or lodging houses.

While the revitalization of Boston's downtown area has been successful, private investment failed to spread throughout the city, a supposition upon which the New Boston movement was based. On the contrary, Boston in 1985 was troubled by persistent poverty, pockets of unemployment, and a serious shortage of decent, affordable housing units. In 1980, 20.2 percent of the city's residents lived below poverty income levels, with the greatest percentage living in traditional working class and minority neighborhoods. In 1985, 28 percent of the black population and 50 percent of the Hispanic population were living in poverty.[12] Unemployment and underemployment continued to plague willing and able adults, especially minorities and teenagers. Although much of Boston's housing stock had been rehabilitated, net new units had not kept up with the burgeoning demand. Private investment flowed to commercial projects or to luxury rental and condominium units and market-rate units that were beyond the means of much of Boston's population. Too often, downtown investment, with the new jobs and increased demand for housing it created, resulted in displacing neighborhood residents who could not keep up with rising rents.

Another turning point occurred in 1983. Four-term Mayor Kevin H. White, who had overseen much of the building of the New Boston, decided not to run for another term. In the subsequent mayoral campaign, in which the needs of neighborhoods resurfaced as the prime campaign issue, Raymond A. Flynn emerged as the victor, promising to spread prosperity to the neighborhoods. Unlike James M. Curley, however, Mayor Flynn set out to work in cooperation with private businesses and with business leaders.

Bunker Hill Street in the Charlestown area is a typical residential street in Boston.

[12] Research Department, Boston Redevelopment Authority, and Neighborhood Development and Employment Agency, 1985 Household Survey conducted by the Center for Survey Research, March 1985.

Ashwani Vasishth and Shakeel Hossain

SOURCES OF REVITALIZATION IN DOWNTOWN BOSTON

The sources of downtown renewal in Boston were multiple. National economic trends, public investment, public mechanisms for private development, and an evolution of planning within fiscal constraints were the primary means that shaped the downtown.

Economic Trends

Boston's local initiatives depended on national trends that created many of the investment opportunities in the city. From Boston's standpoint, the most significant national trend was the shift in the economy and employment toward a broad range of services. A complex set of factors transformed the national economy from production of goods to provision of services.[13] In 1949, some 33 percent of all workers were employed in manufactur-

[13] T.J. Noyelle and T.M. Stanback, *The Economic Transformation of American Cities* (Totowa, New Jersey: Rowman & Allenheld, 1984).

ing, 12 percent in services, and 25 percent in broadly defined services. (See Figure 2-12.) By 1984, the national economy looked very different: services had captured 22 percent of total employment; manufacturing, 21 percent; and broadly defined services, 34 percent.

Warehouses were converted into condominiums on Long Wharf on Boston's waterfront.

FIGURE 2-12
WAGE AND SALARY EMPLOYMENT IN THE UNITED STATES: SELECTED YEARS 1949–1984

NUMBER OF EMPLOYEES IN THOUSANDS

Year	Manufacturing	Services[1]	Broad Services[2]	Total
1949	14,441	5,240	11,069	43,754
1959	16,675	7,087	13,647	53,268
1969	20,167	11,169	19,123	70,384
1979	21,040	17,112	27,223	89,823
1984	19,591	20,661	31,496	94,155

PERCENT DISTRIBUTION OF EMPLOYMENT

Year	Manufacturing	Services[1]	Broad Services[2]	Total
1949	33.0%	12.0%	25.3%	100.0%
1959	31.3	13.3	25.6	100.0
1969	28.7	15.9	27.2	100.0
1979	23.4	19.1	30.3	100.0
1984	20.8	21.9	33.5	100.0

[1] Service industries include health, educational, business, social, professional, repair, amusement, lodging, and personal services.
[2] Broad services comprise transportation, communications, public utilities, finance, insurance, and real estate services, as well as the services listed above.
Source: Economic Report of the President, 1985, Table B-37.

Steadily, the nation took up "new ways of producing and marketing final commodities [consumer goods], involving a move towards operating production facilities and penetrating consumer markets largely on a national . . . scale, and resulting in a significant reorganization of the geography of goods and services production."[14] This national trend was one of the inducements to manufacturers to shift from cities to suburban and nonmetropolitan areas, where space was cheaper. Cities became increasingly specialized in providing and exporting high-level services.

Although Sunbelt cities grew rapidly and took considerable investment away from northern regions of the nation, cities that had a diverse base of services and did not rely primarily on manufacturing held a better economic position.

Boston has had a diverse economy throughout the last 50 years. Manufacturing amounted to only 20 percent of the total earned income in 1929. Wholesale and retail trade was the specialty at that time, commanding 32 percent of the total earned income, while services (with 14 percent) and broadly defined services (with 34 percent) constituted large sectors. (See Figure 2-13.) Boston's economic base of business services, banks, law firms, accountants, insurance companies, hospitals, universities, and transportation facilities positioned the city to take advantage of the national surge in services activities. Therefore, when the urban crisis of the mid-1960s evoked grim outlooks for older, manufacturing-based northeastern cities, underlying economic changes were preparing Boston to resurge as an economic center.[15]

The recessions of the 1970s hit the Boston area hard, with workers

[14] Ibid, p. X-1.
[15] Alexander Ganz, "Where Has the Urban Crisis Gone?" *Urban Affairs Quarterly*, Vol. 20, No. 4, June 1985, pp. 449–68.

BOSTON'S DEVELOPMENT AGENCIES

Boston's primary development agencies are the Boston Redevelopment Authority and the Economic Development and Industrial Development Corporation of Boston. The Neighborhood Development and Employment Agency and the Public Facilities Department have also played important roles in the development process in downtown, and the commonwealth of Massachusetts has contributed significantly.

THE BOSTON REDEVELOPMENT AUTHORITY (BRA)

Established in August 1957 at the request of the mayor and city council, the Boston Redevelopment Authority is responsible for the city's urban renewal and planning activities. Its administrative budget is appropriated from Boston's consolidated budget. Various federal and state sources and income from leasing property provide the remainder of its funds.

In 1960, when the city planning board was abolished, its staff was transferred to the BRA. The functions, duties, and responsibilities for general city planning and development were consolidated in this one agency, which was empowered by state law as the city's redevelopment authority. As such, the BRA is authorized through U.S. Department of Housing and Urban Development (HUD) contracts to finance slum clearance, urban renewal, open space programs, urban beautification, and other programs designed to prevent the spread of urban blight.

The BRA manages the process of development in the city. As the city's planning agency, it functions as economic coordinator and expediter for development projects. Moreover, the agency is responsible for analyzing and monitoring development, and for assuring that development activity produces the jobs, economic benefits, and tax revenues that strengthen the local economy. The departments of the Authority that are organized to implement this role include Community Planning and Development, Development and Urban Design, Environmental Review, Land Use and Environmental Policy, Research and Policy Development, and Zoning. The Authority has offices at the Charlestown Navy Yard and Dudley Station in Roxbury, as well as its main offices in City Hall.

ECONOMIC DEVELOPMENT AND INDUSTRIAL CORPORATION OF BOSTON (EDIC/BOSTON)

Established in 1971 by state legislation, the Economic Development and Industrial Corporation of Boston is mandated to stem the loss of industry and industrial jobs in Boston, to revitalize underused land, and to enhance the tax base. As a public authority, EDIC draws on a variety of local, state, and federal resources—often in combination with private investment—to implement its programs.

Because the agency's efforts are largely targeted to neighborhood industry, EDIC works closely with Boston's Neighborhood Development and Employment Agency (NDEA). As the local administrator of both the Community Development Block Grant program and employment training funds, NDEA provides assistance for many of EDIC's neighborhood industrial development projects, for EDIC's revolving loan fund, and for the Boston Technical Center—a skills training program.

Boston's private sector plays a key role in the development process. Local banks are active participants in EDIC's financial programs; they have financed numerous development projects and have actively promoted the city as a location for industrial development. Real estate brokers have collaborated with EDIC to create comprehensive real estate listings of industrial sites in the city for sale or lease. A cooperative private sector has significantly expanded Boston's potential to offer new manufacturing opportunities and new jobs and has reinforced EDIC's ability to improve and market over 10 million square feet of land.

As owner and operator of three industrial parks—one each in South Boston, Roxbury, and Dorchester—EDIC has established over 220 acres of industrially zoned property for more than 30 companies employing nearly 2,000 people. The services that EDIC offers to businesses deal with real estate and land development, financial assistance, job training, client relations, and relations with locally based community development corporations. EDIC's research department also provides statistics on Boston and its workforce and on manufacturing companies and their employees, as well as listings of available land for sale or lease in the city. The agency's functions have expanded to include work with the mayor's office geared toward marketing Boston's opportunities on a regional, national, and international scale.

in manufacturing and trade bearing the brunt of job losses. The surviving core was all the more oriented toward providing high-level services, many of which were exportable throughout the New England region, the eastern United States, and beyond. By 1985, 37 percent of Boston's salaried employees were working in services, 58 percent in broadly defined services, and only 8 percent in manufacturing. While the number of manufacturing jobs in textiles, food processing, and leather products was decreasing, high-technology manufacturing was growing in Boston's suburbs. The importance of scientific and computer-related knowledge and financial and legal information to these new manufacturing operations meant that firms in the city would be called upon for a variety of services.

During the national recovery after 1975, Boston began to expand its economic base. From 1976 to 1980, its employment grew by 10 percent while national employment grew by 14 percent. Boston grew

FIGURE 2-13
PERCENT OF TOTAL EARNED INCOME BY SECTOR IN SUFFOLK COUNTY: SELECTED YEARS 1929–1984

Sector	1929	1940	1950	1959	1967	1975	1980	1984
Total Nonfarm	100.0	100.0	100.0	100.0	100.0	100.0	100.0	100.0
Private[1]	91.9	86.0	85.8	83.0	83.6	82.5	81.4	84.0
Construction	6.1	4.2	5.5	4.7	5.1	4.9	2.6	2.8
Manufacturing	19.8	15.2	19.8	19.5	15.0	11.2	10.9	9.3
Transportation and Public Utilities	10.2	9.1	9.0	9.8	8.8	10.2	10.7	10.0
Trade	31.6	34.6	28.7	20.8	21.1	16.1	13.1	13.0
Wholesale				10.6	10.6	8.5	6.8	6.2
Retail				10.2	10.5	7.6	6.3	6.8
Finance, Insurance, and Real Estate	10.2	10.2	9.7	12.7	13.9	14.0	14.8	17.3
Services	13.7	12.5	12.9	15.4	19.6	26.1	29.3	31.5
Government and Government-Related Enterprise	8.1	14.0	14.2	17.0	16.4	17.5	18.6	16.0
Civilian	1.8	5.2	6.4	7.2	6.6	5.7	5.0	4.4
Military	0.3	0.8	2.2	1.7	1.3	0.3	0.4	0.4
State and Local	5.9	8.0	5.6	8.1	8.5	11.4	13.2	11.2

[1] Agricultural services, and forestry, fishing, and mining industries are included in total private employment.
Source: Regional Economics Information System, Bureau of Economic Analysis, U.S. Department of Commerce, 1986.

another 5.3 percent during the national recession and recovery from 1980 to 1984 while the nation's employment growth rate was 4.1 percent.

Public Investment

The premise of the New Boston movement of the 1950s was that Boston's blight, economic stagnation, and population loss could be stemmed by a massive public investment program that would spur even greater private investment. The strategy used to implement the movement was to "renew"—with public funds—central areas of the city, which would then become attractive to private developers, offering them opportunities to construct or rehabilitate office buildings, hotels, and residences. The 1960s brought, in particular, Government Center, a massive project that included the redesign of street patterns, a new city hall, and an expansive plaza. Thirty buildings, valued at more than $260 million in 1970, eventually occupied the 60-acre development.[16]

Initially, urban renewal emphasized the rebuilding of public buildings and housing in blighted areas. In the 1970s, the focus of public investment moved toward improvements in infrastructure—streets, utilities, bridges, and other structures—that improved the setting for private investment. The federal government underwrote most of the public improvements in Boston.

Public Mechanisms for Development

Urban renewal was the largest public redevelopment program of those funded primarily by the federal government. Boston used the program extensively, designating 14 urban renewal areas and spending hundreds of millions of dollars from federal funds from the 1950s through the 1970s.[17] Typically, the

city used funds to acquire land, demolish structures, clear land, rebuild streets, and improve infrastructure. A related public mechanism was the power of eminent domain, vested in the Boston Redevelopment Authority (BRA), which gave the city considerable leverage in acquiring land. In many cases, the BRA assembled contiguous parcels of land that were then sold to private developers. In the 1970s, it began to lease property to developers to provide a steady source of income to the agency or the city. As public money for redevelopment diminished, land assembly and leasing became much more important to the city.

The federal government represented a vital force in the downtown revitalization process. In addition to underwriting urban renewal, it sold surplus property to the city, subsidized construction of over 20,000 housing units under Section 8 of the Housing and Urban Development Act, supported key public/private ventures with Urban Development Action Grants, and sent millions of dollars to Boston in other categorical grants over the last 25 years.

Planning within Fiscal Constraints

Planning in Boston has evolved under the influence of local circumstances and opportunities. In the 1960s, federal funds were available for large redevelopment projects. Boston skillfully tapped these resources and laid the foundation for reviving the downtown as an economic center. In the 1980s, when the federal government's role in development all but disappeared, the lack of a federal urban policy and the sharp reductions in federal support for housing construction forced a new orientation in Boston's planning. At the same

time, local property tax limitations, without significant tax reform, put a severe strain on the city's budget. Although state aid took up part of the slack, the city was forced to postpone indefinitely projects requiring large amounts of capital. Without stronger public policies, those parts of Boston that had enjoyed minor benefits in the New Boston era were unlikely to be reached by the private investment occurring in downtown. Coupled with this persistent gap between downtown and the neighborhoods, concern regarding the congested downtown environment required that Boston shift gears in its plans for redevelopment.

The BRA continued its monitoring and design review of private development projects, but in 1984, it expanded its role by beginning a master planning process. Its current strategy is to approve suitable development projects under new guidelines for physical characteristics, as well as to approve revised zoning regulations and new requirements that will spread the benefits of development to neighborhoods outside the downtown. While limiting the environmental impacts of further downtown developments, the city is also helping areas of Boston that have not benefited from previous development; this is being done partly through a linkage program and through a policy that favors Boston residents for construction jobs. Under the linkage program, the city requires development projects larger than 100,000 square feet to pay $5 per square foot for 12 years. The proceeds go to a housing trust that will be used for construction of affordable housing or to other uses that will directly benefit the neighborhoods.

Under Mayor White's executive order of 1979, declared constitutional by the U.S. Supreme Court in 1983, and under Mayor Flynn's executive order of 1985, the city now requires that the composition of construction crews be 50 percent Boston residents, 25 percent minority workers, and 10 percent

---

16 Tom O'Brien, Research Department, Boston Redevelopment Authority, "A History of Boston's Government Center," 1970.

17 Frederick Pikielek, Research Department, Boston Redevelopment Authority "Planning in Boston: The Historical Record," Draft Report, 1972.

women. In 1985, the city began a policy of negotiating hiring goals with developers to assure that these same percentages would apply to new permanent jobs.

The BRA also plans to attract private development, jobs, and income to areas that have not previously attracted investments. One aspect of this plan is parcel-to-parcel linkage. Under this program, the city or state would link the disposal of publicly owned sites downtown to less attractive neighborhood sites. For example, a developer would obtain a downtown commercial site from the city while creating enterprise and job opportunities in a neighborhood of Boston that has not participated in private development activity.

The revitalized parts of downtown, on the other hand, are attracting an abundance of private developers. Although the office market is fairly tight due to much new construction, rents are high, as are hotel occupancy and room rates. Clearly there is money to be made in the downtown. Now, without massive public funds to redevelop other parts of Boston, the city is working to influence the location and magnitude of private development. Planning, zoning, public/private cooperation, and incentives to locate in particular areas represent the public mechanisms currently being used.

ECONOMIC IMPACTS OF DEVELOPMENT

The sources responsible for economic revitalization have been broad and diverse. No attempt is made here to attribute a specific share of the investment, income generated, and other benefits to Boston's own development effort. But summaries of annual spending on construction, of related employment, of changes in total assessed property value and tax revenue, and of special initiatives provide tangible indications of the rewards of the city's development effort to date.

From 1975 to 1985, new construction, rehabilitation, and conversions amounted to over $6 billion in Boston. As shown in Figure 2-7, construction was centered in a variety of private and public structures, with the heaviest investment in office, medical, and residential categories. Annual construction and development surged from 1981 through the present (as shown in Figure 2-14), along with expectations for the next few years.

Construction activity supported many jobs in the metropolitan area. From 1981 through 1985, the average number exceeded 12,000 full-time-equivalent construction jobs annually (see Figure 2-15), which is a substantial number compared with the 8,000 Boston residents who were employed in the construction industry in 1980, according to the U.S. Census.

The number of permanent jobs associated with the new and refurbished structures ranged from 6,000 to 32,000 per year. (See Figure 2-16.) From 1975 to 1985, 160,000 jobs were added or retained due to development projects

FIGURE 2-14
CONSTRUCTION, REHABILITATION, AND CONVERSION IN BOSTON BY TYPE: ACTUAL 1975–1985 AND PROJECTED 1986–1989[1]

Year	Office (Sq. Ft.)	Retail (Sq. Ft.)	Medical (Sq. Ft.)	Educational (Sq. Ft.)	Recreational and Cultural (Sq. Ft.)	Parking and Transportation (No. of Cars)	Industrial (Sq. Ft.)	Hotel (Sq. Ft.)	Exhibition (Sq. Ft.)	Residential (No. of Dwelling Units)
1975	5,322,380	136,000	–	99,000	–	–	105,000	698	–	1,058
1976	1,478,500	75,000	841,630	32,500	–	585	26,000	–	–	1,724
1977	1,255,754	140,000	–	1,674,000	–	–	–	–	–	1,217
1978	350,000	585,000	832,000	127,000	–	–	773,100	–	–	1,549
1979	896,800	77,500	–	–	–	–	562,600	900	–	1,264
1980	463,915	74,099	860,500	56,000	–	–	377,690	–	–	1,216
1981	2,613,747	113,269	287,000	129,000	132,000	–	1,391,337	710	–	1,303
1982	2,105,840	226,775	396,096	10,000	100,000	1,135	949,300	1,350	–	1,305
1983	1,036,740	253,409	426,000	322,062	26,000	1,125	1,803,210	804	205,000	3,076
1984	5,503,951	920,000	425,038	253,000	2,600	3,267	1,165,000	1,145	50,000	1,716
1985	1,789,670	365,236	211,600	35,000	106,500	2,081	786,000	1,310	–	1,609
1986	4,552,733	530,791	–	186,100	32,000	6,442	777,200	105	820,000	3,827
1987	2,746,313	597,128	114,000	94,900	10,000	3,532	295,000	220	–	3,117
1988	4,157,733	254,500	700,000	60,000	–	6,594	1,131,000	250	701,500	1,396
1989	3,400,000	130,000	250,000	–	49,000	2,256	–	250	–	2,937
Totals	37,674,076	4,478,707	5,343,864	3,078,562	458,100	27,017	10,142,437	7,742	1,776,500	28,314

[1] Development is listed by year of actual or anticipated completion. Square foot figures represent net leasable space.
Source: Research Department, Boston Redevelopment Authority, 1986.

FIGURE 2-15
FULL-TIME EQUIVALENT CONSTRUCTION JOBS IN BOSTON:
ACTUAL 1975–1985 AND PROJECTED 1986–1989[1]

Year	Office	Retail	Medical	Educational	Recreational and Cultural	Parking and Transportation	Industrial	Hotel	Exhibition	Residential	Totals
1975	1,595	335	693	510	51	–	61	533	–	2,257	6,035
1976	1,367	529	1,170	663	200	82	27	–	–	1,754	5,792
1977	814	639	453	605	150	–	–	–	–	1,420	4,081
1978	484	724	875	289	221	–	1,987	114	–	1,349	6,043
1979	1,270	99	528	334	247	–	1,935	114	–	1,060	5,587
1980	1,664	100	769	268	290	–	1,913	1,045	–	1,590	7,639
1981	3,615	168	896	177	398	–	3,001	2,245	–	1,945	12,445
1982	3,932	652	1,285	278	289	878	670	1,883	151	1,972	11,990
1983	3,613	941	1,204	578	288	1,466	1,201	1,388	151	2,036	12,866
1984	6,387	1,056	841	266	167	965	459	1,525	51	1,678	13,395
1985	4,848	431	738	57	235	1,047	585	923	674	1,958	11,496
1986	7,666	669	297	294	438	1,192	606	239	1,119	3,772	16,292
1987	8,479	1,043	563	288	317	1,151	715	524	675	3,607	17,362
1988	6,255	518	532	529	188	950	634	358	675	2,156	12,795
1989	2,734	278	406	–	49	464	–	122	–	1,992	6,045
Totals	54,723	8,182	11,250	5,136	3,528	8,195	13,794	11,013	3,496	30,546	149,863

[1] These figures assume a 1985 construction wage of $27,760. They also assume that 45 percent of new construction cost and 55 percent of rehab and conversion construction cost represent payroll for commerical projects. Payroll for new and rehab conversion residential projects is taken as 50 percent and 60 percent of construction costs, respectively. Jobs on larger projects are spread over two, three, or four years.
Source: Research Department, Boston Redevelopment Authority, 1986.

FIGURE 2-16
PERMANENT JOB EXPANSION AND RETENTION IN BOSTON THROUGH DEVELOPMENT:
ACTUAL 1975–1985 AND PROJECTED 1986–1989[1]

Year	Office	Retail	Medical	Educational	Recreational and Cultural	Parking and Transportation	Industrial	Hotel	Exhibition	Residential	Total Jobs
1975	24,190	340	165	248	–	–	210	465	–	13	25,631
1976	6,720	188	4,208	81	–	2	52	–	–	21	11,272
1977	5,708	350	325	4,185	–	–	–	–	–	15	10,583
1978	1,591	1,463	4,160	318	–	–	976	–	–	20	8,528
1979	4,076	194	194	–	–	–	1,125	600	–	16	6,205
1980	2,108	185	4,303	140	–	–	755	–	–	15	7,506
1981	11,881	283	1,435	323	132	–	2,784	473	–	16	17,327
1982	9,572	567	1,980	25	100	4	1,899	900	–	16	15,063
1983	4,713	634	2,130	805	26	4	3,020	536	205	26	12,099
1984	25,018	2,301	2,125	633	3	11	1,455	763	50	21	32,380
1985	8,135	913	1,775	88	107	7	1,010	873	–	20	12,928
1986	20,695	1,327	675	466	32	21	984	70	820	48	25,138
1987	12,483	1,493	688	238	10	12	590	147	–	39	15,700
1988	18,898	637	3,554	150	–	22	1,462	167	702	16	25,608
1989	15,455	325	1,250	–	49	8	–	167	–	37	17,291
Totals	171,243	11,200	28,967	7,700	459	91	16,322	5,161	1,777	339	243,259

[1] Estimates of jobs are based on the following factors by type—one job per: 220 sq. ft., office; 400 sq. ft., retail; 200 sq. ft., medical; 400 sq. ft., educational; 1,000 sq. ft., recreational and cultural; 300 cars, parking and transportation; 500 sq. ft., industrial; 1.5 hotel rooms; 1,000 sq. ft., exhibition; 80 dwelling units, residential.
Source: Research Department, Boston Redevelopment Authority, 1986.

in Boston—a net gain of about 85,000 jobs. The development projects were key to the transformation and expansion of Boston's economic base. In particular, large established firms in finance and services were able to expand into new office space, while old office space became available to new or smaller businesses.

Not all of the new jobs went to Boston residents. According to the census, commuters held about six of every 10 jobs located in the city in 1980. Even so, with four out of 10 jobs and the related income going to Boston residents, the new jobs indirectly generated additional local jobs and income.

In the three years following a re-evaluation of the city's taxable property, the assessed taxable value increased by more than $1 billion annually. From January 1, 1982, to January 1, 1984, the total assessed taxable value rose 25 percent,[18] and the record year for construction completions in 1984 probably expanded the base by as much as 20 percent.[19] Estimates of actual and projected increases in property taxes, under tax limitation provisions, indicate that development will yield over $200 million in property tax increases, or 60 percent of the total, during the fiscal period from 1985 through 1995. (See Figure 2-17 for growth data.)

The relationship between the magnitude of development and the economic benefits that nine downtown projects will bring to the city in the near future are presented in Figures 2-18, 2-19, and 2-20, which summarize the jobs, tax revenues, and other characteristics associated with the developments. These benefits, as well as special initiatives funded by developers (Figure

FIGURE 2-17
BOSTON PROPERTY TAX YIELD INCREASES: ACTUAL FY 1985 AND PROJECTED FY 1986–FY 1995
(Millions of Dollars)

	From Development	From Growth in Value	Total
FY 1985 Actual	$ 22	$ 8	$ 30
FY 1986[1]	$ 15	$ 9	$ 24
FY 1987[1]	$ 14	$ 10	$ 24
FY 1988[1]	$ 14	$ 10	$ 24
FY 1989–1995[2]	$150	$100	$250
FY 1985–1995	$215	$137	$352

[1] Estimated by the city of Boston, Assessing, Treasury, and Budget Departments, March 22, 1985.
[2] Projected by the Research Department, Boston Redevelopment Authority, March 28, 1985.
Source: Research Department, Boston Redevelopment Authority, 1986.

[18] City of Boston, Official Statement, August 15, 1985, p. 36.
[19] Estimate made by the Research Department, Boston Redevelopment Authority; a reevaluation process in FY 1986 has delayed compilation of the January 1, 1985, total assessed taxable value.

FIGURE 2-18
CHARACTERISTICS OF NINE LARGE DEVELOPMENT PROJECTS IN BOSTON

Project	SIZE						COST
	Total Area (Thousands of Square Feet)	Rentable Area (Thousands of Square Feet)		Floor/ Area Ratio[1]	Height		Total Development[2] (Thousands of Dollars)
		Office	Retail		Stories	Feet	
75 State Street	840	700	15	8.51	29	395	$ 240,000
Rowes/Foster Wharf	655	340	13	4.00	16	182	150,000
International Place	1,657	1,471	70	14.37	46	600	414,000
150 Federal Street	510	475	10	13.71	26	348	90,000
101 Federal Street	505	469	15	16.50	28	382	101,000
One Franklin Place	416	340	46	16.50	20	273	80,000
99 Summer Street	264	239	10	12.50	20	282	39,600
Arlington/Haddassah	486	112	45	12.60	12	130	80,000
500 Boylston Street	1,379	1,200	100	9.56	25	330	289,000
Totals	6,732	5,346	324				$1,483,600

[1] Total above-grade floor space by site area.
[2] Total cost of the project as estimated by the developer.
Source: Research Department, Boston Redevelopment Authority, 1986.

FIGURE 2-19
ESTIMATED ECONOMIC BENEFITS FROM NINE LARGE DEVELOPMENT PROJECTS IN BOSTON

Project	REVENUES (Thousands of Dollars)			JOBS	
	Additional Revenues[1]	Net New Taxes[2]	Linkage Payments[3]	Construction[4]	Permanent[5]
75 State Street	$ 8,000	$ 6,700	$ 3,100	1,400	3,220
Rowes/Foster Wharves	–	3,618	2,085	1,118	1,590
International Place	25,000	10,390	7,785	3,500	7,200
150 Federal Street	–	1,523	1,925	1,500	2,170
101 Federal Street	–	2,029	1,920	975	2,265
One Franklin Place	–	1,952	1,411	800	1,800
99 Summer Street	–	1,008	645	416	1,200
Arlington/Haddassah	–	1,411	355	975	620
500 Boylston Street	7,766	6,841	6,000	3,000	5,705
Totals	$40,766	$35,472	$25,326	13,684	25,770

[1] Proceeds to the city from the sale of surplus garages.
[2] Increase in the city tax revenue after development completion, as estimated by the BRA and the city assessor for fiscal year 1990.
[3] Development Impact Project Plan payments to the Neighborhood Housing Trust, paid in 12 equal annual installments beginning at project completion or two years after construction start.
[4] Full-time year-long jobs created by project construction, as estimated by the developer.
[5] Office and retail employees with jobs in the project.
Source: Research Department, Boston Redevelopment Authority, 1986.

FIGURE 2-20
PROJECTED TAX REVENUES: NINE DOWNTOWN PROJECTS COMPARED WITH OTHER BOSTON REALTY TAX RESOURCES[1]

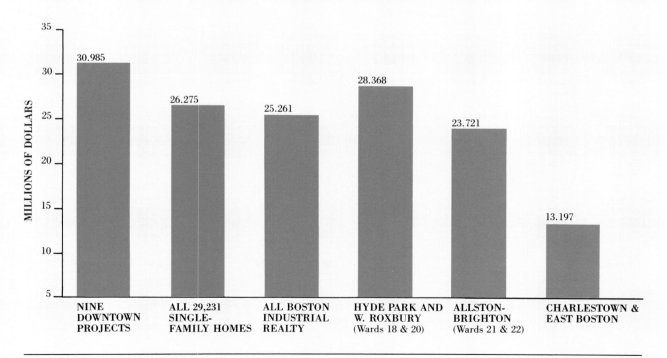

[1]Projected taxes from nine downtown projects include the estimated net increase in annual tax payments upon completion in 1990. Other taxes shown are Fiscal Year 1984 figures. Actual neighborhood taxes were somewhat less than amounts listed here due to the effect of homeowner exemptions.

FIGURE 2-21
SPECIAL INITIATIVES IN BOSTON
FUNDED BY PRIVATE DEVELOPERS

Project	Amount	Program
Arlington/Hadassah	$665,000	Low- and moderate-income housing
	$ 75,000	Maintenance of the Public Garden and Boston Common
500 Boylston Street	$500,000	Construction of Copley Place
International Place	$300,000	Boston athletic scholarship fund
	$100,000	Boston schools' jobs training program
101 Federal Street	$300,000	Neighborhood Development Bank
One Franklin Street	$250,000	Neighborhood Development Bank
150 Federal Street	$200,000	Neighborhood Development Bank
99 Summer Street	$150,000	Neighborhood Development Bank
75 State Street	$200,000	Neighborhood Development Bank

Source: Research Department, Boston Redevelopment Authority, 1986.

FIGURE 2-22
DESIGN BENEFITS IN BOSTON
PROVIDED BY PRIVATE DEVELOPERS[1]

Project	Public Amenities
Post Office Square Park	1.56-acre park, restaurant, pedestrian walkway, and clock tower.
75 State Street	Fifth-story pedestrian arcade and landscape improvements linking Quincy Market to the financial district.
Rowes/Foster Wharves	6,400-square-foot courtyard, water taxi terminal, marina and 30-foot walkways, and eighth-floor public observatory deck.
International Place	25,000-square-foot "Crystal Court" with indoor public eating area, and walkway connecting financial district to Dewey Square.
150 Federal Street	Preservation of United States Building, interior retail arcade.
101 Federal Street	Snow Place Walk, a major pedestrian link between Downtown Crossing and financial district bus drop-off, and retail arcade.
One Franklin Place	Snow Place Walkway with access to subway concourse (including access for the handicapped), preservation of Kennedy's facade, three-level retail atrium, development of MBTA concourse, and adjacent building and pedestrian improvements to Summer Street.
99 Summer Street	Major pedestrian improvements to Summer Street, and skylighted interior arcade with fountain.
Arlington/Hadassah	Improvements to Park Square fountain and to first-floor retail arcade.
500 Boylston Street	Two public courtyards lined with retail stores on Boylston Street.

[1] All projects have appropriate new treatments of sidewalks, including landscaping and trash receptacles. Maintenance of these public improvements will remain a private responsibility.
Source: Research Department, Boston Redevelopment Authority, 1986.

2-21) and design benefits also funded by developers (Figure 2-22), will clearly improve the fortunes of some Bostonians.

Who benefits from this growth has become an issue of concern to the city. Although some segments of the economy have prospered, data clearly indicate that the advantages of development have not been widespread; a large segment of Boston's population has not benefited from the New Boston.

In 1970, 16 percent of Boston's residents lived below the federal poverty level. By 1980, the rate had risen to 20 percent. In spite of the recent development and job growth, one out of every five residents was living in poverty in 1985.[20] The city's recent increase in population apparently included many indigent families and individuals. Further, the incidence of poverty was concentrated among specific population groups. According to the 1980 census, one out of every four families in Boston with children under 18 years of age had an income below the poverty level. For households headed by women with no husband present and with children under six years of age, the poverty rate reached 66 percent.

This trend was not limited to Boston. The national poverty rate rose from 11.1 percent in 1973 to 15.2 percent in 1983, and the average poverty rate in the central cities of metropolitan areas increased from 15 percent in 1975 to 19.9 percent in 1982.[21]

A substantial number of "working poor" have jobs that pay too little to provide an adequate standard of living. Part of the problem lies with Boston's high cost of living—the second highest of the 38 largest metropolitan areas in the contiguous United States—which is not factored into statistics on pov-

[20] Research Department, Boston Redevelopment Authority, "Boston and Its Neighborhoods," 1982; also Boston Redevelopment Authority, 1985 Household Survey, op. cit.
[21] Ganz, op. cit., p. 461.

erty.[22] Yet, even by national standards, the incomes of Boston workers who earn minimum or somewhat higher wages are below the poverty level. Even a successful state program, Employment and Training Choices (ET), which provides job training and placement for public welfare recipients, cannot pull clients out of the "working poor" category. ET graduates who recently found full-time jobs were earning an average of $9,800 a year, which was below the 1984 poverty line for a family of four and only $1,500 above the poverty level for a family of three.[23]

Many others in Boston have no jobs. Despite an unemployment rate that is at its lowest in 20 years, jobless rates continue to be unacceptably high for youths, blacks, and other nonwhite residents. In a 1980 survey, although the citywide unemployment rate was 6 percent, the rates were 9 percent for nonwhites, 12 percent for teenagers (16 to 19 years old), and 17 percent for minority teenagers.[24]

Pressure on the city's housing market caused by growth and development often results in higher shelter costs or displacement. In 1985, Boston suffered from a serious shortage of affordable housing due, in part, to the fact that the public and private sectors had failed to invest in the construction of low- or moderately priced units in the 1980s. At best, the rise in housing costs pulled the least advantaged residents deeper into poverty. At worst, some residents were pushed to join the 5,000 homeless people on Boston's streets.

The inequitable distribution of benefits presents challenges that the mayor's office and the city's development agencies are struggling to meet.

---

[22] U.S. Bureau of Labor Statistics, "Annual Cost of an Intermediate Budget for a Four-Person Family," Autumn 1981.
[23] "Poverty Amidst Affluence," *The Boston Globe Magazine*, December 15, 1985.
[24] Boston Redevelopment Authority, 1985 Household Survey, op. cit.

DOWNTOWN CASE STUDY PROJECTS

Five downtown projects that participated in different stages of Boston's redevelopment process exemplify the use of public mechanisms and combinations of public and private funds.

SITE LOCATIONS OF PROJECT CASE STUDIES, CITY OF BOSTON

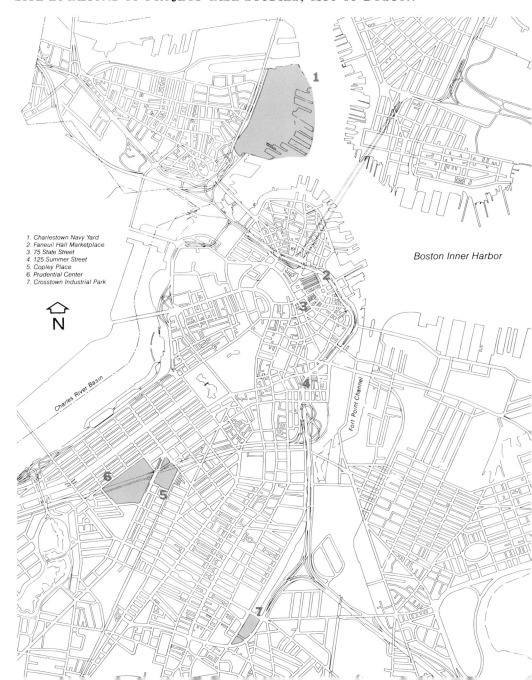

1. Charlestown Navy Yard
2. Faneuil Hall Marketplace
3. 75 State Street
4. 125 Summer Street
5. Copley Place
6. Prudential Center
7. Crosstown Industrial Park

N

Boston Inner Harbor

Charles River Basin

Fort Point Channel

Aerial view of the Prudential Center with the Charles River in the background.

PRUDENTIAL CENTER

Project Type: A 52-story, 1 million-square-foot office tower; a 25-story, 500,000-square-foot office tower; a 29-story, 1,400-room hotel; a shopping mall; three 26-story apartment buildings containing 781 units; and a 3,000-car underground parking garage in the Back Bay area of Boston.

Developer: Prudential Insurance, Inc., Boston, Massachusetts

Architecture: Charles Luchman Associates, New York, New York, and Los Angeles, California.

Construction: Perini Corporation, Boston, Massachusetts; Perini Ltd., Toronto, Canada; Walsh Construction, Inc., Boston, Massachusetts; Turner Construction Company, Boston, Massachusetts; Gilbane Company, Providence, Rhode Island.

Financing: A $250 million project financed privately by Prudential.

Status: The project was completed in August 1971.

THE PRUDENTIAL CENTER

As a pioneering project, the Prudential Center became the first office tower, the first major private investment in the New Boston era, and the first to make use of Chapter 121A of the General Laws of Massachusetts for a commercial project.

Prudential began assembling parcels and planning the project in the early 1950s and started construction in April 1959 on the 31-acre site that had been a Boston and Albany railroad yard and an exhibition building (Mechanics Hall) in the Back Bay between Boylston Street and Huntington Avenue. The development consisted of the 52-story, 1 million-square-foot Prudential tower; a 25-story, 500,000-square-foot office tower; a 29-story, 1,400-room hotel; a shopping mall including two anchor department stores; three 26-story apartment buildings containing 781 units; and three levels of underground parking for 3,000 cars. When construction started, the project was planned to be the largest commercial complex in the world. Prudential began occupying the office tower in 1964. Construction of the complex was completed in August 1971.

The $250 million project was financed privately by Prudential, which owns and manages the entire complex, except for an auditorium built with $12 million of public funds. The John B. Hynes Auditorium has been owned and managed by the Massachusetts Convention Center Authority since the city sold the property in 1982.

The novel feature of the development process was the public accommodation of a private project through special legislative and judicial actions. Because the city's only significant local source of revenue is the property tax, tax rates were high at the time and would continue to increase. Boston was willing to set a lower tax rate for Prudential, which the company had requested, if doing so ensured that the project would be built. At any rate, the railroad yard had generated minimal tax revenues, and the site had no other development prospects at the time.

Prudential and the city of Boston negotiated a 40-year payment-in-lieu-of-taxes agreement whereby Prudential would pay the city 20 percent of its gross rental income with a minimum payment of $2,082,000 per year.[25] A public hearing was held, and after the BRA Board accepted the plan, the mayor reviewed and approved it. From 1961 through fiscal year 1983, the Prudential Center paid $79 million to Boston; payments totaled $6.7 million in fiscal year 1983. Prudential was the first developer to enter into a 121A agreement for nonhousing development.

Chapter 121A of the General Laws of Massachusetts had been in effect since 1946 for the purpose of promoting housing development in blighted areas. In 1960, while construction of the Prudential Center idled, the state legislature amended Chapter 121A to allow for commercial development in blighted areas. The act provided that no subsequent legislative act could change the parts of Chapter 121A that would affect Prudential. The state's Supreme Judicial Court upheld the amended chapter on the basis that Prudential Center had a

limited life (40 years) that would not unreasonably preclude future legislative acts.[26]

A rider to the act abolished the Boston City Planning Board and entrusted its functions to the Boston Redevelopment Authority. This gave Mayor John Collins a reorganized, strengthened redevelopment agency with an aggressive planner, Edward Logue, as its director. Therefore, the 121A amendment not only gave Prudential the incentive it sought to complete the project, but it also opened the door for Mayor Collins's "90 Million Dollar Development Program" for Boston.[27]

In 1985, 14 years after completion of the project, a major redevelopment of Prudential Center is in the planning stages, including possible additions of office, retail, hotel, and residential development.

[25] Research Department, Boston Redevelopment Authority, "The Prudential Center," Parts One and Two, 1969.
[26] *Dodge* v. *Prudential Insurance Co. of America* (1962) 179 N.E. 2nd 234, 343 Mass. 375; Opinion of the Justices to the Senate and House of Representatives (1960) 168 N.E. 2nd 858, 344 Mass. 760.
[27] Whitehill, op. cit., p. 202.

FANEUIL HALL MARKETPLACE

Project Description

Faneuil Hall Marketplace consists of three parallel buildings on 6.5 acres behind historic Faneuil Hall near the waterfront, east of Government Center, between Congress Street and Atlantic Avenue. The Quincy Market building, containing 75,000 square feet of retail space, is flanked by the South Market building (with 80,000 square feet of retail and 90,000 square feet of office space) and the North Market building (with 60,000 square feet of retail and 80,000 square feet of office space).[28]

The renovated buildings opened one at a time in the summers of 1976 to 1978. The structures contain 70 shops and restaurants, and outdoor space accommodates dozens of small carts. The cost of renovation was $30 million, with an

[28] Research Department, Boston Redevelopment Authority, "Faneuil Hall Marketplace," 1978.

Strategically located to serve as the centerpiece of Boston's downtown redevelopment, Faneuil Hall Marketplace houses a variety of shops in three converted market buildings.

additional public investment of $12 million. In 1984, retail sales amounted to $85 million.

Construction of the marketplace in 1826 was an early "urban renewal" project. Under Mayor Josiah Quincy, the city filled in the town dock, creating land for the two-story, granite market house and two parallel granite warehouses, designed by Alexander Parris. Included in the $1.1 million

project were six new streets. By the 1950s, the marketplace, though active, was run-down and was surrounded by older, deteriorated commercial and industrial structures. The area limited access to Boston's waterfront and had a blighting influence on the adjacent central business district.

Development Process and Team

The city began plans for the Waterfront Urban Renewal Area in 1961. From 1967 through 1969, the Boston Redevelopment Authority employed Architectural Heritage Incorporated to study the feasibility of renovating the market buildings; during this time it also applied to the U.S. Department of Housing and Urban Development (HUD) for a $2 million restoration grant. Although the city of Boston owned the Quincy Market building, the North and South Market buildings were privately owned. The

BRA, vested with the power of eminent domain, negotiated purchase of the buildings. It then relocated 400 businesses, including wholesale produce dealers; installed new utilities; restored the exterior facades to the original design of Alexander Parris; and improved streets.

The city subsequently transferred the Quincy Market building to the BRA in order to simplify the leasing of the buildings to a developer. In 1973, the BRA designated the Rouse Company as developer and manager of the market buildings, leasing the buildings to Rouse for 99 years for $1 per year. The prime incentive in the deal was a tax letter of agreement in which the city gave the Rouse Company a three-year property tax abatement, after which property taxes would be set at 25 percent of the gross rental income. Although this would be a giveaway by today's standards, the circumstances at the time called for a strong incentive to the private developer. Retail trade in Boston had been dwindling for years, and the waterfront was underused and in poor condition. Arguably, the area needed a dramatic project, and Faneuil Hall Marketplace fit the bill.

Development Financing[29]

Substantial public financing was used to develop this project, in return for which the city shares in the overall profits of the Marketplace. The Rouse Company manages all day-to-day aspects of the Marketplace as outlined in its contractual agreement with BRA. Federal funds were used to pay for public improvements in the market area, such as upgrading of streets, sewers, and other utilities. Private construction and permanent mortgage financing were arranged by the Rouse Company to pay for the costs of construction. In lieu of

---

FANEUIL HALL MARKETPLACE

Project Type:	A festival marketplace consisting of three parallel buildings east of Government Center. It includes Quincy Market with 75,000 square feet of retail space, South Market building with 80,000 square feet of retail space and 90,000 square feet of office space, and the North Market building with 60,000 square feet of retail space and 80,000 square feet of office space.
Owner:	The Boston Redevelopment Authority.
Developer:	The Rouse Company, Columbia, Maryland.
Architecture:	Benjamin Thompson & Associates, Inc., Cambridge, Massachusetts.
Financing:	The Boston Redevelopment Authority leased the building to the Rouse Company for $1 per year for 99 years. Private development costs totaled over $30 million, including all improvements.
Status:	The project opened August 26, 1976.

---

[29] This section is excerpted from ULI– the Urban Land Institute, *Downtown Retail Development: Conditions for Success and Project Profiles* (Washington, D.C.: author, 1983), pp. 51–52.

The Rouse Company manages all day-to-day aspects of the Marketplace, endeavoring to make it a total shopping environment.

property taxes and conventional lease terms, the city acted as a limited development partner, sharing a percentage of the center's net cash flow. In 1981, Faneuil Hall generated $72 million in gross sales.

Private development costs totaled over $30 million, inclusive of all improvements and an additional 143,000 square feet of office space belonging to the project.

Status

The project opened on August 26, 1976. Basic rents now range between $30 and $45 per square foot in the North and South Markets and between $50 and $100 per square foot in the Quincy Market building, far exceeding initial projections. During its first decade of operation, Faneuil Hall Marketplace became a prime tourist attraction, generating significant unanticipated sales. Perhaps more important, the marketplace gave suburban households an exciting downtown shopping option and provided a safe daytime and evening place for young people.

COPLEY PLACE

Project Description

Copley Place is a 3.7 million-square-foot mixed-use complex, the largest of its type in Boston. The complex is located on 9.5 acres of land and in air rights space over the Massachusetts Turnpike and three railroads. The site is near Copley Square, south of Huntington Avenue, west of Dartmouth Street, east of Harcourt Street, and north of the Southwest Corridor, in the city's Back Bay area. Copley Place consists of a 370,510-square-foot retail center including a specialty department store (Neiman-Marcus), gallery shops, restaurants, theaters, and a health club; 845,000 leasable square feet of low-rise office space in four seven-story towers; an 804-room Westin Hotel; a 1,147-room Marriott convention hotel with extensive meeting facilities; 100 units of housing, one quarter of which is available for households of low and moderate income; and en-

The largest mixed-use complex in Boston, Copley Place is a 3.7 million-square-foot facility comprising two high-rise hotels, four interconnected office towers, a 100-store shopping gallery, and 104 residential units (not shown).

closed parking for 1,432 cars. Public improvements on the site included relocation of a turnpike ramp, relocation of a major water main, modifications and relocations of adjacent streets, development of glass-enclosed pedestrian bridges and related landscaping, and improvement of ventilation and lighting. The Urban Investment Development Corporation (UIDC), the developer, holds a 99-year lease on this state-owned property and manages the complex.

Development Process and Financing

The total cost for the project was $530 million. The Boston Redevelopment Authority received a $19.7 million Urban Development

Action Grant from the Department of Housing and Urban Development for site preparation and unforeseen construction costs. Fifteen million dollars of that grant was used as a mortgage loan to UIDC at 5 percent for seven years, then at 10 percent for an additional 20 years. Funds repaid under the loan agreement will go into a revolving loan fund that will provide financial assistance to community development organizations in neighborhoods of Boston. For the first four years, UIDC's rent will be $250,000 per year; in years 5 through 9 it will be $500,000; in years 10 through 14 it will be $750,000; and in year 15 it will increase to $950,000.[30]

Financing Copley Place was challenging. Because Copley Place was built on air and land rights leased for 99 years with certain subordination uncertainties, it was critical to make the lease "financeable." To eliminate any monetary defaults, all rent was prepaid (at $11.5 million), and the lease became acceptable for financing.

Each major component—the Westin Hotel, the Marriott Hotel, and the central area (retail, office, and parking)—was separately financed initially with eight- to 13-year construction loans. Permanent financing was not considered feasible at the outset because of unfavorable interest rates. Fixed-rate financing without the lender's participation was subsequently obtained for each component.

Equity for the hotel was initially provided equally by the developer and its hotel operator partners. The developer joined an equity partner for the Marriott Hotel but retained full interest in the Westin Hotel. It brought an institutional partner, one of JMB Realty's public

limited partnerships, into the office/retail component in 1983. Currently, the developer owns 50 percent of the Westin Hotel, the office/retail component, and 20 percent of the Marriott Hotel.

The residential component of Copley Place, which is comprised largely of for-sale cooperative units, was internally financed during construction with takeout commitments available to purchasers.[31]

The public sector participated to a greater extent in Copley Place than it has in any development project in Boston to date. The commonwealth of Massachusetts played a key role in developing the blighted, underused, untaxed property. In 1977, the state decided to use an iterative planning process involving community organizations and to work with a single developer instead of requesting competitive development proposals. The Office of State Planning organized the Copley Square Citizens Review Committee (CRC) in May 1977 to identify design, environmental, and other concerns of the community. The CRC also studied physical design, land use, jobs, pedestrian circulation, traffic, housing, wind and shadows, and economic impacts to prepare recommendations for project guidelines. In 1977, the state selected the Urban Investment Development Corporation to develop the challenging, complex site.

One of two hotels in the complex, the Westin Hotel includes 804 rooms.

The Citizens Review Committee issued project guidelines in September 1977 that included major revisions of UIDC's initial plan. The state used these guidelines as negotiating points for the air rights lease with UIDC. The developer completed a redesign plan in 1978 that became the basis for an environmental impact statement. Lease negotiations in 1978 resulted in a requirement that 20 percent of the construction jobs at the site go to minority workers, with financial penalties for noncompliance. Fifty percent of the construction jobs were to be set aside for Boston residents and 10 percent for women. The lease also established goals for permanent jobs in the complex: 30 percent were to be reserved for minorities, 17.2 percent for area resi-

[30] John F. Kennedy School of Government, Harvard University, "Citizen Participation at Copley Place," 1983.
[31] The previous four paragraphs were excerpted from ULI–the Urban Land Institute, *Mixed-Use Development Handbook* (Washington, D.C.: author, 1987), p. 268.

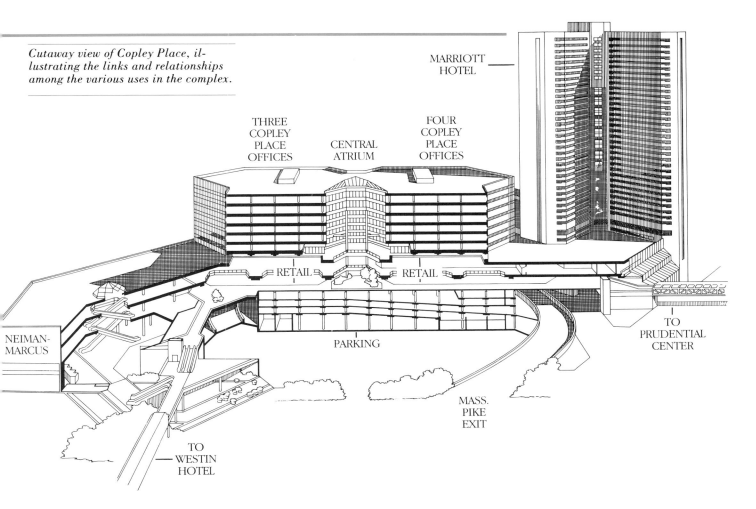

Cutaway view of Copley Place, illustrating the links and relationships among the various uses in the complex.

MARRIOTT HOTEL

THREE COPLEY PLACE OFFICES

CENTRAL ATRIUM

FOUR COPLEY PLACE OFFICES

RETAIL

RETAIL

NEIMAN-MARCUS

PARKING

TO PRUDENTIAL CENTER

MASS. PIKE EXIT

TO WESTIN HOTEL

dents affected by the development, 50 percent for women, and 50 percent for Boston residents; also, good faith efforts were to be made to employ physically impaired people. And the lease required that UIDC set aside 20,000 square feet of retail space for community-based tenants at below-market rents.

A change in prospective tenants led to another round of studies, reviews, and negotiations. In 1980, a design review subcommittee of the CRC and a BRA-appointed Design Advisory Group reviewed the details of the project and were involved in the final approval and the lease agreements of the complex.

As a result of this process, the developer made costly and dramatic changes in its plans: it developed the entire site at once instead of in stages as originally planned, added pedestrian bridges for easier access from the neighborhoods, and moved back the hotel towers

COPLEY PLACE

Project Type:	A 3.7 million-square-foot mixed-use complex, including 370,510 square feet of retail (which includes a specialty department store, gallery shops, restaurants, theaters, and a health club), 845,000 leasable square feet of office space, an 804-room Westin Hotel, a 1,147-room Marriott Hotel, 100 units of housing, and a 1,432-space parking garage.
Developer:	Urban Investment Development Corporation, Chicago, Illinois.
Primary Architecture:	Architects Collaborative, Cambridge, Massachusetts.
Construction:	Perini Corporation, Boston, Massachusetts; Turner Construction, Boston, Massachusetts; Morse, Diesel, Inc., Boston, Massachusetts.
Financing:	The total cost was $530 million, including a $19.7 million Urban Development Action Grant.
Status:	The project was completed in April 1985.

The two-level shopping gallery includes an atrium that provides views from the offices above. The shopping gallery contains a Neiman-Marcus specialty department store and the 845,000-square-foot office section of Copley Place.

on the site to reduce their visual impact and wind problems. Only the interior architecture of Copley Place was truly under the developer's control.[32]

Status

Completed in April 1985, the complex is expected to generate over $5 million a year in revenue from property taxes for the city and provide 6,280 new permanent jobs. Construction jobs averaged 650 per year for three years. The complex will also generate $15 million annually in sales and meals taxes, hotel room occupancy taxes, and income taxes from new permanent employees from the varied markets the project serves.

[32] This paragraph was excerpted from ULI–the Urban Land Institute, *Mixed-Use Development Handbook*, p. 267.

75 STATE STREET

This project exemplifies Boston's change of circumstances in the mid-1980s. In the case of 75 State Street, a private developer will take over a municipal service (public parking), make off-site improvements (installing paving, lighting, and crosswalks), and construct a first-class office complex without public funds or tax incentives.

Project Description

The Kilby Street parking garage and parcels adjacent to it make up the 60,000-square-foot site of the 75 State Street project. Among the buildings that were demolished on the site was the 14-story Fiske Building at 87–95 State Street, which will be replaced by a six-story, 78-foot-high structure that will have rounded corners similar to existing old buildings in the vicinity.

The six-story structure will form the base for a 31-story, 390-foot-tall, stepped tower set back one-half block from the street. The base will include an atrium with 15,000 square feet of retail space on the ground level and office space on the five floors above. A pedestrian walkway along a skylit court will connect the office tower to Merchants Row and the Faneuil Hall Marketplace. Office space on the site will take up 685,000 square feet.

The architects specified brick and granite for the structure, and the base will be finished in marble and accented with gold leaf. Demolition of old structures and the setback design of the tower will open up the view from State and Congress Streets to the historic Custom House Tower.

A five-level, subsurface parking garage will accommodate 700 cars, 250 more than the old Kilby Street garage. The city discontinued the use of Doane Street as a public street to make room for a depressed ramp leading into the garage.

Development Team and Financing

The 75 State Street project is being developed as a joint venture of the Beacon Companies of Boston and Equitable Real Estate, an affiliate of the Equitable Life Assurance Society of the United States. The two firms—both highly experienced with projects in the Boston area—joined forces as the 99 State Street Limited Partnership. The Beacon Construction

75 STATE STREET

Project Type:	Development of a 31-story office tower over a six-story base designed to be similar to the surrounding buildings.
Developers:	Beacon Companies, Boston, Massachusetts; and Equitable Real Estate.
Architecture:	Graham Gund Associates, Cambridge, Massachusetts; and Skidmore, Owings & Merrill, Chicago, Illinois.
Construction:	Beacon Construction Company, Boston, Massachusetts; and Turner Construction Company, Boston, Massachusetts.
Financing:	Total cost of $240 million, privately financed.
Status:	Construction began in fall, 1986; completion expected in summer, 1988.

Company, a subsidiary of the Beacon Companies, and the Turner Construction Company will build the project, with Graham Gund Associates and Skidmore, Owings & Merrill of Chicago as the architects, and Cosentini Associates as the mechanical engineers. Equitable Real Estate will finance 75 State Street, whose total cost is estimated at $240 million.

Development Process

In the early 1950s, Boston faced an out-migration of population and a shift of retail trade to suburban cities and towns. The rising popularity of the automobile put Boston, with its narrow streets and limited parking spaces, at a disadvantage with suburban towns and their emerging shopping centers. The city built four public parking garages in the downtown area in the early 1950s, hoping to attract mobile shoppers. The garages served their purpose for a time, but by the 1980s, they were outmoded and inefficient. In addition, as development in the downtown area intensified in the 1970s and early 1980s, the value of the garage sites rose far above their value as parking facilities.

Meanwhile, demand for private office space was strong in the early 1980s. The number of employees in private office space increased from 167,000 to 188,000 between 1980 and 1985, while occupied office space expanded from 33.6 million square feet in 1980 to 38.6 million square feet in 1985. When Boston's city council voted in 1983 to sell the garage sites as surplus property, prospective developers were eager to obtain such prime downtown locations. For the city, sale of the garage sites would raise much-needed revenue, foster downtown development, and potentially increase the number of parking spaces in the downtown area. For developers, the location and price were right.

The Kilby Street garage was the key parcel in the 75 State Street project. The developer was able to assemble adjacent parcels into a large enough site to make a first-class office complex feasible—and approvable in the public review process.

Five development teams submitted proposals to the Boston Redevelopment Authority in 1983 in response to the first-stage guidelines issued by the Authority. Three of the proposals called for a 500-foot tower. After evaluating the proposals, the BRA issued second-stage guidelines that included a 260-foot height limit (which, during negotiations, was eventually raised to 390 feet). The prospective developers submitted revised proposals that were reviewed by the BRA and the Boston Society of Architects. The winner of the competition was

A 31-story office tower to be constructed of brick and granite, the 75 State Street project exemplifies the new public/private cooperative effort.

the 99 State Street Limited Partnership, whose proposal included adjacent parcels of land. In 1985, the Partnership sought to acquire all of the adjacent parcels. Skidmore, Owings & Merrill joined Graham Gund as the architects, and the project was renamed 75 State Street.

In the second half of 1985, the BRA held public hearings on the proposed design and on the project's overall impact. Negotiations between the joint venture and the BRA resulted in design modifications and agreements on off-site improvements and "linkage" payments. Subsequently, the BRA

Board of Directors approved the following:

- Design plans—schematic, design development, and final drawings;
- Environmental Impact Report— how the project would affect air quality, microclimate, and traffic;
- Development Impact Report— how the project would affect downtown residents, property values, and housing in neighborhoods;
- Planned Development Area—designation for particular zoning relief; and
- Recommendation of final designation of developer.

Other public actions include the Public Facilities Commission's final disposition and deed transfer, the Boston Air Pollution Control Commission's parking permit approval, the Massachusetts Environmental Protection Agency's review, and the city archeologist's review. The Zoning Board of Appeals granted a conditional use permit consistent with the designation as a Planned Development Area. Because the development involved public property, the Public Improvement Commission and the Real Property Department also participated in the review process.

The archeological review went particularly smoothly. Unlike a number of other American cities in which a developer must adhere to strict guidelines, Boston has no ordinances relating to archeology. Therefore, provisions for archeological digs are left up to the discretion of the developers. The development team for 75 State Street was especially cooperative in following a review process that included an environmental notification form, archeological testing for the final Environmental Impact Report, and archeological monitoring of construction. The city archeologist and the Massachusetts Historical Commission reviewed the environmental documents and recommended additional testing; as the site rests on the Shawmut Peninsula's original shoreline, significant archeological findings were

possible. However, landfill and construction of wharves in the 18th century and building construction in the 19th century had apparently already disturbed any significant archeological resources.

The city will eventually receive $6.7 million annually in property taxes from the 75 State Street project and a total of $3.1 million in linkage payments over 12 years. The latter will be placed in a housing trust and used to develop neighborhood housing.

Private Issues Resolved

Two private legal issues are notable regarding the 75 State Street project. The owners and tenants of adjacent buildings valued their window views enough to become involved with the design process. They negotiated with the developers to change the design of the office tower to increase the distance between it and existing office buildings and, less important, to limit the new building height to 395 feet (390 feet will be the actual height). In addition, covenants were signed that will limit building height and the floor/area ratio (total floor space to site area) in adjacent parcels, in order to achieve conformity in the block if other buildings are constructed.

Status

The BRA Board approved the final design in June 1986. Construction of 75 State Street began in the fall of 1986 and is scheduled to be completed in the summer of 1988.

125 SUMMER STREET

The 125 Summer Street project presents another example of the recently expanded role of private development in providing public amenities and distributing economic benefits.

Project Description

The project will consist of a 22-story office building with ground-floor retail and services areas and parking space for 350 cars on five

levels below grade. Of the 448,445 square feet of gross floor area, approximately 421,000 square feet will accommodate first-class office use and the balance will include first-floor lobbies, retail stores, and a vaulted arcade providing a passageway through the block for pedestrians. The office tower, atop a five-story base, will rise to 300 feet. The project's proposed floor/area ratio is 14 to 5.

Lincoln Street will provide access to parking and three off-street loading bays. The project is designed to allow room for trucks to maneuver so that they will cause minimal disruption of vehicular and pedestrian traffic in the area.

Located on the edge of Boston's financial district, the site contains approximately 31,100 square feet. It is made up of the properties at 115–117, 119–121, 123–129, 131–135, and 137–141 Summer Street; at 13–23 South Street; at 16–20, 22–24, and 26–32 Lincoln Street; and the vacant land at 34–38 Lincoln Street.

The developer will make approximately $700,000 in landscape improvements and will construct a park on adjacent city- and state-owned land. In addition, the developer will restore the facades of four 19th century granite buildings on Summer Street, as part of the 125 Summer Street Project.

Development Team and Financing

The developer is Perry/Jaymont Venture, a joint venture between A.W. Perry, Inc., and Jaymont Incorporated. The architect is Kohn Pedersen Fox Associates. Perry/Jaymont Venture will own and manage the new building. The total development cost of $115 million will be financed privately.

Development Process

Boston's expanding economy continues to provide opportunities to develop first-class office space. Beginning in 1978, declining office vacancies and a rise in office rental

rates spurred the rehabilitation of a large amount of older commercial space. Construction of new office space peaked in 1984, when over 3 million square feet of space was completed. Demand for space kept up with the construction surge. In mid-1986, when the 125 Summer Street project was nearing approval from the Boston Redevelopment Authority, the office vacancy rate in Boston was around 8 percent, which was lower than all major markets except those of New York and Washington, D.C. Given the strong demand for more office space, office development in Boston is expected to add another 7 million square feet of space between 1986 and 1990.

In this context, Perry/Jaymont Venture assembled 10 properties and prepared plans for a new office complex. Any large building proposed in Boston typically requires relief from the city's zoning regulations. In this case, 125 Summer

Two views of the model of 125 Summer Street, which will be a 22-story office building.

125 SUMMER STREET

Project Type:	A 22-story office building with ground-floor retail and service areas and parking for 350 cars below grade.
Developer:	Perry/Jaymont Venture, Boston, Massachusetts.
Architecture:	Kohn Pedersen Fox Associates, New York, New York.
Management:	Perry/Jaymont Venture.
Financing:	Total cost of $115 million, privately financed.
Status:	Construction is scheduled to begin 1987 and to be completed 1989.

Street lies in an M-8 (restricted manufacturing) zoning district under the Boston Zoning Code. The proposed building would violate the maximum allowed floor/area ratio in that district. In addition, the site is in a restricted parking district.

To obtain zoning relief, Perry/Jaymont Venture requested approval of a development impact project plan to construct the 125 Summer Street project. As part of the plan, in accordance with Article 26A-3 of the Boston Zoning Code, the developer entered into a development impact project contribution agreement, the first approved by the BRA. Perry/Jaymont Venture agreed to contribute approximately $1.7 million through the housing creation option. The developer formed a partnership with the Chinese Consolidated Benevolent Association in order to build housing units in Chinatown, adjacent to the 125 Summer Street site. Because of a shortage of housing for a growing Asian population in Chinatown, this proved a timely agreement.

In accordance with Article 26B-3, the developer will also enter into an agreement to provide a jobs contribution grant of approximately $348,000. The developer also will submit to the BRA a resident construction employment plan and employment opportunity plan. Each plan will set goals for hiring Boston residents, minorities, and women for construction jobs and for positions in the finished office complex. These agreements will spread some of the development benefits—investment, jobs, and income—to Chinatown and to residents of other neighborhoods.

As standard elements in the development process, the developer prepared a draft environmental impact assessment and submitted schematic plans and a transportation access plan to the BRA. The latter plan included measures to mitigate the impact of the project on the city's already-congested traffic flow. An archeological review did not recommend testing for resources because construction over the last century had disturbed the site.

Public Participation

Public participation included review of the environmental impact assessment by the Massachusetts Historical Commission, the city archeologist, the city's traffic and parking department, and various state agencies. The BRA and the developer also held meetings with the Chinatown Neighborhood Council and other interested groups and persons from Chinatown and downtown areas.

Status

The 125 Summer Street project was under final BRA review in December 1986 after receiving approval from the Zoning Board of Appeals earlier that month. Construction was scheduled to begin in the first quarter of 1987 and is expected to be completed in the first quarter of 1989.

PROJECTS OUTSIDE DOWNTOWN

Development outside of the downtown area has become increasingly important as the link between investment in the downtown and jobs and income in the neighborhoods increasingly weakens. Two projects that have set important precedents in Boston are the Charlestown Navy Yard and the Crosstown Industrial Park.

CHARLESTOWN NAVY YARD

Project Description

Redevelopment of the Charlestown Navy Yard is an extensive, multidimensional undertaking in which 133 acres of surplus government property are being transformed into homes, shops, offices, historic attractions, and public spaces. The restoration and adaptation of buildings and land, when completed, will make up the largest redevelopment project in the United States. Investment in the project will eventually total more than $700 million.

When finished, the Navy Yard will, in effect, take its place as a new town in Boston. With some 7,000 residents, it will have a population larger than half of the towns in Massachusetts, and it will provide more jobs than approximately 70 percent of the towns in the state. The Navy Yard represents a vital element in Boston's plans to rejuvenate its harbor, to bring development closer to residents who need jobs and income, and to create new housing without the strains of displacement.

Map of the Charlestown Navy Yard, delineating the development areas.

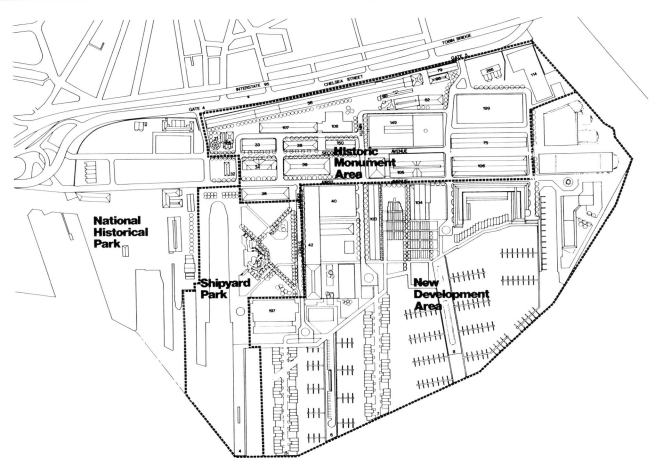

An aerial view of the Charlestown Navy Yard, where over $700 million will eventually be invested.

Located north of the downtown area across from Boston's Inner Harbor, the site is separated from the rest of Charlestown by a major elevated highway, Route 1. The Navy Yard consists of four main areas: the Shipyard Park, the Historic Monument Area, the New Development Area, and a 30-acre portion of the Boston National Historic Park. The latter, located at the southern end of the yard, includes the U.S.S. *Constitution*, docked there. The entire Navy Yard is listed on the National Register of Historic Places because of its general historic and architectural significance.

The Navy established the Charlestown Yard in 1800 and built the first United States warship there in 1813. Eventually 141 ships were built in the yard. Most of the yard's 86 structures were built in the 19th century, including solid granite workshops and warehouses and the 1,360-foot-long Ropewalk building where, for 135 years, the Navy made all of its hemp and manila rope.[33] From 1926 to 1974, the Navy Yard manufactured its standard anchor chain in the forge shop. This industrial complex employed as many as 50,000 workers during World War II and still maintained a workforce of 5,000 when the yard closed in 1974. When the U.S. Navy decommissioned the

yard, the General Services Administration sold the land and structures to the BRA.

The New Development Area comprises 57 acres of land, piers, and water, and contains both rehabilitated buildings and new construction. Developments in that area include:

- Building 42, converted in 1982 to 367 rental apartments—known as Constitution Quarters—at a cost of $28 million.
- Building 40, converted to a 367-car parking garage costing $2 million.
- The Anchorage, formerly Building 103, transformed into 112 subsidized apartments for the elderly in 1985 at a cost of $6.9 million.
- Building 197, currently being converted into 154 condominium units, 13 of which will be newly constructed townhouses, along with an adjacent 165-car parking garage, at a total development cost of $25 million.
- The Shipways, a $9.2 million building containing 21 condominiums built in 1984 and 27 condominiums, nine offices, and a 92-car garage constructed in 1986.
- Pier 6, refurbished in 1982 into Shipyards Quarters Marina I, with slips for 150 boats, at a cost of $3.5 million.
- Pier 8, a $4 million rehabilitation creating a second marina, including slips for 200 boats.
- Pier 7, the site for 64 townhouse condominiums, with parking space for 110 cars, which will be completed in 1987 and will cost $19 million.
- Parcel 4A, the site for 39 below-market-rate condominiums and outdoor space for 39 cars, to be completed in 1987 at a cost of $3.7 million.
- Parcel 5, which includes Pier 11, will eventually contain a complex of apartments, shops, a garage, and a restaurant or yacht club that will cost around $200 million.
- Piers 4 through 10 will encompass 11 more projects of varying size and scope—nine of which will involve mixed developments of housing, offices, retail space, and

---

[33] National Park Service, "Report on the History of the Proposed Boston Naval Shipyard National Historic Site," 1973, p. 5.

parking—for an undetermined cost.

The 30-acre Historic Monument Area will be devoted primarily to office and retail projects. Of the 22 buildings available for development, 12 will be devoted all or in part to offices, seven will be devoted all or in part to retail and service uses, two will be used as residences, and one will be converted to a parking garage. Four notable projects in the Historic Monument Area are:

• Building 34, the Parris Building, which, in 1986, was renovated into 36,000 gross square feet of office space and 13,000 square feet of retail space at a cost of $4.5 million.
• Building 105, the Chain Forge, which—with the exception of 30,000 gross square feet that will be used for displaying large equipment—is to be converted into a $15.6 million complex of office and retail space by 1988.
• Building 149, which, in 1987 and 1988, will be converted into office, medical laboratory, and retail space. The adjoining Building 199 was converted into a 1,388-car parking garage at a total cost of $61 million.
• Building 106, the Basilica, which is being recycled into 92 condominium units—nine of which will be subsidized units for elderly residents—including an 84-car garage, at a total development cost of $9.5 million.

Development Teams

The primary developer of the Charlestown Navy Yard is Immobiliare New England, formed in 1976 by two Italian firms—Societá Generale Immobiliare and ICOS construction company. RCC International, headed by Neil St. John Raymond, purchased Immobiliare and ICOS in July 1986. Immobiliare is the designated developer for the entire New Development Area and is developing some of the buildings in the Historic Monument Area, which are individually available to developers. The archi-

tect for Constitution Quarters in the New Development Area was Anderson Notter Feingold. Other architects in the New Development Area included Jordan Gruzen Partnership (Building 197), Childs, Bertman, Tseckares and Casendino (Shipyard Quarters and Pier 8), Anderson Associates (Pier 6), and Notter Feingold Alexander (Pier 7).

As the developer of Buildings 149 and 199, the Congress Group of Boston had the second largest investment in the Navy Yard. The architects of the buildings were Huygens and DiMella. Immobiliare bought these buildings in 1986 and is leasing them to Massachusetts General Hospital.

The Bricklayers and Laborers Non-Profit Housing Corporation and Immobiliare are codeveloping Parcel 4A. Basilica Associates, whose general partners are Paul May and NAGE Housing, Inc., of Boston, is developing Buildings 106 and 75, with Vitols Associates as the architect.

Navy Yard Plaza Development Associates, Inc., of Boston, is a joint venture of Kenney Development Co., Joseph Flaherty, and the First Charlestown Development Group. The latter is composed of business people from the Charlestown neighborhood. The Associates developed Building 33 (the Billings) and Building 34 (the Parris Building), with The Architectural Team, Inc., as the architect.

Immobiliare and the Congress Group formed a joint venture to bid for and gain designation as the developers of Building 105, the Chain Forge. The architects will be the Architects Collaborative. Immobiliare and the Barken Companies formed a joint venture to convert Building 103 to apartments, with Bruner Cott as the architect.

Financing

Redevelopment of the Charlestown Navy Yard has relied on innovative, complex financing from private and public sources. In 1977, the Boston Redevelopment Author-

ity paid the General Services Administration $1.7 million to purchase the New Development Area. Concurrently, the designated developer for the New Development Area, Immobiliare New England, loaned $1.7 million to the BRA. As the BRA conveys parcels of land to Immobiliare, the value of the parcels is deducted from the loan. The parcels will revert to the BRA after 99 years, with the exception of those that have been developed into condominiums. Immobiliare pays the BRA 4 percent of the gross sales price of the condominiums and another 4 percent of the price is deducted from the New Development Area mortgage held by Immobiliare.

The BRA made site improvements on streets, sidewalks, lighting, and landscaping, with a total of $7 million obtained from the Economic Development Administration, the Bureau of Outdoor Recreation, the Land and Water Conservation Fund, the Massachusetts Coastal Zone Management Coastal Facilities Improvement Program, the city of Boston, and the U.S. Department of Housing and Urban Development through an Urban Development Action Grant (UDAG). The BRA has spent an additional $1.6 million on site improvements and will spend $2.1 million in 1987 on a third phase of improvements.

In developing the Anchorage apartments for the elderly (Building 103), the joint venture obtained a UDAG for $1.6 million, supplemented by a grant of $175,270 from the State Housing Assistance Rental Partnership (SHARP) program. The Massachusetts Housing Finance Agency, which administers the SHARP program, provided lower interest rates for the venture's bank loans, and Immobiliare placed $450,000 in escrow as a rent moderation fund. The combination of these four elements has kept rents at moderate levels.

The below-market-rate condominiums in Parcel 4A were financed with the help of a donation of land development rights from

Immobiliare and the BRA and a contribution of $500,000 from Immobiliare.

Otherwise, the redevelopment projects in the Navy Yard to date have been privately financed. Because the Navy Yard is listed on the National Register of Historic Places, developers of buildings within the yard have been eligible for the tax advantages related to historic buildings defined in the Federal Tax Reform Acts of 1976, 1981, and 1986.

Development Process

The development process began with the closing of the Navy Yard in 1974. The loss of jobs and the historic value of the site motivated the city to begin creating new resources for employment while also preserving the historic character of the area. After negotiations and reviews involving the National Park Service, the Navy, the Bureau of Outdoor Recreation, the General Services Administration, and the Boston Redevelopment Authority,

the land and buildings became available for redevelopment in 1976. The Bureau of Outdoor Recreation sold the Shipyard Park site to the BRA for $1 on the condition that it be used only for public recreational purposes. The General Services Administration transferred the 30-acre Historic Monument Area, including 22 buildings, to the BRA for $1, contingent upon the buildings' being preserved, developed, and maintained according to strict guidelines. The guidelines were formed in an agreement between the BRA and the National Advisory Council on Historic Preservation.

The BRA incorporated the Navy Yard into the Charlestown urban renewal plan in 1976 after preparing a tentative development plan the year before. Anderson Notter Feingold, under contract to the BRA, drew up a second master plan for the Navy Yard in 1978. At present, the Navy Yard is included in the BRA's Harborpark Plan, which seeks to combine private development with public benefits

along the entire length of Boston's waterfront. Current Navy Yard plans emphasize housing in the New Development Area with provisions for low- and moderate-income residents. The Historic Monument Area remains targeted for office and commercial uses.

Development in the Navy Yard was a challenge because the area had been off limits to the public for generations and therefore had low visibility. Rather than forging ahead on an extensive development program, Immobiliare New England renovated and constructed buildings in phases in the New Development Area, using revenues from early phases to kick off subsequent phases while testing the market for housing, offices, and retail space. The presence and early success of Immobiliare in the New

Captain's Quarter, an example of the 19th century architecture in the Charlestown Navy Yard.

Lively events are scheduled in the Charlestown Navy Yard to familiarize the public with the area. Harborpark Day has now become an annual Boston event.

Development Area encouraged other developers to invest in the Historic Monument Area. The pace of development was slow in the early 1980s, but as Immobiliare moved into a second phase and other developers began their projects, construction accelerated in 1985 and 1986. In the latter year, projects amounting to $66.2 million in construction costs were completed.

As part of the development process, the BRA received commitments for linkage payments of $3.5 million from the two large developers in the Historic Monument Area. It will set aside this money in a housing trust to support construction of affordable housing. Also, smaller developers in the area will contribute $0.50 per square foot of development to a fund for community projects in Charlestown.

Public Participation

Public participation in the Navy Yard redevelopment began with an advisory committee comprising Charlestown residents and other interested parties. The committee played an early role in the plans and guidelines set by the BRA. Although the committee is currently inactive, the BRA holds several public meetings annually concerning the project. The Harborpark Advisory Committee also reviews plans for the Navy Yard.

Involving the community is an important goal of the development program. The BRA designated a group of Charlestown merchants to develop two buildings in the Historic Monument Area. The BRA required one of the larger developers to provide space for an employment recruiting office through which merchants will seek residents of Charlestown and other parts of Boston as employees for commercial tenants. In addition, the Charlestown Community Development Corporation operates, under a four-year lease, a marina that produces revenue for further development.

Status

By the end of 1986, private developers and the BRA had invested nearly $240 million in the New Development Area and in the Historic Monument Area. Net new taxes totaled $4,390,200. Lease payments to the BRA amounted to $1,171,782 a year, plus a percentage of the operating revenue from commercial projects and a percentage of the sales price from condominiums. Developers had committed payments of an additional $3,813,700 to the linkage/community fund. Construction jobs totaled 3,502, measured in person-years. The project will eventually support around 5,400 jobs in offices, research facilities, retail stores, restaurants, hotels, and other commercial activities.

Construction, planning, and review were proceeding at a steady pace as 1986 ended. Total development investment appeared likely to reach $700 million early in the 1990s.

CROSSTOWN INDUSTRIAL PARK

The Crosstown Industrial Park is a 38-acre site in the Roxbury section of Boston. It straddles Albany Street, is crossed by Melnea Cass Boulevard, and is across from Boston City Hospital. The Economic Development and Industrial Corporation of Boston (EDIC/Boston) and the Community Development Corporation of Boston, Inc. (CDC of Boston—a minority-owned, community-based, nonprofit organization), jointly developed the park in 1978 for light industrial manufacturing. Thus, it provides another example of public investment paving the way for private investment in a project that generates jobs.

The project was conceived in 1975 to shore up Boston's severely eroded manufacturing base, attract new industry to the inner city, and provide accessible, skill-enhancing jobs for inner-city residents. The development process on the first section began in 1978 with EDIC/Boston's assembly of parcels of land owned by the Boston Redevelopment Authority, the city of Boston, and the state's Department of Public Works. With a $2.07 million Title I grant from the Economic Development Administration (EDA)

49

Ashwani Vasishth and Shakeel Hossain

The USS Constitution is moored at the Charlestown Navy Yard.

of the U.S. Department of Commerce, $500,000 from the city of Boston, and $350,000 from the Community Development Block Grant program, EDIC/Boston cleared land and relocated streets, utilities, and commercial businesses. The CDC of Boston also received a $213,000 Technical Assistance Grant from EDA for feasibility studies and planning. The state constructed an $8 million roadway, Melnea Cass Boulevard.

In 1979, the Digital Equipment Corporation leased a seven-acre site in the first parcel and constructed a 62,000-square-foot, $2.9 million manufacturing plant on part of the site, creating 150 jobs by 1980 and 200 more to date. The company has an option to buy the property and has plans to expand the facility by another 62,000 square feet. The significance of this project is compounded by the fact that two other high-technology companies followed Digital Equipment Corporation's lead by locating

The Crosstown Industrial Park occupies 38 acres located in the Roxbury section of Boston.

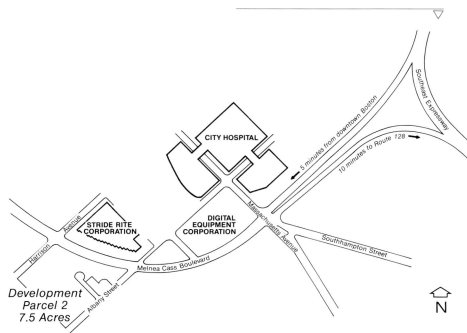

parts of their operations on the outskirts of the downtown, near neighborhood labor forces.

Development of 7.5 acres in the second parcel includes an old factory building—the four-story, 46,000-square-foot Baltimore Brush Building. CDC of Boston is rehabilitating the factory for light industry and research and development at a cost of $2.75 million. The project is funded by a $1.5 million public works grant from EDA, $500,000 from the Community Development Finance Corporation, a $500,000 loan guarantee from the Cities Neighborhood Development

The Digital Equipment Company was one of the first companies to locate in the Crosstown Industrial Park.

Fund, and $250,000 from the Local Initiatives Support Corporation. Construction began in spring 1987 and is scheduled to be completed in fall 1987.

In 1985, Morgan Memorial Goodwill Industries purchased 6.23 acres of land for $575,000, on which it will construct a 130,000-square-foot, single-story building as its headquarters. The $6 million cost of the project will be funded privately, mostly from Morgan Memorial's sale of its buildings elsewhere in Boston. The development will retain 240 jobs while creating 80 additional jobs. Morgan Memorial trains for jobs more than 300 disabled clients annually and intends to gear its services to take advantage of the new and longstanding manufacturing plants in the vicinity. The city stands to gain about $250,000 in tax revenue from the sale of Morgan Memorial's old buildings.

In addition, the M. Abelman Company, a local paint and painting supply distributor, will construct a 12,000-square-foot building on 1.23 acres of land in parcel 2. The $350,000 project will be funded by the Boston Local Development Corporation, which will contribute $105,000, and by private sources.

Crosstown Industrial Park has not generated as many new jobs as it might have if companies outside of Boston had located operations there. Nevertheless, the project has proved laudable in accommodating local employers who are expanding and in providing local residents with jobs and training opportunities. The nearby Hubert H. Humphrey Occupational Resource Center and an underemployed, minority labor force lend strength to the location of the Crosstown Industrial Park and increase the potential that its tenants will expand.

LESSONS LEARNED

Foremost, the development process in Boston has demonstrated that public investment and initiatives can generate a more than equal amount of private investment in developments that benefit the public to varying degrees. The city of Boston and the commonwealth of Massachusetts expended substantial public resources on improvements to infrastructure in projects like the Prudential Center and Copley Place. The city also made tax concessions for projects such as the Prudential Center and Faneuil Hall Marketplace, all of which were key incentives for development. Those concessions may be considered a cost of development, measured in tax revenue forgone in initial and later years. The public resources, spent or forgone, were well invested, however, in light of the ultimate scale of development and job growth that they helped bring to Boston's downtown, as well as the incentives they provided to private investment generally.

The expenditures and the planning efforts of Boston, its development agencies, and the state and local community development organizations were vital to the development of the downtown and adjacent areas. In particular, the city's and state's abilities to assemble parcels of land and conduct orderly, publicly reviewed development encouraged private investment in the 1970s and, in the mid-1980s, may have slowed development, thus preventing the overbuilding seen in some cities.

Planning, design guidelines, and historic preservation go hand-in-hand with the monitoring of the private office and hotel markets to maximize the success rate of approved development projects. Had Boston and its citizens not influenced the size, appearance, type, and location of private development, the city could have looked much different in 1985. Even so, Bostonians have harshly criticized the design, height, and function of a number of approved development projects.

The federal government's role in Boston's development process was immense in the 1960s. Federal agencies bankrolled the city's extensive urban renewal program and the creation of Government Center. Federal grants in the 1970s were in-

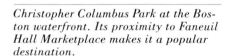

Christopher Columbus Park at the Boston waterfront. Its proximity to Faneuil Hall Marketplace makes it a popular destination.

Ashwani Vasishth and Shakeel Hossain

FIGURE 2-23

CHANGES IN FEDERAL AID TO THE CITY OF BOSTON:
FY 1980–1985 IN CONSTANT FY 1985 DOLLARS
(Millions of Dollars)

Federal Revenue Source	FY 1980	FY 1985	Difference Number	Percent
Community Development Block Grants	$ 34.4	$22.4	$ −12.0	$ −35
General Revenue Sharing	30.9	18.5	−12.4	−40
Jobs and Training			−59.9	−91
CETA (FY 1980)	65.9	–		
JPTA (FY 1985)	–	6.0		
Urban Development Action Grants	31.0	22.6	−8.4	−27
Economic Development Administration	9.1	0.1	−9.0	−99
Housing			−16.8	−82
Sections 8 and 312 (FY 1980)	20.5	–		
Rental Rehab and HoDAG (FY 1985)	–	3.7		
Total	$191.8	$73.3	$−118.5	$ −62

Source: City of Boston, Office of Intergovernmental Relations, various reports, 1983–1985.

strumental in developing Copley Place and Crosstown Industrial Park. After the closing of the Charlestown Navy Yard, the federal government gave the city the yard's valuable land and structures, which have since been extensively redeveloped. Aside from its support in the construction of industrial and commercial structures and public facilities, the federal government invested hundreds of millions of dollars in housing for Boston's residents from the 1950s through the 1970s. While the benefits of downtown development did not reach all parts of Boston, housing development—public housing and subsidized units—was concentrated in the neighborhoods where it was most needed.

The shift in the federal budget toward a military buildup in the 1980s, coupled with cutbacks in domestic urban programs, drastically reduced aid to economic development in Boston. Measured in fiscal year 1985 dollars, federal receipts in Boston for six major programs in fiscal year 1981 were $192 million. (See Figure 2-23.) By fiscal year 1985, those programs amounted to only $73 million, a drop of $119 million, or 62 percent. The reduced federal role created major fiscal obstacles for the city

and the state in the development process and weakened the link between development benefits and the neighborhoods.

In the 1980s, as private investment in downtown Boston expanded rapidly, with less need for public incentives, another lesson became clear: private developers alone could not meet public needs. In the midst of a serious shortage of affordable housing in Boston, private development money flowed toward commercial projects, which yielded much larger returns. Although many Boston residents were unemployed or underemployed, private developments created jobs that typically required considerable skills and education or, alternatively, that paid low wages with little chance for advancement.

Parking spaces, open space, and public access are important elements of development projects and must be made available in adequate amounts to the public. Consequently, Boston increasingly is negotiating with developers to provide privately funded public needs and amenities as part of development projects.

Overall, the returns of the development process to Boston have been tremendous. Hefty increases

in jobs, income, and tax revenue have benefited many of the city's residents. Particularly fortunate were young adults whose skills and education qualified them for many of the newly created jobs, and, in turn, allowed them to buy the ever-more expensive real estate and to enjoy the improved cultural and entertainment offerings of Boston. Many of those who benefited lived outside the city and carried their earned income home with them. Property owners, in general, prospered as development drove up property values.

Those who did not gain from the redevelopment activities were residents of Boston's neighborhoods who could not take advantage of the new opportunities. Most notably, they have been the working poor who rented residential units and were displaced as property values rose when their neighborhoods were redeveloped. To spread the benefits of development, the city must establish guidelines for private development, negotiate with developers for the provision of public amenities, and continue to initiate solutions to the problems of housing shortages, underemployment, and lack of equal access to economic opportunities for a large proportion of its residents.

LOUISVILLE

LOUISVILLE
A COMMENTARY

R eading George Yater's highly accurate account of the developments in Louisville from the late 1960s to date was for me like a trip down memory lane. Born and raised in Louisville, I had enjoyed, as a youth, the old pre–World War II Louisville with its vibrant downtown and pleasant residential areas, all of which were within easy reach of the central business area. Shopping was done downtown. The major restaurants, theaters, cinemas, and hotels were all downtown. High school students from all parts of the community went downtown for weekend fun. Little did we realize as teenagers that our city would in the next 20 years (from 1944 to 1964) undergo radical change.

The secret of Louisville's success has been the joint efforts of talented, dedicated, and tenacious business and government leaders.

Leaving Louisville in 1944 to enter military service, I did not return to live there permanently until 1955. During those 11 years, I had lived for periods in New Haven, Connecticut, New York City, and Washington, D.C. I had also visited London, Paris, Rome, and other cities in Europe. With this exposure and with the memory of an earlier Louisville, I returned to Louisville to start my private law practice, totally unprepared for the substantial and devastating changes that the city had undergone during my absence.

Yater chronicles the causes and the results of these changes. Downtown Louisville was dying while the suburbs and their shopping centers were prospering. Many of us felt that without the resurrection of our downtown, Louisville, as we had known it, would also die. The city could not compete for economic growth without a viable downtown. Fortunately, this feeling was shared by several older Louisville leaders and by many who returned to the city after World War II to assume positions of prominence and power in the business and government sectors.

The secret of Louisville's success from 1965 through 1985, as reported by Yater, depended on public/private partnership. And indeed, by working together, many talented, dedicated, and tenacious government and business leaders have turned the city around.

Louisville has always been known as the home of the Kentucky Derby; the challenge was to make it known as the home of thriving large and small companies.

During this period of activity, the city's archaic laws prevented the mayor of Louisville from succeeding himself in office. Thus, with the city's chief executive officer limited to a term of four years, Louisville lacked the continuity of municipal leadership found in Atlanta, Chicago, Milwaukee, and other cities in which strong mayors have led the development of their cities. The governor of Kentucky is also limited to a four-year term; again, this was unfortunate because in Louisville's public/private partnerships, governors have played major roles. Further, Louisville had no single corporate entity that could alone provide new development, such as Ford in Detroit or Hallmark in Kansas City. Because of these obstacles, it was incumbent upon business and private sector leaders to join together to provide the continuity and momentum needed to revitalize the city. Moreover, even though they came and went, elected officials provided the support and leadership needed while in office.

I was fortunate enough to have been actively involved in the redevelopment effort throughout this period. Each segment of George Yater's narrative recalls vivid memories of the struggle to bring each of the projects to fruition—the Fourth Avenue Mall, the Convention Center, the Hyatt Regency, the Galleria, the Kentucky Center for the Arts, and many others. Each project had its own set of problems that demanded solutions. Nothing was easy. But government and business leaders remained united throughout the difficult times.

Although governors, mayors, county judges, and corporate and professional leaders changed through the years, the goal of revitalizing the community remained constant—as did the partnership of federal, state, and local officials with leaders in the business community. Not one of the successes discussed in Yater's report could have been accomplished without the joint efforts of the government and private sectors. From land acquisition to financing, to construction, to completion, the public/private sectors had to function as a unit—not always an easy task, but one that was achieved.

Like most urban communities in the United States, Louisville still has many problems to overcome. Its governmental systems still need revisions, although, through amendment to the Kentucky constitution, the mayor may now serve three successive four-year terms, and, by compact, the city and county governments may operate joint agencies and share tax revenues. Louisville has not been as successful as some neighboring cities in attracting new and expanding white-collar businesses or in replacing lost blue-collar jobs. Public housing needs attention. The riverfront needs to undergo rapid and continuing development. And so on. But I believe the city's strengths far outweigh its weaknesses.

Louisville is today a great place in which to live and to raise a family. Its educational system, from its nursery schools through its

The Galleria brought people back downtown to shop.

colleges and universities, now has (after experiencing some difficulties in the past) excellent ratings. Its arts programs are exemplary and stand as models for the country. Louisville's theater program, symphony orchestra, resident opera and ballet companies, art museums, and other cultural facilities rank with the finest in the nation. Its public parks remain outstanding. Living costs are among the most attractive in the nation. Labor/management relations have never been better. The medical school of the University of Louisville and associated hospitals continue to gain worldwide respect. The city's location remains an asset to growth. And most important of all, the people are among the most hospitable.

If the city can maintain and continue the spirit of the public/private partnership that has been the hallmark of its past successes, Louisvillians, new and old, can look forward to a bright future. "My Old Kentucky Home" is alive and well in Louisville.

Gordon B. Davidson is managing partner with the law firm of Wyatt, Tarrant & Combs in Louisville, Kentucky.

INTRODUCTION

In a 1975 study for the National Tax Association, The Brookings Institution listed Louisville as the 16th "most distressed" city in the United States. Yet in 1985, the *Cincinnati Enquirer* took a look at its downriver neighboring city and found Louisville moving "from Midwestern obscurity to international renown." The *1985 Places Rated Almanac* ranked Louisville as the ninth best city in the nation in quality of life. It is gaining attention for its postmodern architecture, its imaginative adaptive use of its stock of 19th century commercial buildings, the revitalization of its older residential neighborhoods, and its commitment to the performing arts. It is also becoming known as a center for medical research (especially for work in re-attachment of severed limbs and artificial heart implants), and as a leader in downtown redevelopment, with some $1 billion invested since 1970. Its 20-year population decline stabilized in 1982 at about 290,000 and now appears to be rising slowly.

All of this constitutes a rather dramatic departure for a city that a few years ago—according to a chamber of commerce nationwide survey of business executives—registered only a blank image in the American mind. If Louisville was known for anything it was for the Kentucky Derby, and perhaps as the city that produces bourbon whiskey, cigarettes, and Louisville Slugger baseball bats. To understand the dynamics of change, one must know something of the background of Kentucky's largest metropolitan area, which began life during the American Revolution as the farthest western outpost of American settlement.

BACKGROUND

Louisville grew prosperous during the 19th century and by 1850 was America's 10th largest city, due primarily to its strategic location at the Ohio River falls, which created the only natural stop in the flow of navigation on the 1,000 miles of inland waterway between Pittsburgh and New Orleans. The city's economy was built on mercantilism: wholesaling, warehousing, and distribution, with only a scattering of manufacturing. As railroads cut into the profitable river trade and the shipment of goods and people around the falls in the years following the Civil War, Louisville made a deliberate—and successful—transition to a manufacturing economy, plowing its accumulated profits from trade into factories. Wholesale trade and distribution continued to be important, however (and still are), especially in trade with southern markets. Louisville countered competition from cities by building the Louisville & Nashville Railroad with substantial local government participation, pushing it eventually to the Gulf of Mexico. The L&N was, in the words of one historian:

Churchill Downs, site of the Kentucky Derby.

"Louisville's imperial weapon."[1] Although Louisville lost its ranking as the 10th largest city with the expansion of the trans–Mississippi West, it continued its pattern of growth based on its heavy blue-collar employment.

During World War II, the manufacturing sector gained strength through a proliferation of war-related industries, particularly in the fields of metal fabrication and chemical processing. The expansion continued after the war, easily enabling Louisville and Jefferson County to remain the leading industrial center in the Southeast, a position they still hold, despite the erosion of the manufacturing base. In 1983, the city and county jointly were ranked 19th nationally in industrial activity, with output valued at more than $12 million. Oddly, bourbon, tobacco, and baseball bats, although best known, have always constituted only a small segment of industrial products.

Louisville, commonly thought of as southern (an image it once cultivated assiduously as a sales tool in southern markets), is actually a border city. The riverfront looks north across the Ohio River to Indiana, three of whose counties are part of the Louisville seven-county metropolitan statistical area. Today, the city is oriented more to the Midwest than to the South. Local market researchers have found that, as one says: "Most residents . . . don't want to think of themselves as stereotyped Southerners nor to be identified with what they consider the brash pushiness of East Coast cities."[2] As a manufacturing center, Louisville became midwestern in temper and pace, and since the mid-1970s has suffered the same employment decline in smokestack industries that has marked the Midwest, with manufacturing industries becoming se-

verely crippled by foreign imports or moving to lower-wage, open-shop states to the south.

With robotization (which has occurred at General Electric's huge Appliance Park and at Ford Motor's two large truck-assembly plants), factory employment will probably continue to shrink even if production increases. The Louisville area's diversified manufacturing base, however, provides some cushion against the shocks felt by those cities depending largely on one industry. In 1950, a combined total of 65,000 blue- and white-collar workers held manufacturing jobs, representing 40 percent of nonagricultural employment in the city and county. Industrial jobs continued to increase in number, peaking at 107,000 in 1974, then steeply declining to 74,000 in 1980, representing 24.8 percent of non-agricultural employment. There was a slight uptick to 77,000 in 1982 (shown in the last U.S. Census figures available).

Total employment continued to rise, however, from 200,000 in 1960 to 268,000 in 1983, indicating a concurrent increase in other sectors, particularly those of finance, real estate, and insurance, whose share rose from 20 percent of non-agricultural employment in 1960 to 32 percent in 1980. This change underscored the community's shift from a blue collar–dominated to a white collar–dominated workforce, employed primarily in varied professional services.

After reaching a peak of over 390,000 in 1960, Louisville's population began to decline, losing 7.9 percent during the 1960s, and falling into a steeper dive during the 1970s with a 17.5 percent loss. Thus, over a 20-year period, the city lost nearly 100,000 residents, following the pattern of other older, mature cities. (Surprisingly, although it was the frontier of American settlement beyond the Allegheny/Appalachian range, Louisville is only 50 years younger than Baltimore and almost 25 years older than Buffalo.) Departing residents went to suburban areas be-

yond the city's corporate boundaries, where garden apartments, single-family housing tracts, and lower taxes—plus a developing expressway system that made once-remote areas easily accessible—produced a rising population curve. By the mid-1970s, the population in the county outside the city for the first time exceeded that within the city. The Louisville public schools, losing students and operating at a deficit, were forced to merge with the county schools in 1974. The county's population edge continued to widen and by 1980 had reached some 100,000. Although the "city limits" signs are the only visible evidence demarcating the city from the urbanized areas beyond, Louisville is hamstrung by state law limiting the annexation of areas by cities of the "first class" (which applies only to Louisville), and cannot easily expand its boundaries to take in what is actually normal outward growth of the city. Yet, despite being separated politically, the city and county form one geographic and economic unit with a 1980 population of some 685,000. This unit in turn constitutes the center not only of the metropolitan area but also of the 15-county primary marketing area, in which it commands 75 percent of the employment.

As the county urbanized and the city lost population, Louisville's central business district suffered painfully: shopping malls, motels, office buildings, and other facilities that in an earlier era would have been located in an expanding CBD were instead developed in the suburbs. After a major office project was built in 1953, commercial construction in the CBD virtually came to a halt for nearly 15 years. Many downtown stores (including two major department stores) closed, along with hotels, first-class cinemas, restaurants, and other amenities. The number of retail establishments declined from 811 in 1963 to 387 in 1982. (The numbers are somewhat overstated, as the Census Bureau's definition of the CBD encompasses a larger

[1] Leonard Curry, *Rail Routes South* (Lexington, Kentucky: University Press of Kentucky, 1969).
[2] George H. Yater, "Who's Looking at Us and Why," *Louisville* magazine, October 1982, pp. 30–36.

area than does the local definition of 103 square blocks, but the trend is clear.) Many older, often sound, buildings fell to the wrecking ball to make way for parking lots, which peppered the CBD like so many missing teeth. When Maurice D. Johnson (who became one of the key players in the revitalization of downtown) arrived in Louisville to take command of Kentucky's second-largest bank, he found the CBD "gray and growing grayer."

Louisville thus was faced with a set of interrelated problems:
• An economic change that was altering the traditional manufacturing/employment base throughout the city and county.
• An exodus of city residents (generally those who were better educated and earned higher incomes) to suburban areas with a consequent decline of city property values and of property maintenance in some older residential neighborhoods.
• The decline of the CBD, the traditional heart of the metropolitan region.
• A fragmented government structure that did not reflect the fact that urbanization of the county represented normal growth of the city, and that fostered a sense of mutual distrust between the county and the city.

The strategy to deal with these problems evolved slowly (and often painfully) over more than 20 years. Not all the problems have been solved, and two governmental units still exercise jurisdiction over the geographic and economic unity of city and county. However, a city/county compact, agreed to by both government entities and approved by the state legislature in March 1986, took effect January 1, 1987, and is expected to alleviate, at least temporarily, many of the nagging issues. The compact freezes Louisville boundaries for 12 years, putting an end to suburban fears of annexation. The two governments will also share occupational tax income under a complex formula as a step toward ending competition for new jobs and the tax revenue that they generate.

In addition, the county will increase its contribution to joint city/county agencies' funding by nearly $1 million annually, and a joint economic development office will replace the two competing development agencies. The mayor and county judge/executive will appoint the directors of agencies that have hitherto had independent boards, such as the library and transit systems. Although some believe that this change could politicize such agencies in the future, the mayor and county judge believe that tighter controls will enable them to better control budgets squeezed by cuts in federal funding. The Louisville Chamber of Commerce, in a poll of its members, found 76 percent in favor of the compact.

A strong public/private partnership has emerged that takes on major projects requiring coordinated planning. This, in turn, encourages private developers (some of whom were active in suburban areas) to plunge into renovation and rehabilitation work on their own, both in center city and older residential areas.

As it did after the Civil War, Louisville is once again facing the issue of changing its economic direction. Revitalization of the CBD and neighborhoods is seen as part of the overall strategy for keeping the economy healthy by aiding the transition from a manufacturing base to a white-collar base built on the information/service sector. An attractive community with an above-average quality of life will have a strong competitive edge in this transformation.

Thus, Louisville hopes to provide the setting that will nurture local enterprises and attract new ones of this stripe, including regional offices and national headquarters. To do this, the city must provide the lifestyle that urban professionals want: a community strong in the arts and recreational opportunities, which also has excellent schools and quality housing in the urban core. The central city must act as the nucleus of this redevelopment, providing the office space, the cultural amenities, the shopping facilities, and the auxiliary services that one expects in the heart of a metropolitan area with a population of more than 900,000.

This approach would have been more difficult (if not impossible) without the strong services and financial base that were developing as industrial operations were declining. Louisville's banks, which form the core of the region's financial center, helped lead downtown revitalization. Representative of new economic activity are such corporate names as Humana, a private hospital-operating company; Capital Holding, one of the nation's largest insurance holding companies; BATUS, the holding company for Marshall Field, Saks Fifth Avenue, and other properties of British-American Tobacco Company; Mercer-Meidinger, a nationwide employee-benefits consulting firm; Kentucky Fried Chicken; and Chi-Chi's, the Mexican restaurant chain.

These companies join already established corporations, but the new players, headquartered in Louisville and often founded there, have a particularly strong stake in the city's economic health and quality of life and many have readily committed significant amounts of corporate cash to the public/private partnership.

Manufacturing continues to be one of the community's development priorities. New industrial jobs (1,972 in 1984 and 2,415 in 1985) are created annually, slowing—but not reversing—the general downward trend. One of the tools used to stimulate new manufacturing and related activities is the city-sponsored enterprise zone created in 1983—the first to be established in Kentucky and among the first in the nation. Now embracing 6.7 square miles, the zone had its beginning in a 1976 study by the City/County Planning Commission, which found that the average available industrial site in the city offered fewer than four acres, while an average site in the county outside the city offered more than 20 acres. By 1979, the study had triggered a concrete proposal to use land south of Union Station that was no longer used for railroad purposes.

In 1981, when it seemed that federal legislation providing tax incentives to businesses in enterprise zones would be approved, the city purchased 14 acres of vacant land from the Louisville & Nashville Railroad (now part of CSX Transportation) and launched Station Park as an incubator area to stimulate small-scale entrepreneurship. A federal grant from the Economic Development Administration paid the $1.2 million purchase price. The city allocated an additional $750,000 in Community Development Block Grant funds to improve streets and utilities in the area. An adjacent four-acre tract was soon added to Station Park and all 18 acres were sold to new or expanding small businesses within a year, with one purchaser acquiring 11 acres.

Although the expected federal legislation did not materialize, in 1982, the Kentucky legislature authorized local governments to set up enterprise zones with a life of 20 years, which eliminated some state taxes and allowed local jurisdictions to eliminate others. Under the legislation, Station Park became an enterprise zone to which acreage in nearby low-income areas was added to create a 172-acre zone.

In late 1983, the zone was greatly enlarged to encompass its present 6.72 square miles, extending along the railroad corridor from the Ohio River south to the airport. The new zoning category of EZ-1 was established, permitting parcels to be switched between commercial and manufacturing categories without the normally required Planning Commission review and recommendation to the Board of Aldermen. Parcels now zoned for residential use will remain in that category, but will become EZ-1 if sold.

To be eligible for tax benefits, new businesses must draw at least 25 percent of their employees from within the zone, or from among individuals who have been unemployed or have received welfare payments for at least three months. Businesses that were within the zone before it was created can take tax benefits if they launch new activities that generate a 20 percent increase in employment or a 20 percent increase in capital investment.

State tax benefits include exemption from sales tax on purchase

LOUISVILLE DESIGNATED ENTERPRISE ZONE

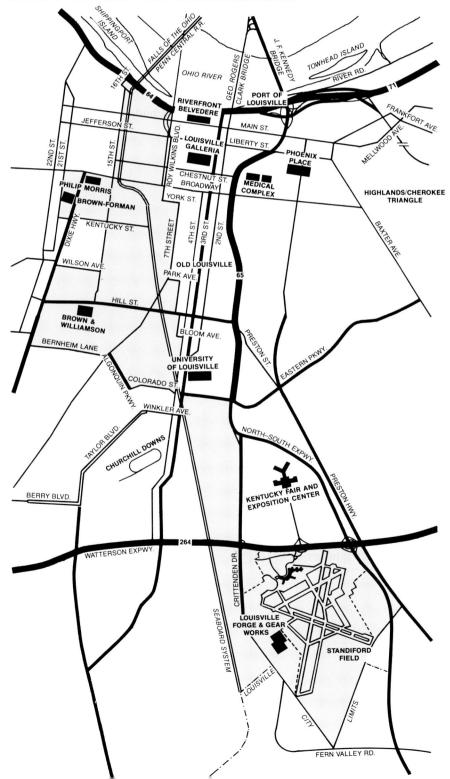

of machinery, equipment, and building materials; waiver of the capital gains tax on sales of real estate and of income tax paid by lenders on the interest from loans made to certified businesses in the zone. City tax benefits include waiver of building permit fees on new structures, a five-year moratorium on property taxes for new manufacturing facilities, and a five-year moratorium on commercial structures that are at least 25 years old and whose improvements and rehabilitation represent at least 10 percent of their assessed value.

A study by the Small Business Administration in 1986 found that although employment in the area now within the zone decreased from 55,822 in 1980 to 46,482 in 1984, the loss was in the larger existing companies (primarily tobacco, textiles, and leather businesses). The new, smaller enterprises had expanded.

Through early 1986, the state had certified 78 companies for tax benefits, of which five are no longer in the program. Of the 73 active enterprises, 38 are new to the zone and 35 have expanded, creating 783 new jobs that generate an estimated $2.15 million in city taxes. In 1986, 40 percent of employment was concentrated in manufacturing, 30 percent in service occupations or wholesaling, and 30 percent in retailing.

Louisville has a number of advantages in dealing with its overall problems. Because it is a city of medium size, issues are manageable. It has a close-knit business community and many young leaders. It has pockets of poverty and blight, but no vast stretches. City government, while operating on pinched budgets at times, has never faced a fiscal crisis. The city's bonded debt of $49 million in 1975 was reduced to $27.3 million in 1985, and the occupational tax (producing $49.5 million in 1985) was more than 15 times the principal and interest payments ($2.5 million in principal and $1 million interest in 1985).

LOUISVILLE DEVELOPMENT ORGANIZATIONS

LOUISVILLE CENTRAL AREA, INC. (LCA)

LCA's purpose is to promote the economic growth and development of downtown Louisville. Supported by corporate funding, LCA works closely with the public sector, serving as a forum to identify strategies for CBD revitalization, to select annual priorities for action, and to achieve mutual goals.

LOUISVILLE CHAMBER OF COMMERCE

The Chamber serves as the lead unit in economic development throughout the Louisville area, working closely with state and local government development agencies, private developers, site finders, and others.

LOUISVILLE AND JEFFERSON COUNTY OFFICE FOR ECONOMIC DEVELOPMENT

This joint city/county office has an active business retention program, provides financial advice for business expansion, handles issuance of both city and county IRBs, oversees the urban renewal process (through the Urban Renewal Commission), and handles administration and development of the enterprise zone.

CITY OF LOUISVILLE LANDMARKS COMMISSION

This agency protects historic and architecturally significant buildings and districts (which may or may not be on the National Register of Historic Places) through official recognition of their landmark status, and prepares nominations to the National Register of Historic Places. It also provides design and technical assistance for the rehabilitation of historic structures with particular emphasis on the use of local and federal tax incentives.

JEFFERSON COUNTY OFFICE OF HISTORIC PRESERVATION AND ARCHIVES

This office identifies county historic resources outside the city of Louisville as a guide to development planning, reviews individual landmarks, prepares nominations to the National Register of Historic Places, and provides design and technical assistance including use of tax incentives.

PRESERVATION ALLIANCE OF LOUISVILLE AND JEFFERSON COUNTY

The Alliance is a nonprofit coalition of neighborhood associations, historical societies, and public agencies with an interest in historic preservation. It serves the community through demonstration, education, and advocacy programs.

CITY OF LOUISVILLE DEPARTMENT OF INSPECTIONS, PERMITS, AND LICENSES

This department reduces red tape by coordinating construction plan review involving a large number of agencies issuing permits and licenses. It also handles building, housing, and environmental inspection services.

The city owns 100 percent of the stock of the Louisville Water Company, which also serves the suburban areas, and receives about $5 million annually in dividends. More recently, water company bonds were refinanced to produce a $15 million special dividend, most of which is being used for redevelopment in the CBD and nearby areas.

Against this background the long process of coming to grips with the city's problems has matured. This process included the dedicated dollar involvement of the private sector in the arts, in education, and in other community needs, particularly in rebuilding the center city. The first problem that demanded attention was the decline of the CBD.

DOWNTOWN BLUES: CHALLENGE AND RESPONSE

The central business district began to show the first symptoms of distress in the mid-1950s with slowing retail sales. Blighted areas to the east and west of downtown presented a bad image to shoppers passing through and discouraged the new investment needed to brighten up the CBD. Federal urban renewal funds were becoming available at this time, but Mayor Bruce Hoblitzell, frustrated by the red tape, abandoned that approach. Typical of the innocence of the times was another city effort to brighten the CBD: baskets of plastic plants were hung on blue painted street lights on Market

Downtown Louisville in 1964. Fourth Avenue is at the center, and the 800 Apartments can be seen in the left foreground.

Street, and concrete benches were placed at bus stops. Needless to say, this had no noticeable effect on retail sales. Although private investors rehabilitated a handful of housing units around the CBD investment under the mayor's urging, it was soon evident that this effort, too, was doomed. Housing contractors were more interested in the high profits to be found in suburbia.

The Chamber of Commerce proposed a solution: issue $5 million in city bonds to acquire and clear these blighted areas. They would then be developed as a medical center on the east and a civic center for new local government buildings on the west. Mayor Hoblitzell, a fiscal conservative, was eventually convinced—by the city's previous failures—that such large-scale action was called for; a $5 million bond issue was put on the ballot and approved in 1957. This marked the entrance of the initially reluctant city into large-scale restructuring of the built environment, which was to result in the 10-square-block Medical Center. The private sector's involvement was minimal.

The downtown became home to the University of Louisville medical and dental schools, six hospitals, research institutes, medical office buildings, and a variety of related functions. Total investment in public and private funding currently runs at more than $300 million. The civic center never materialized, however. Neither city nor county government felt comfortable committing the dollars needed to move their operations to new structures. The area was later redeveloped with subsidized low- and high-rise housing and office structures after urban renewal began in earnest.

Unfortunately, the main thrust of this first redevelopment effort—to encourage private investment in the CBD—was a dismal failure. Shoppers continued to abandon downtown for the new and multiplying suburban shopping centers. As it became obvious that downtown needed more than a sanitized outer perimeter to maintain its health, the Chamber of Commerce's Downtown Committee was transformed in 1959 into the independent, nonprofit Louisville Central Area, Inc., to focus on the problems of the CBD and to pro-

The University of Louisville School of Medicine, located east of the central business district.

pose imaginative solutions. One of its first reports, showing a demand for quality downtown apartments, spurred one local investor to erect an apartment tower on the south end of the CBD, the first such project since the late 1920s. At 29 stories, the 800 Apartments (named for its Fourth Street address) was the tallest building in the city and provided 247 units having one to four bedrooms. With its liveried doorman, balconies, blue-anodized aluminum cladding, the 800 Apartments building made a colorful punctuation mark on the skyline, but was slow to fill. Some of the apartments were leased by national corporations with local operations as temporary housing for new executives transferred to Louisville; some were rented for office space. The better part of a decade had passed before the major part of the space was leased to bona fide residential tenants, many of them older retirees. The investor had trouble making payments on the $6 million, FHA-insured loan.

One of the lessons learned was that although many people expressed a desire to live downtown, that wish was apparently conditioned on downtown providing the full complement of varied activities and facilities associated with a vital CBD. The performing arts were just beginning their phenomenal rise when the 800 Apartments building opened; downtown festive events that now are common had not yet been launched; and the CBD was on a visible decline. Inducements to live in the CBD were not strong. As the CBD's attractiveness has increased, so have rentals in the 800 Apartments building.

One of the factors prompting construction of the 800 Apartments building was the prospect of a dramatic revitalization of the historic riverfront area at the north end of downtown. In 1960, Reynolds Metals (later joined by the General Electric Pension Fund) proposed a $20 million complex of high-rise office and apartment towers surrounding a marina. The redevelop-

ment of the riverfront had been proposed as early as 1930 by the St. Louis planning firm of Harland Bartholomew and Associates, consultants to the Louisville Planning Commission. The proposal was put on the back burner during the Depression and World War II. Later, with a full-fledged Urban Renewal Agency (Mayor Hoblitzell's successors were not averse to dealing with the federal bureaucracy to secure redevelopment funding), the proposal for what was to become the Riverfront Project was revived.

Reynolds Metals, intrigued by the potential profit in nationwide CBD renewal as federal funds fueled urban renewal and by the emerging planning philosophy that espoused downtown living, envisioned up to 1,000 apartment units in the three-square-block development, as well as motel and other amenities—in addition to office space and the marina. It was an exciting prospect, with the planning firm of Doxiadis and Associates, based in Athens, Greece, called in as chief designer. The project was predicated upon city participation in acquiring land through the urban renewal process. As it turned out, although this particular project was never built, laying the groundwork for it precipitated a crisis that proved the catalyst both for large-scale renewal and renovation in the heart of the CBD and for the public/private partnership that has characterized center city redevelopment in Louisville.

Federal approval for urban renewal funding was not received until 1963, and as the rather cumbersome process of acquiring land for the Reynolds Metals project began, technical snags arose. This was the renewal agency's first venture into higher-priced property, in which many of the buildings, although aging, were generally well maintained. Disputes over property valuation were rife and the acquisition process seemed interminable. Another problem was the state's decision to route a segment of the interstate highway system along the

riverfront, which forced a revision of design. In 1967, Reynolds—discouraged by what it saw as the spotty record of similar projects in other cities—hurriedly withdrew. That left the city in a quandary with much property acquired, demolition begun, and no developer.

After the initial shock, urban renewal planners, building on the Doxiadis design, revised the plan with underground parking (the sloping land from Main Street to the river facilitated this) topped by a public open space (the plaza with a higher belvedere that would extend over the expressway), plus a major hotel as the anchor to encourage the development of office buildings. Proposals were solicited from developers nationwide, but the silence was deafening. It took a local builder/developer to sense the possibilities, including the headstart advantage of having an expressway exit nearby. Al J. Schneider had made his appearance on the downtown scene in the early 1960s with a 12-story motor hotel on Broadway at the south end of the CBD. By the mid-1960s, he was erecting two new buildings on Broadway for financial institutions.

Schneider agreed in 1968 to build the hotel (Galt House) if construction of the 1,600-car garage and the Plaza/Belvedere were assured. This resulted in—after some sticky financial problems had been solved—the beginning of public/private partnership in rebuilding the center city. Ironically, in 1969, the head of the Center City Committee, a consortium of public and private interests set up to oversee the formulation of a general plan for CBD redevelopment, would bemoan "the absence of a coalition of powerful and enlightened public and private leadership." Such a coalition was taking shape even as he spoke.

The comment was based on the experience of the 1960s following the 1962 publication of Louisville Central Area, Inc.'s *Design for Downtown*. As a blueprint for CBD redevelopment, the publication suggested numerous new facilities, including a convention center, a performing arts hall, and the conversion of Fourth Avenue (the major retail shopping thoroughfare) to a pedestrian mall. But because no mechanism existed for implementing or coordinating the proposals, each special interest group waved its own banner independently. The performing arts supporters were skeptical of the need for a convention center and the Convention Bureau considered a performance hall an unnecessary bauble. The Crime Consortium gave the county jail top priority, and so forth. Downtown redevelopment became a battleground for competing fiefdoms. In this municipal disarray, the Center City Committee helped set priorities and the Riverfront Project created the public/private partnership that proved to be the mechanism that was needed.

Since then, over a 15-year period, the CBD has experienced its greatest changes. All the goals enumerated in *Design for Downtown* have been achieved, and the public/private partnership has moved on to projects undreamed of in those early days. Office space increased from 4 million square feet of net leasable space in 1971, with a 21 percent vacancy rate, to 6.9 million leasable square feet in 1985 (most of it new or renovated), with an 11.3 percent vacancy rate. The rate declined from 14.5 percent in 1984, even with the addition of 525,000 square feet of space. (Figured on gross square footage and including buildings fully occupied by their owners, the vacancy rate was only 9.8 percent of 91.3 million gross square feet.)

Between 1968 and the mid-1980s, center city employment increased from 45,000 to over 60,000, the property tax base from $176.7 million to $610 million, the city's share of property tax revenue from $1 million to $3.4 million, the occupational tax revenue from $4.9 million to $13.9 million, and the number of new or renovated hotel rooms from 2,291 to 3,265.

Outside developers, who showed no interest in the Riverfront Proj-

FIGURE 3-1
LOUISVILLE OFFICE SPACE VACANCY RATES: CBD DEVELOPMENT COMPARED WITH SUBURBAN DEVELOPMENT[1]

Year	CBD Space Available (Square Feet)	Percent Vacant	Suburban Space Available (Square Feet)	Percent Vacant
1971	4,047,850	21.0%	229,219	25.6%
1976	4,216,252	16.3	805,947	30.6
1981	5,249,188	10.1	1,144,638	26.0
1985	6,935,480	11.3	4,559,382	17.2

[1] Based on net square feet of rentable space.
Source: Research Department, Louisville Chamber of Commerce.

FIGURE 3-2
OCCUPATIONAL TAX INCOME: LOUISVILLE COMPARED WITH JEFFERSON COUNTY[1]

Year	City	County
1971	$20,282,499	$ 9,920,321
1976	28,616,457	16,180,202
1981	41,404,985	26,677,646
1985	49,584,561	34,835,330

[1] Based on 1.25 percent of gross wages and net business profits.
Source: Research Department, Louisville Chamber of Commerce.

FIGURE 3-3
RETURN ON COMMUNITY INVESTMENT IN DOWNTOWN LOUISVILLE

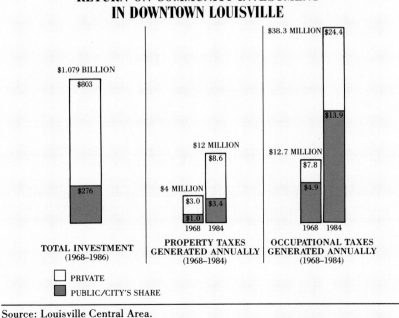

Source: Louisville Central Area.

ect in 1968, today respond quickly to offered opportunities and sometimes seek opportunities independently. The city's 1985 offer to make a surface parking lot adjacent to city hall available for high-rise office structures elicited rival offers from three prominent national development partnerships. Another outside development group is planning to develop office structures on East Main Street—where further commercial and residential development is likely—extending the development that has already occurred in the West Main Street historic preservation district.

Louisville Central Area, Inc., points out that, based on past experiences, this new space will drive up the vacancy rate temporarily, but that the new space will soon be absorbed. A 1985 example is the $60 million, 27-story Humana Building, headquarters of one of the city's corporate superstars. The company expected to occupy only part of the building and lease the remainder. Instead, it occupies the entire building and

also leases space in a new building adjacent to its headquarters.

While the CBD has been rebuilding, the suburban corridors of development have not been idle. Suburbia today is no longer simply the quiet retreat of the American dream; it is also the site of vast commercial development that in a pre-expressway/pre-beltway era would have taken place in the center city.

While new office buildings went up downtown, they also appeared in increasing numbers in suburbia. In Louisville, this development has been particularly marked to the east of the city limits, where a suburban activity center has developed. From 1971 through 1985, when CBD net office space grew by a respectable 57 percent, suburban office space registered a 74 percent gain, from 896,960 to 4,559,382 net square feet.

The suburban vacancy rate, however, is consistently higher than in the CBD, despite the fact that most space was recently constructed and rental rates are lower. In 1972,

when Louisville's vacancy rates were their highest, the CBD posted a 21.6 percent rate, while the suburbs had a 30.7 percent rate. In 1985, the CBD rate was 11.5 percent, compared with a suburban rate of 17.2 percent. The highest rental rate for suburban office space in 1985 was $14.50 per square foot, much lower the downtown's top rate of $20. The average 1985 rental rate in the suburbs was about $10 per square foot compared with about $12.50 in the CBD.

Future development of the Louisville urban core vis-a-vis the suburban peripheries will be influenced by changes in the federal tax laws, the direction of the national economy, and the CBD power structure's continued commitment to revitalization. But, having provided the attractions and facilities that make downtown a place worth living, the city must next provide the housing that will appeal to middle- and upper-income groups. That process, now underway, is one of the topics discussed in the case studies that follow.

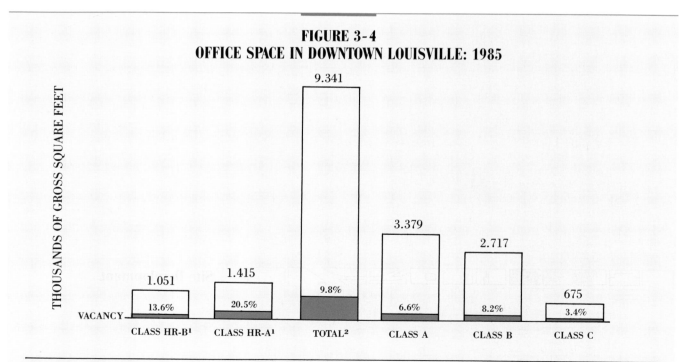

FIGURE 3-4
OFFICE SPACE IN DOWNTOWN LOUISVILLE: 1985

[1]HR stands for historic renovation.
[2]Includes owner-occupied space. Vacant space is a percent of gross available space.
Source: Louisville Central Area.

CENTRAL BUSINESS DISTRICT PROJECTS

RIVERFRONT PROJECT

Louisville's downtown riverfront and wharf parallel Main Street, which is a block from the wharf and some 40 feet higher. Once the commercial and financial heart of the city, the area had lost its prestigious standing by the early 20th century. The commercial area spread to the south and the river gave way to railroads as the dominant means of transportation. As early as 1913, when the "City Beautiful" movement was in full flower nationally, suggestions were made to redevelop the area. In 1930, planning consultants prepared designs for redevelopment, which were shelved with the onslaught of the Depression and, later, World War II. Not until the federal urban renewal program emerged in the 1950s were the mechanism and the funding available to trigger rebuilding.

History

The decision of Reynolds Metals Company in 1967 to withdraw from the redevelopment of the riverfront led directly to the present Riverfront Plaza/Belvedere and its accompanying complex of new buildings. After the redesign of the project, discussed previously, the city agreed to construct the 1,600-car underground garage. With that assurance, a local developer agreed to erect the hotel, choosing the name Galt House to commemorate an earlier famed Louisville hostelry. Other developments soon followed.

Louisville Trust Company (since merged with Liberty National Bank) announced that it would be the principal tenant in a 22-story office building to be erected by the hotel developer. In 1970, First National Bank decided to move its headquarters to Main Street as principal tenant in a 40-story tower to be built on land cleared by the Urban Renewal Agency just across from the Plaza/Belvedere. In 1971, American Life and Accident Insurance Company, displaced by the Riverfront Project, announced its intention to construct a new headquarters building as part of the developing complex. Developments since have included the Kentucky Center for the Arts and a second hotel—both built on land cleared as a result of urban renewal—and two high-rise office buildings nearby.

Site Development

The 30-acre site, extending three blocks between the river and Main Street, as well as some land along one block south of Main Street, was purchased and cleared by the Louisville Urban Renewal Agency for the abortive Reynolds Metals/G.E. Pension Fund project. The

DOWNTOWN LOUISVILLE

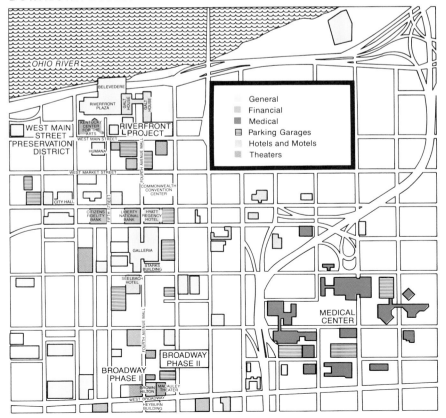

OHIO RIVER

BELEVEDERE

RIVERFRONT PLAZA

GALT HOUSE

GALT HOUSE

KENTUCKY CENTER FOR THE ARTS

RIVERFRONT PROJECT

WEST MAIN STREET PRESERVATION DISTRICT

WEST MAIN STREET

HUMANA

WEST MARKET STREET

CITY HALL

COMMONWEALTH CONVENTION CENTER

CITIZENS FIDELITY BANK

LIBERTY NATIONAL BANK

HYATT REGENCY HOTEL

GALLERIA

STARKS BUILDING

SEELBACH HOTEL

FOURTH AVENUE MALL

MEDICAL CENTER

BROADWAY PHASE II

BROADWAY PHASE I

BROWN HILTON

MACAULEY THEATER

WEST BROADWAY

HEYBURN BUILDING

General
Financial
Medical
Parking Garages
Hotels and Motels
Theaters

RIVERFRONT PROJECT

Project Type: Redevelopment of CBD wharf area with open space, hotel, offices, and underground parking garage.

Developers: City of Louisville; Al J. Schneider Company, Louisville; and American Life & Accident Insurance Company, Louisville.

Construction Supervision: Garage and Plaza/Belvedere: Lawrence P. Mellilo, architect, Louisville.

Hotel and office building: Al J. Schneider Company.

Insurance company corporate headquarters: Office of Mies van der Rohe, Chicago.

Architecture: Concept: Doxiadis Associates, Athens, Greece.

Parking garage: Lawrence P. Mellilo and Jasper Ward, Louisville.

Hotel: Lawrence P. Mellilo.

Office building: Nolan & Nolan, Louisville.

Insurance company corporate headquarters: Office of Mies van der Rohe, Chicago.

Landscape Architecture: Plaza/Belvedere, Simonds & Simonds (now Environmental Planning & Design), Pittsburgh; and Lester Collins, Washington, D.C.

Financing: Total project cost: $33 million. Financing components were: parking garage, $10 million bond issue plus $3.5 million cash from city of Louisville; hotel, $10.5 million, long-term mortgage financing from Louisville Trust Company; office building, $6 million in long-term financing from Louisville Trust Company; American Life & Accident Insurance Company headquarters, $3 million in long-term financing.

Status: Construction began in 1970; Plaza/Belvedere and buildings completed in 1972.

---

buildings demolished were, with rare exceptions, 19th century commercial structures, including the 10-story 1889 Columbia Building, the city's first "high-rise." Because the property is made up entirely of river sand (though well compacted), footings for the high-rise buildings had to extend down 30 feet or more below the surface for adequate support. Construction began in 1970 and all of the initial building projects were completed during 1972.

Planning and Design

A primary goal of the Riverfront Project was to make easily visible the Ohio River, which is one mile wide at Louisville, and to create the Plaza, a pleasant open space set atop the underground garage and about five feet higher than Main Street. The Belvedere, five feet higher than the Plaza, extends over the elevated, six-lane Riverfront Expressway, providing a view

of the river, as well as of the dam that has tamed the Ohio River falls.

The site posed some development problems in that Main Street is about 40 feet higher than the riverbank, which, also meant however, that only minimal excavation was necessary for the three-level, 1,600-car garage. The Plaza/Belvedere, occupying about seven acres of the total site, includes trees and other plantings, reflecting pools, fountains, cascades, an ice-skating rink, sculpture, and roofed-over areas. Because part of the area is subject to flooding, floodwalls (which are part of an extensive Louisville flood control system) were incorporated in the garage; therefore, a major flood would put the lower level of the garage under water.

The Riverfront Commission supervised the design of the public open space, but the structures around its south and east perimeters were designed under contract to the developers involved. These designs had to be approved by the commission and by the Louisville Urban Renewal Agency (LURA). The American Life and Accident Insurance Company chose the well-known Mies van der Rohe firm to design its five-story, Cor-Ten steel structure. Later, the Kentucky Center for the Arts was designed by Caudill Rowlett Scott of Houston, a firm experienced in such projects elsewhere.

Financing and Development Costs

Federal urban renewal grants provided the $11.5 million needed to acquire the site, clear it, and relocate utilities. The city government and private sources bore all further costs of site redevelopment. Cooperation between the public and private sectors solved some of the early problems.

Although the city agreed to issue bonds to cover the bulk of the cost of building, it was feared that the issue would be difficult to market because of the existing 7 percent interest rate limit set by the state on government bonds. To assure that construction would not be delayed and thus jeopardize the hotel project, Louisville's five largest banks together loaned the city $7.5 million and persuaded Chemical Bank of New York to purchase $2.5 million in short-term notes in anticipation of the city issuing bonds. Chemical Bank's participation was based on assurance that the 1970 Kentucky legislature would lift its 7 percent interest rate limitation and, after adroit lobbying, it did. In 1970, the city issued $10 million in bonds and provided $3.5 million in cash to build the underground garage. The city's total contribution of $13.5 million also covered the costs of developing the Plaza/ Belvedere and rebuilding the historic wharf to provide docking for the *Belle of Louisville*—owned jointly by the city and county—and for other passenger boats.

To pay the bond issue, the city dedicated all revenue from CBD parking meters (about $1 million annually) plus revenues from the Galt House air rights lease. Air rights fees amount to 4 percent of the hotel's room rentals and 2 per-

A typical winter's day at the Riverfront Plaza/Belvedere ice skating rink.

cent of its beverage and food sales, averaging $225,000 to $250,000 annually. (Galt House grosses about $4 million a year.)

After rescuing the garage project, the financial institutions again had their mettle tested when the hotel developer, faced with a tight money market, had difficulty raising construction funds for the 23-story Galt House. The deadline for these funds was December 24, 1969, the expiration date of the contractors' bid on the garage. Because the hotel was leasing air rights from the city, the foundation work on the hotel and garage construction had to proceed simultaneously. Moreover, the hotel was essential to the viability of the garage. Five banks and six savings and loan associations stepped in to provide an interim construction loan while negotiations were underway for $10.5 million in long-term financing.

The office building was erected simultaneously with the hotel and

garage as an integral part of the complex. The Louisville Trust Company, the principal tenant, financed the $6 million project, which includes its own underground garage separate from but adjacent to the public garage. The American Life & Accident Insurance and First National Bank headquarters buildings were erected at a cost of $38 million in conventional loans.

Management and Maintenance

The overall design and construction management were entrusted to the Riverfront Commission established by the city in 1964. With its mix of public officials and CBD leaders and headed by a retired industrialist, the commission paved the way for the private sector to participate in the financing of downtown renewal.

For a few years after opening the Plaza/Belvedere, the Riverfront Commission was responsible for maintenance. The commission was later consolidated with another

The Louisville downtown riverfront as of 1985. Galt House East and Galt House can be seen on the left and the Humana Building on the right.

The Riverfront Plaza/Belvedere provides a popular meeting place and setting for lunch during the summer months.

agency with similar responsibilities for the Fourth Avenue Mall, and eventually, the two became the Parking Authority of River City. The city's Department of Public Works now handles maintenance.

Status

All of the varied elements were completed during 1972, transforming what had been a desolate area of the city into a showcase that gave Louisville a new skyline. The plethora of 1.67 million square feet of new office space (including the 1972 Citizens Plaza a block away) caused the CBD vacancy rate—mostly in older buildings—to increase to 21.6 percent in 1973, but by 1978, that figure had dropped to 6.8 percent.

In addition to the initial spurt of redevelopment, the Riverfront Project triggered other activity: the West Main Street Historic Preservation District, the Kentucky Center for the Arts, and the Humana Building. The first two represent a mix of public and private financing

and are discussed in the case studies that follow. The Humana Building, headquarters of one of Louisville's fastest-growing corporations, is entirely private. Financed by Humana, the $60 million, 27-story postmodern structure with retail space on its lower two floors was designed by Michael Graves.

The Galt House has been deemed an unqualified success; the developer expanded the project by building Galt House East in 1985—a 14-story, 500-room hotel with underground parking for 1,500 cars. It is connected to the original Galt House by a skywalk across Fourth Avenue and is built on urban renewal land purchased by the developer. Convention trade accounts for approximately 80 percent of the occupancy of the two hotels.

The new hotel is part of a complex that includes 200 riverfront apartments and two five-story office buildings and one 15-story office tower (under construction in 1986). The developer has not disclosed his investment to date, but it is estimated that the entire complex will be in the range of $70 million. Of this, $20 million is in the form of city-issued industrial reve-

Galt House at the Riverfront Plaza.

The Humana Building, located at Fifth and Main streets, was designed by Michael Graves.

nue bonds and $50 million in a combination of self-financing and mortgage loans from Louisville financial institutions. The Riverfront Project marked the beginning of the revitalization of Louisville's CBD, which has been on an upward curve ever since.

FOURTH AVENUE MALL

Fourth Avenue is the heart of Louisville's downtown retail shopping district. The retail decline of the 1960s had its most visible impact on Fourth Avenue as shoppers deserted the CBD for the elaborate new shopping malls springing up beyond the city boundaries. Vacant stores, closed movie palaces, hotels struggling to survive or shutting down, and a creeping air of desolation characterized this once-vibrant thoroughfare.

History

In the search for solutions, the 1962 planning document Design for Downtown had recommended turning three blocks of the street into a pedestrian mall with lanes for buses, taxis, and emergency vehicles only. (As one block is extremely long, the effect would be four blocks of mall.) Such pedestrian malls had been tried—with some success—in other cities facing the same CBD problems.

By the late 1960s, as the retail situation continued to worsen, merchants and building owners had grown receptive to the pedestrian mall proposal. Louisville Central Area, Inc., organized trips for business and political leaders to inspect downtown malls in other communities. Although funding was an issue, the city and business interests had formulated a program by 1967.

Site Development

As a principal north/south thoroughfare that extends nearly one mile through the CBD, Fourth Avenue is home to downtown's finest shops, department stores, hotels, and related amenities. Although converting three blocks of it into a pedestrianway required no site clearance, the area was closed for some time while the redevelopment was underway.

Removing old streetcar rails that had been embedded in thick concrete slabs and covered by asphalt paving proved the most time-consuming task. Utilities were rearranged to serve fountains, reflecting pools, and relocated fire hydrants and light standards, as well as to allow for landscaping. Commercial gas and electric services were moved to alleys behind stores fronting the mall. At the same time, these alleys were widened where possible to permit rear door delivery of merchandise. The thoroughfare also had to remain usable for pedestrians while all work was in progress.

Work on the mall began in 1972 with the hope that the three blocks (covering one-half mile) could be completed by the Christmas season of that year. Although one block was finished by early December, the other two had far to go and were not completed until August 1973.

Planning and Design

Earlier proposals that the mall provide public service and emergency vehicle access were abandoned in favor of a pedestrian-only design. With a width of 60 feet, the Fourth Avenue Mall was not considered wide enough for both vehicular and pedestrian traffic. A winding path was constructed for

Fourth Avenue before the mall was developed. The buildings on the right have been replaced with new structures.

Fourth Avenue Mall in 1986, with the Seelbach Hotel on the right.

fire and other emergency vehicles, and served also as part of the pedestrianway. The final design included brick paving and numerous raised landscaped areas, as well as trees, benches, fountains, pools, covered shelters, open areas for street events, play areas for children, and provisions for adding fu-

ture amenities. In 1974, the mall won an award for urban design from the American Society of Landscape Architects.

Financing and Development Costs

The development plan called for the city to condemn and purchase property along Fourth Avenue to sell to private developers, and for property owners along the street to pay a special assessment to cover the cost of transforming the street into a pedestrian precinct. Approval by the state legislature was necessary to give the city the power of eminent domain. Such powers had previously been restricted to federal urban renewal projects. Fourth Avenue, although economically adrift, was not designated physically blighted and therefore did not qualify as an urban renewal area.

The 1968 legislature, however, rejected the proposal. Mall backers, concentrating on winning the support of Louisville legislators,

had not reckoned on opposition from other legislators who represented small communities throughout the state, and who feared that the provisions might be extended to their bailiwicks. Although the bill was amended to apply only to Louisville, the move came too late. Learning the lesson, proponents returned to the 1970 legislature with a bill that eliminated the condemnation powers of the city and trimmed the size of the special assessment district, which originally included property extending a full block from the mall. This time the effort was successful, and Fourth Avenue was given the opportunity to pull itself up by its own bootstraps in what mall supporters called "private urban renewal."

To finance construction, the city issued in 1972 $1.5 million in 20-year bonds that are being retired through assessments on land (not improvements) extending back 210 feet on either side of the mall. The yearly assessments ($129,146 in 1984) vary to cover the cost of any maintenance of the mall that exceeds the normal cost of maintaining it as a traffic thoroughfare; these assessments have no upper limit. In addition, the city appropriated $400,000 from general funds to widen alleys.

Because the bond issue fell $217,000 short of the amount needed to complete the mall as originally designed, some cutbacks were planned. In 1973, however, the city applied for and received an open spaces grant from the U.S. Department of Housing and Urban Development, which permitted the original design to be carried out.

Status

The simultaneous opening in the summer of 1973 of the Fourth Avenue Mall and the Riverfront Project boosted hopes that the CBD's retail heart would regain a large measure of its old vigor. But the retail mall did not fulfill this hope. Although stores at the cross street intersections benefited, with some even reporting increased sales, those re-

FOURTH AVENUE MALL

Project Type: Conversion of three blocks of the main thoroughfare of the CBD into a pedestrian mall.

Developer: City of Louisville.

Construction Supervision: Ryan, Cooke & Zuern, Architects, Louisville.

Architecture: Ryan, Cooke & Zuern.

Landscape Architecture: Johnson, Johnson & Roy, Ann Arbor, Michigan.

Financing: Total project cost: $1.7 million, financed by a $1.5 million city bond issue retired by assessments on adjacent property, and by a $217,000 open spaces HUD grant.

Status: Construction began May 1972; one block was completed and opened December 1972; the remainder was completed and opened August 1973.

tailers in midblock did not fare so well. Stores continued to close, as well as two of Louisville's grand old hotels—the Brown and the Seelbach. The management of one store was blunt about its decision to close: the mall "was no help and may have hurt."

With experience, some of the mall's shortcomings could be pinpointed:
• No low-rate parking facilities giving direct access to the mall had been constructed, in part because the city lacked condemnation powers. Motorists were forced to park some distance from the mall.
• The lack of public transportation worked against the mall. Fourth Avenue extends one mile from the Riverfront to Broadway. The half-mile length of the mall itself created what one observer called "a tunnel" for pedestrians.
• The south (Broadway) end of the mall lacked a firm anchor. The closing of the Brown Hotel at that intersection and the redevelopment of the riverfront pulled activity to the north end of the CBD. By 1974, pornography shops and X-rated movie houses

were appearing at the south end of the mall.
• At night, the mall was dead—bereft of activity, people, and traffic.

But a residuum of positive aspects has, in the long run, outweighed the negative side. The mall became a factor in the city's gaining state support for building the Commonwealth Convention Center/Hyatt Regency Louisville; it made possible the Galleria, the CBD's first successful retail revitalization project; and it stimulated the development of Theater Square on the south end of the mall as part of the Broadway Renaissance. Along the one-mile stretch of Fourth Avenue in the CBD, 59 percent of the buildings existing when the mall was opened in 1973 had been replaced by new structures by 1985, and many others had been totally renovated.

After three years of study and debate, the Transit Authority of River City (TARC) voted in May 1986 to implement plans for a shuttle bus service to tie the Broadway Renaissance to the Riverfront Project along the mall. The buses will

be replicas of old trolleys. As no provision was made for a transit-way in the original mall design, plantings and street furniture must be relocated to make space for it. By providing transit, the mall will become more functional. The costs of the bus service, estimated at $4 million for mall improvements and $1.5 million for nine buses, is expected to be 80 percent funded by the federal Urban Mass Transportation Administration, with the remainder supplied by city and county governments and by TARC's reserve fund.

COMMONWEALTH CONVENTION CENTER/HYATT REGENCY LOUISVILLE

The Commonwealth Convention Center and the companion Hyatt Regency Louisville hotel, built as a single project, resulted from plans developed by Louisville Central Area, Inc. By the late 1960s, a need clearly existed for better convention facilities and more first-class hotels to accommodate convention attendees. Downtown business executives with strong ties to the state government persuaded the state to fund the convention center and the major cost of the hotel, demonstrating that the private/public partnership can extend beyond local government.

History

Conventions have long been important to Louisville's economy and attendance has consistently grown through the years. By the middle 1960s, the then-existing downtown convention center, operated by Jefferson County, could no longer attract desirable conventions. Neither the county nor the city, then engaged in the Riverfront Project and the Fourth Avenue Mall, had the resources to undertake construction of a new convention center. Fortunately, the state of Kentucky had an interest in developing economic activity in Louisville and came to the rescue. In August 1971, the governor announced the

COMMONWEALTH CONVENTION CENTER

Project Type: Convention center.

Developer: Commonwealth of Kentucky through State Fair Board.

Construction Supervision: Luckett & Farley Architects, Engineers & Construction Managers,Inc., Louisville.

Architecture: Luckett & Farley.

Financing: Total project cost: $21.2 million, financed by a state bond issue for that amount.

Status: Construction began in 1975; the project was completed and opened in 1977.

state's commitment to build a new convention center.

While preliminary planning for the Commonwealth Convention Center was proceeding, the same group of downtown business leaders, supported by the city administration, launched a corollary project involving the development of a hotel adjacent to the center. They were able to convince state officials that the center could not stand alone. With three major downtown hotels closing, the CBD was short of the rooms needed to draw large conventions, despite the new 710-room Galt House and the clutch of new motels that had sprung up on urban renewal land on the east fringe of downtown. The state agreed to help acquire land for a hotel and to build a 615-car parking garage for the hotel.

Site Development

Facing Fourth Avenue immediately north of the pedestrian mall termination, the site selected was to serve as a link between the mall and the riverfront. Because of the strong commitment of important members of the business community to the revitalization of the CBD, no location outside that area was considered.

The state chose the Kentucky State Fair Board (which operates

the Kentucky Fair and Exposition Center in Louisville) as the government agency to oversee construction of the center and parking garage and to operate them when completed. In turn, the State Fair Board designated the Louisville Urban Renewal Agency to serve as the contracting agent in acquiring the property and clearing the site. Land acquisition began in June

A view from the top of the atrium of the Hyatt Regency Louisville.

1973 and was completed a year later with no problems.

Meantime, the State Fair Board picked a local architectural firm to design the center and named a 21-member citizens' advisory committee to provide input—a recognition of the role of the private sector in initiating the project. In 1974, clearance began of the hotel and garage site south of the convention center (and separated from it by a major east/west thoroughfare), and by July of that year, after inviting hotel bid proposals from developers, the board received three serious responses.

The Hyatt Corporation's offer was accepted in May 1975. Although, financially, it was the least attractive offer, the prestige of the Hyatt name plus the luxury facility proposed convinced board members (and the business community) that it was the best choice. Construction began in the fall of 1976 and was completed two years later.

Planning and Design

The Commonwealth Convention Center occupies one large square block and the Hyatt Regency Louisville and attached garage occupy the adjacent, but smaller, square block. A second-level skywalk connects the hotel with the convention center. As part of the overall design, the two blocks of Fourth Avenue that pass in front of the hotel and convention center became part of the pedestrian mall, making the mall five blocks in length.

The Citizens' Advisory Committee was dissatisfied with the original design of the convention center, unveiled in March 1974. The block-like monolith presented blank facades on both its north and south sides. Committee members had hoped for a more graceful design and for the provision of some retail space on these two sides. Alternative designs were prepared—all minor variations on the original design. But the committee members discovered that the state, as the developer, retained ultimate authority in making decisions. With delays pushing up construction costs and the governor wanting groundbreaking to occur before he left office at the end of 1974, state authorities kept the original design.

Although architecturally bland, the convention center, built of reinforced concrete, is quite functional on the inside. Its 427,800 square feet includes an exhibit area of 100,000 square feet of column-free space with a ceiling 32 feet high. The center—which can handle conventions of up to 12,000 delegates—provides 37 meeting rooms, ample storage and dock space, and on-floor delivery of exhibit materials.

The 18-story Hyatt Regency Louisville is of typical Hyatt design, with a 17-story atrium around which 400 guest rooms are grouped. A revolving restaurant/lounge caps the Indiana limestone structure. The state-owned garage was constructed at the same time as the hotel.

Financing and Development Costs

The state financed the entire $21.2 million cost of developing the Commonwealth Convention Center (including land acquisition, site clearance, and construction)

through a bond issue. It also issued $3.2 million in bonds to acquire land for the hotel—and to construct the retail space on the first floor—and for a parking garage. The Hyatt Corporation leases the land from the state at a minimum of $275,000 annually. Should 2 percent of room rentals and one-half percent of food and beverage sales exceed this figure, the excess would be paid to the state. As of 1985, this level had not been reached. The hotel also pays its guests' overnight parking charges, which range from $11,000 to $12,000 a month.

The $18.5 million construction cost of the hotel was financed by a $15.5 million loan from Equitable Life Assurance Society and $1.275 million in short-term construction loans from Louisville banks. Seven Louisville investors (IHR Partnership) added $1.5 million, which gives them 50 percent control for the first 12 years. Hyatt contributed $250,000 in equity. The Louisville investors can obtain two-thirds control by reimbursing Hyatt $250,000 in 1990.

The Hyatt Regency Louisville contains 400 rooms and serves the Commonwealth Convention Center.

HYATT REGENCY LOUISVILLE

Project Type:	Hotel to serve Commonwealth Convention Center.
Developer:	IHR Partnership (formed by seven Louisville investors), Louisville.
Construction Supervision:	Morse Diesel Company, New York City.
Architecture:	Welton Becket & Associates, Chicago.
Financing:	Total project cost: $21.7 million. Financing components were $1.275 million in short-term construction loans from Louisville banks; $1.5 million in equity from IHR Partnership; $250,000 in equity from Hyatt; $15.5 million in long-term financing from Equitable Life Assurance Society; and a $3.2 million state bond issue for land acquisition, garage construction, and retail space in hotel.
Status:	Construction began in 1976; the project was completed and opened in 1978.

Skywalks connect the Commonwealth Convention Center with the Hyatt Regency Louisville.

Status

In 1984, six years after the Commonwealth Convention Center opened, Louisville became the 10th largest convention city in the nation in attendance. Its 406,000 convention delegates and visitors that year were up from 383,543 in 1977, the year the center opened. Growth rates since then have been in the 5 to 8 percent range annually.

Although the center has been responsible for much of the growth, numerous new, smaller private facilities scattered throughout the metropolitan area, which are usually part of a hotel or motel complex, have also contributed their share. Convention center usage has increased from 126 days of conventions and trade shows in 1977 to 283 in 1984—good, but not yet good enough to make the facility self-supporting. Usage declined to about 230 days in 1985, principally because several regular conventions are held every other year and 1985 was a "skip" year. An expanded marketing program, however, is expected to make the facility self-supporting by 1988, or possibly 1987.

Meanwhile, the center plays an important role in CBD revitalization through the business that convention delegates generate for nearby hotels and retailers, especially the Galleria mixed-use complex, which is connected to the Hyatt Regency and the convention center by a skywalk. Although the Hyatt Regency does not reveal occupancy rates, it probably ranks second to the Galt House.

THE GALLERIA

The Galleria, a $143.5-million, mixed-use development of shops, restaurants, and two high-rise office towers in the heart of downtown, has been instrumental in halting the long-term decline of retail shopping in Louisville's CBD, changing a block with many vacant stores into the centerpiece of downtown revitalization. It also illustrates how the private sector can act as the coordinating factor in public/private development.

History

The 1973 development of the Fourth Avenue Mall—a three-block pedestrian mall filled with retail shops downtown—had failed to stem the loss of retail sales to suburban shopping centers. In 1975, at the suggestion of the mayor, an informal working group, headed by a retired CEO and composed of private sector executives, developed a plan for a mixed-use project emphasizing retailing. The working group maintained a close relationship with city and state governments while formulating the plan and choosing a developer.

Selected as the developer in early 1977, Oxford Properties, Inc., is the U.S. subsidiary of the Oxford Development Group of Edmonton, Alberta, Canada. Oxford was chosen following exhaustive studies that included trips by a group of government officials and executives of CBD-headquartered businesses to projects built by the developers under consideration.

Site Development

The site was occupied by a diverse array of older buildings, some approaching the century mark and showing it. The Louisville Urban Renewal Agency, charged with acquiring and clearing the property, encountered only one problem. The owners of the site selected for the anchor department store, a surface parking lot west of Fourth Avenue, declined to sell. Although the Urban Renewal Agency possessed condemnation powers, the decision was made not to press a suit because of the delay entailed, and instead, to change the site plans.

The northernmost office tower was shifted east across Fourth Avenue, and the department store repositioned to fill the vacated tower site. This not only required moving the parking facility underground where the department store was originally planned, but also sparked a battle with Louisville's well-entrenched preservation movement. The new site for the tower required that an 1876 landmark be demolished. A coalition of preservationists sought to convince Oxford to incorporate the building into the Galleria complex, but the site was on a prime corner and the issue was not negotiable.

As the controversy grew heated, the preservation coalition—charging that federal environmental and preservation legislation had been ignored—tried to block an $8 million Urban Development Action Grant to construct the department store. The imbroglio brought the full weight of the public/private partnership (including Kentucky's two U.S. Senators) to bear on the issue, and the Federal Preservation Advisory Council ruled that the UDAG funding could not be obstructed. Formal groundbreaking took place in December 1979 and the project opened in September 1982.

Planning and Design

The Fourth Avenue pedestrian mall became an ideal feature around which the new construction was grouped; a portion of the mall was enclosed in an all-glass, climate-controlled atrium soaring to a height of 110 feet. Thus, retail outlets have open shopfronts, creating an informal atmosphere that is inviting to shoppers. The developer sought a mix of retail tenants, as well as amenities such as restaurants and service establishments.

Retail space is on two levels linked by escalators, with both levels connected to the city-built, 750-car parking garage. The brick-paved open atrium provides a spacious and hospitable atmosphere, and Louisvillians often use it as a

THE GALLERIA

Project Type:	Mixed retail and office development.
Developers:	Oxford Properties, Inc., and City of Louisville.
Construction Supervision:	Oxford Properties, Inc., Ltd.
Architecture:	Skidmore, Owings & Merrill, Denver office.
Financing:	Total project cost: $143.5 million. Financing components were $81 million in long-term financing from Teachers Insurance Annuity Association to Oxford Properties, Inc.; $8 million in UDAG funding to the city for construction of the department store; $8 million from the state for public spaces; a $6.5 million city bond issue for construction of the parking garage; and $40 million in short-term loans to Oxford Properties to cover inflation-based cost overruns.
Status:	Construction began December 1979 and was completed in August 1982; the project opened in September 1982.

meeting place. As the atrium spans the Fourth Avenue Mall, many pedestrians bound elsewhere pass through and often stop for impulse shopping. The two 26-story office buildings—one at the north end of the Galleria, and the other at the south end—act as beacons defining the location of the project.

With the exception of the adaptive use of the 1903 Kaufman-Strauss Building (which exemplifies the Chicago School of architecture) the Galleria is new construction, of which 58,000 square feet is in retail space and 65,000 square feet in office space. The buff-brick facade of the five-story Kaufman-Strauss Building set the color tone for all new brick work. The new construction provided 187,000 square feet of leasable retail space; in addition, the anchor department store—built with UDAG funding and owned by the city—contains 90,000 square feet. The two office towers contain 634,000 square feet of leasable space.

The atrium of the Louisville Galleria.

79

Financing and Development Costs

A combination of private, city, state, and federal funds financed the Galleria's development. The private sector provided $121 million of the total $143.5 million cost. The Teachers Insurance and Annuity Association provided $81 million in long-term mortgage financing, which was expected to cover the cost of land acquisition and construction. However, the sharp inflation and spiraling interest rates of the early 1980s increased the cost by another $40 million, which Oxford Properties paid.

A city bond issue of $6.5 million funded land acquisition, clearance, and construction of the parking structure. Fees are kept low for short-term parkers who shop in the Galleria, and parking is free on Saturdays and Sundays. The garage ran at a deficit the first two years, but by the end of 1986 had reached the break-even point. The state provided $8 million for the Galleria's public spaces—principally the atrium and the skywalks to adjacent buildings—which it owns and maintains.

An $8 million UDAG was approved in 1979 for land acquisition, site clearance, and construction of the department store, which is leased by Bacon's, a locally owned chain. The grant stipulated that the store pay 3 percent of gross sales to the city as rent, with that amount going to create a minority venture-capital corporation, which receives about $300,000 annually.

Because many developers shy away from the large upfront costs of preparing invited proposals for projects that are, in effect, competitions, an informal working group of Louisville's local business and government leaders agreed to underwrite these costs. The developer chosen would repay the sum advanced; the other candidates would not. Proposal expenses were offset with $500,000 raised from private sources ($50,000 of the total expenses for invited proposals came from city funds).

THE SEELBACH HOTEL

The most immediate and visible byproduct of the Galleria was the renovation and reopening of the 10-story, 350-room Seelbach Hotel, Louisville's finest hotel when it first opened in 1905. Since its closing in 1975, however, the hotel had sat like a stately ghost. Its reopening in 1982 not only revived a popular Louisville landmark but also helped refocus activity to an important CBD hub.

HISTORY

Built by the brothers Otto and Louis Seelbach, who came to Louisville during the heavy German immigration of the 19th century, the Seelbach immediately became the hotel of choice of visiting dignitaries. Its Beaux-Arts elegance, its lower-level rathskeller (whose walls are covered with Rookwood tiles), its specially commissioned murals, and its fine food made the Seelbach a household word among Louisvillians and knowledgeable travelers.

When the hotel first opened, the city's most elegant shopping area was moving south along Fourth Avenue and away from the river. The Seelbachs chose the corner of Fourth and Walnut streets (now Muhammad Ali Boulevard) for their enterprise, and their faith in the inland location was justified. Within a few years, the intersection had become Louisville's busiest, and today it remains one of the principal nodes of the downtown scene.

The hotel weathered competition from newer arrivals like the Brown Hotel, but with the spread of suburbia after World War II and the proliferation of motels in both the CBD and the city's outer fringes, grand hotels like the Seelbach began to lose customers and prestige. Service and maintenance suffered and finally, in 1975, the hotel closed its doors.

PLANNING AND DESIGN

An empty 10-story hotel was not an attractive neighbor to the new Galleria. When a Baltimore developer failed to secure financing to reopen the Seelbach, representatives of the city's key banks asked two Louisville developers to take on the renovation, promising construction loans and assistance in finding permanent long-term financing. The developers agreed and purchased the property in December 1978.

As part of the redevelopment, the city agreed to acquire a nearby parking structure and to enlarge it to accommodate 1,000 automobiles so that hotel guests would have convenient parking. With the reopening of the hotel, the restriction was eased that had limited the

Performance

Because of increased construction costs resulting from inflation, the Galleria did not generate the positive cash flow expected by the end of 1985. (It would have done so, had the original $81 million estimate of costs remained firm.) Still, results have been impressive, especially in light of the dismal CBD retail picture before the Galleria made its entrance.

The leased retail space (excluding Bacon's department store) averaged $162 in gross sales per square foot the first year; sales increased to $178 the second year and approached $200 in 1985, with 148,000 square feet of retail space leased out of the available 187,000

use of the mall to pedestrians. The developers were allowed to build a 20-foot-wide, granite-block-paved drive in front of the hotel for arriving and departing guests. Tunnels through the ground level of a building adjacent to the Seelbach provided access to the garage.

The developers had one prevailing concept: to restore the hotel to its original elegance. This required undoing all of the previous alterations, most of which dated from the 1930s and the 1950s. False ceilings were removed from the lobby, revealing beautifully detailed ornamental plaster; plate-glass windows at street level were replaced with new cut-stone work to restore the original arched effect; mahoghany and walnut woodwork was stripped of paint and restored to its natural finish; and all other unacceptable alterations were removed.

At the same time, utilities were reworked and updated; central air conditioning was installed; kitchen equipment was replaced; and rooms were refurbished with traditional furniture. Retail space was returned to its original appearance and only high-fashion shops sought as tenants. The hotel reopened in April 1982, nearly six months before the Galleria opened.

FINANCING AND DEVELOPMENT COSTS

The estimated cost of renovating the project was $20 million, of which the developers provided $5 million in equity. They experienced some difficulty in finding long-term financing, but in January 1981, the Metropolitan Life Insurance Company offered a $15.5 million mortgage at 13.5 percent interest, plus a 50 percent equity interest. The Galleria project was an important deciding factor in the insurance carrier's commitment. The city financed the municipal garage with $6.5 million in revenue bonds.

Because of the unusual care given to the quality of the hotel restoration, the total cost came to $24 million. This cost overrun, plus the high interest rate, resulted in a default on mortgage payments in 1983. In 1984, Metropolitan Life purchased the local developers' share of the project for $12.7 million, gaining 98 percent ownership. (Currently, the Radisson Hotel chain operates the Seelbach.)

STATUS

Advertising has made the Seelbach nationally known. Before the mortgage default, the occupancy rate was reported at 60 percent or higher. Although Metropolitan Life has not made public recent figures, the rate has likely improved. The synergism between the hotel and the adjacent Galleria has restored the old vitality to the intersection of Fourth and Muhammad Ali.

The Fourth Avenue Mall runs through the Louisville Galleria.

By attracting more shoppers to the downtown area, the Galleria has been a major factor in halting the decline in the CBD retail base. Surveys covering 30-day shoppers before and after the opening of the project by Louisville Central Area, Inc., show there were 95,000 shoppers in 1981, 181,000 in 1983, and 201,000 in 1985. Peak shopping hours, however, are at noon and after offices close, indicating a heavy reliance on office clientele.

This project has also spurred adjacent retail development. A $3 million remodeling has created a second-floor retail area with a 14-story atrium in the 15-story Starks Building, connected to the Galleria by two skywalks. L.S. Ayres, a high-quality department store, also connected to the Galleria by a skywalk, has been remodeled at a cost of $6.5 million. Without the Galleria, Ayres (formerly Stewart's)

square feet. The department store's sales have been lower, although they increased from $125 per net square foot the first year to around $150 for the last half of 1985, and they continue to move upward.

Office space leasing in one Galleria tower lags. (The other tower was sold for $33.5 million to Brown & Williamson Tobacco Corporation as its headquarters.) With rents up to $20 per square foot (which is the limit in the Louisville market) the 26-story structure must compete with other new office buildings of comparable quality, as well as a large amount of space in older renovated buildings leasing at much lower rates.

undoubtedly would have closed, leaving the CBD without a single department store.

Property values and tax revenues have been immensely enhanced. In 1979, the land on which the Galleria is located had an assessed value of $4.5 million, generating only $70,000 in state and local property taxes. Today, it is assessed at $110 million, and tax revenues have increased nearly twentyfold to some $1 million annually.

KENTUCKY CENTER FOR THE ARTS

During the past 30 years, Louisville's emphasis on the arts, especially the performing arts, has attracted national attention. It is a medium-sized city where dancer Mikhail Baryshnikov and tenor Luciano Pavarotti can be counted on to fill the hall, where Actors Theater of Louisville (ATL) has transcended its regional role to become internationally prominent, where the Louisville Orchestra has gained recognition throughout the music world for its recordings of specially commissioned contemporary pieces, and where the local opera and ballet companies have loyal followings. Thus, the arts have become a tool in Louisville's economic development.

With this large increase in audience size (outstripping, proportionately, population growth), came the need for a building to house the various performing arts.

History

A former downtown cinema, the Macauley Theatre had been the home of the performing arts since 1962. Though elegant, it seated only 1,435 patrons, requiring multiple performances to accommodate all who wished to attend, which pushed up production costs and ticket prices. By 1970, ticket prices were approaching the $25 range. Lack of funding in 1969 thwarted attempts to construct a new facility. In 1974, the Center City Commission, a public/private group, un-

veiled plans for a new 2,400-seat hall, and proposed that public funds (the majority to come from the state) be used to construct it.

Although the state agreed to fund the center, the extent of local government participation was complicated by divided authority and conflicts between city and county officials. Some of the arts groups also had differing agendas and did not operate together smoothly. A new start was made in 1975, with the state agreeing to participate if local problems could be solved. In the spring of 1977, a task force of local arts and business representatives came up with a proposal that the mayor and the county's chief executive both endorsed. The state approved the proposal and named a 17-member committee including prominent local citizens to carry out the project. The state also allocated $400,000 from the governor's contingency fund to start the process moving.

Site Development

The site selected is in the Riverfront Project, where an empty parcel adjoining the Plaza/

Belvedere still remained. The Louisville Urban Renewal Agency had already cleared the site and relocated utilities. The Kentucky Center for the Arts was to face Main Street and have direct access at the rear to the Plaza/Belvedere. Construction of the arts center began in early 1982 and was completed in November 1983.

The developer of the nearby Galt House hotel had been negotiating to erect an apartment building on the property but agreed to accept another large site in the Riverfront Project area, where he later built a second hotel and apartments and is currently building two office structures.

Management and Maintenance

Two operating entities were set up in 1980: Kentucky Center for the Arts, Inc., a state-sponsored

The Kentucky Center for the Performing Arts houses two performance halls—one with 625 seats and the other with 2,400 seats for symphonic performances, touring Broadway shows, and other large productions.

nonprofit corporation to operate the center; and Kentucky Center for the Arts Endowment, Inc., to manage the endowment funds contributed by private corporations. Originally, a blue-ribbon committee was to oversee design and construction while the University of Louisville, a state institution, was to manage the completed arts center. But because of the cost increases and a change of state administrations, the private sector became more involved and the two present operating and management entities were created. The Kentucky Center for the Arts, Inc., is headed by the chief operating officer of Humana, Inc., who was instrumental in solving the problems plaguing the project. (The University of Louisville, which had feared that any operating deficits of the arts center might come out of its budget, did not object to the change in plans.)

Planning and Design

In addition to considering the design of the performance hall, the state-appointed committee assessed the possibility of commercial development on the opposite side of Main Street facing the hall. Gerald D. Hines Interests of Houston prepared a design scheme that would convert some of the existing Victorian commercial buildings into uses for the visual arts, including galleries, a school of fine arts, and high-rise office buildings that could generate revenue to help meet the arts centers' operating costs. A skywalk across Main Street was to link the performance hall, designed by Caudill Rowlett Scott of Houston, with the visual arts facility.

But signs of national recession, reduced state revenue, skyrocketing inflation, and the change in state administrations forced costs to be trimmed and brought about a change in plans. The visual arts component was dropped, not only because of cost but also because the Galleria project was moving forward at the same time. Hines

An interior view of the Kentucky Center for the Performing Arts.

Interests was advised in late 1978 not to pursue efforts to attract tenants for the office towers as that could interfere with efforts to lease space in the two office buildings that were to be part of the Galleria complex. At the same time, the arts center was redesigned to reduce construction costs. The completed design retained two performance halls: one with 625 seats to meet the needs of arts groups, such as the opera, desiring an intimate theater; and one with 2,400 seats for symphonic performances, touring Broadway shows, and other large productions.

Financing and Development Costs

The 1978 Kentucky legislature approved a bond issue of $23.5 million—the estimated cost for construction of the arts center—to be issued when construction started; the state advanced funds to begin architectural design in the interim. With inflation steadily pushing costs upward, the state increased its commitment to $35 million. It advanced $345,000 from the governor's contingency fund and began hurried preparations to issue $35 million in bonds, fearing that a new administration would not be favorably inclined toward the project.

The new administration did indeed have reservations about the state's large commitment and delayed sale of the bond issue. Ultimately, the state provided the $23.5 million initially approved by the 1978 legislature, but it covered no construction cost overruns nor future operating deficits.

In January 1980, the new governor issued a challenge to the Louisville business community to come up with $6 million in endowment funds, using its income to cover the arts center's operating deficits. Eventually more than $14 million was raised, but $8.5 million of this had to be used to supple-

ment state construction funds, as the final construction cost of the performance hall amounted to $33.75 million. This use of private funding to support a state project was a first for Louisville. Because the income from the endowment was not likely to cover the entire operating deficit, the governor and the Louisville corporate executive he had named to head Kentucky Center for the Arts, Inc., proposed a 3 percent increase in the Jefferson County hotel/motel room tax normally used to fund convention and tourist promotion.

Local hoteliers voiced opposition; the local legislative delegation was cool toward the proposal; and other legislators opposed the whole idea of the arts center. But after certain compromises were made, a 1 percent tax was adopted. As with the private funding, this use of local tax money to help support a state project was unusual. Helping in the legislative effort was the city of Louisville's commitment to provide the $2 million site and to build a $2.5 million, 330-car garage as part of the center.

Despite the redesign to cut costs, the construction bids were as much as $4.5 million over estimates. Humana, Inc., provided a $5.9 million interest-free loan to save the project. The smaller hall

KENTUCKY CENTER FOR THE ARTS

Project Type: Performing arts center.

Developer: Commonwealth of Kentucky.

Construction Supervision: Humana, Inc., Louisville.

Architecture: Caudill Rowlett Scott, Inc., Houston.

Financing: Total cost of project: $33.75 million. Financing components were a state bond issue of $23.5 million, $8.5 million in corporate gifts, and $1.75 million from ticket sales at the opening ceremony. Operating budget shortfalls are covered by a hotel/motel room tax of 1 percent (averaging $600,000 annually) in the Louisville area and by a $600,000 annual contribution from the state.

Status: Construction began in April 1981; the project opened in November 1983 and was completed in February 1984.

was not completed when the center was formally opened, and the $750 charged each person attending that event produced nearly $1.75 million with which to finish the work.

The endowment fund, minus the $8.5 million used in construction, stood at $4.3 million in 1985, generating about $400,000 annually for the operating budget. Payment of outstanding pledges increased the endowment to about $5.1 million at the end of 1986. The 1 percent hotel/motel room tax brings in about $600,000 annually for the operating budget, while a 6 percent surcharge on gross income of user groups, rentals by user groups (rents have deliberately been kept low), and other concession income generate another $1.45 million. These three sources produce about $2.45 million annually for the operating budget, short of the $2.9 million spent from 1984 through 1985.

Status

The Kentucky Center for the Arts has triggered other development on Main Street. Victorian commercial buildings are now being adapted not only for office space but also for housing. The de-

cision by Humana, Inc., to erect its corporate headquarters on Main Street was undoubtedly influenced by its nearness to the arts center.

Attendance at the wide variety of events (bluegrass music, classic music, arts and crafts shows) runs at more than 400,000 annually. All arts groups using the center reported increases in ticket sales during the first season (1984–1985). The Louisville Theatrical Association, which brings Broadway shows to the city, showed a 33 percent increase with a subscription audience of nearly 6,400. The Louisville Ballet increased subscriptions 20 percent, and Stage One: The Children's Theatre, 200 percent. This upward trend has continued, and sales of tickets for one-performance events have also increased. Some single performances brought to Louisville by the arts center itself have not fared as well, however. The center is still fine-tuning its own programming.

The operating budget shortfalls have required use of some endowment funds. Despite the state's earlier stricture that it would not cover operating budgets, the 1986 Kentucky General Assembly voted $600,000 in appropriations for the

center's 1986–1987 biennium. This action was taken when attempts to raise the necessary funds by increasing the Jefferson County hotel/motel room tax was strongly opposed by local hoteliers. Once such funding is introduced into state budgets, it is likely to remain, although the level of funds may change.

BROADWAY RENAISSANCE

The southern end of the Louisville CBD, centering on Fourth Avenue and Broadway, is in the midst of an ongoing revitalization. Groundwork for the Broadway Renaissance, prepared in 1978, resulted in a full-scale private/public partnership. The first phase, costing $34.4 million, has been completed. The initial construction of the second phase—market-rate housing—began in 1986 at an estimated cost of $27.5 million. This will be the first new market-rate housing in the CBD in a quarter century.

History

In February 1971, the Brown Hotel, one of Louisville's leading hotels since its opening in 1923, closed its doors—another victim of the CBD's waning vitality. It had been the cornerstone of the Fourth and Broadway intersection since the year after its opening. In 1927, one Louisville newspaper called it the "magic corner," referring to the transformation of the immediate area from one of mixed residential and marginal commercial uses to a new center of activity. But little of the magic was left in the 1970s.

The Broadway Renaissance area not only suffered from the general malaise afflicting downtown but also from the redevelopment of the riverfront taking place one mile to the north. The Fourth Avenue Mall of 1973 did not help the situation. By the time the state of Kentucky agreed in 1977 to provide funding for the Center for the Arts in the riverfront area, the future of the Broadway area seemed gloomier than ever. The new center usurped the position of the Macauley Theatre, neighbor to the Brown Hotel, as the centerpiece for the local performing arts.

Capital Holding Corporation, one of the nation's fastest-growing insurance-holding companies located in its own 23-story corporate headquarters at Fourth and Broadway, was not happy about the decline of its business neighborhood. The corporation teamed up with Louisville Central Area, Inc., in 1978 to form the Broadway Group. This broadly based task force of downtown business leaders began looking for ways to infuse new life into the area. With $30,000 from the governor's contingency funds, Zuchelli, Hunter & Associates of Annapolis, Maryland, was commissioned to do the initial planning and feasibility studies, which were completed in December 1979.

Because a developer to handle the entire project would be impossible to find, as was the case with the Galleria, a nonprofit operating entity—the Broadway Project Corporation—was formed in early 1980 to oversee the overall execution of the plan and to find developers for individual components.

Site Development

The Broadway Renaissance involved a mix of new buildings and adaptive reuse of existing structures. To return the Brown Hotel to its original use, the Fourth Avenue Mall had to be reconstructed to permit vehicular access to the hotel entrance. To demolish five older buildings along the mall to make way for new construction required changes in the utility services for the new low-rise structures con-

taining office and retail space. In contemplation of a shuttle bus service along the mall to reach the north end of the CBD, a portion of the mall was repaved with granite Belgian blocks stockpiled from earlier reconstruction projects on Louisville streets. With no unusual problems to be solved, the first phase of the Broadway Renaissance began in mid-1983. The Brown Hotel, the central focus of the project, was reopened in January 1985, with the construction of the project's new buildings completed in the summer of that year.

Planning and Design

Although the proposed design underwent changes as the project actually got underway, the plan from the first called for a mix of new buildings and adaptive use of

The master plan for the first phase of the Broadway Renaissance.

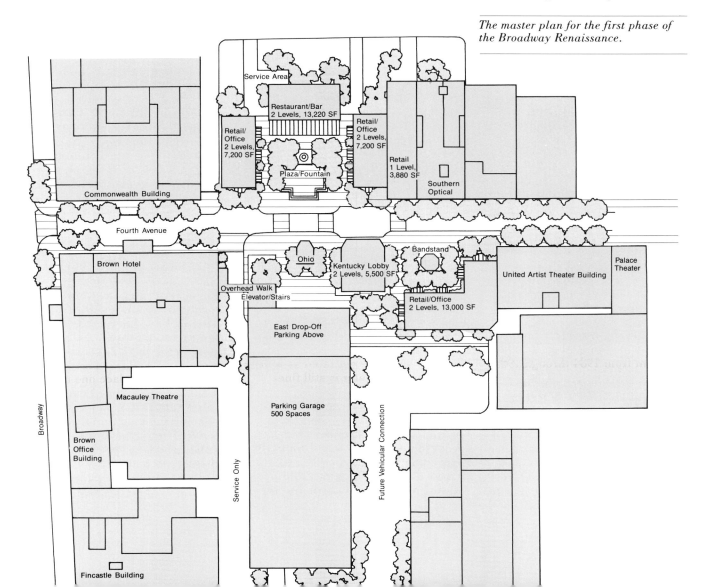

The Fourth Avenue Mall after the Broadway Renaissance. The Brown Hotel is at the left.

many existing structures. The target area, encompassing five square blocks, is large; therefore, planners divided the redevelopment process into three phases. The emphasis is on creating a new and radically different environment as a southern anchor to downtown, where restaurants, shops, and top-quality housing thrive amid landscaping and open spaces.

An important element in the planning was to make the area attractive as a place to live for the growing number of professionals employed in the CBD. The Broadway Renaissance culminates the rebuilding of downtown over the past 15 years, bringing it to life 24 hours a day with a significant population of higher-income residents.

The original planning scheme was regarded as a guide; changes have been made as circumstances required. For instance, some buildings originally marked for demolition have been retained. The Kentucky Theater has been retained as the home for the *KentuckyShow*, a $1.2 million multimedia presentation on Louisville and Kentucky. Another building designated for clearance was saved after the owner/occupant (Southern Optical), which objected to moving, proposed instead to renovate the building and to restore it to its original 1915 appearance by removing an anodized aluminum screen installed in the 1950s.

The first phase of the Broadway Renaissance called for reopening the Brown Hotel, renovating the adjacent Brown Office Building (originally an office building, but later converted to a school), constructing a 475-car parking garage, and transforming the pedestrian mall north of the Brown Hotel into what is now Theater Square. The two developers chosen to undertake this phase—Cranston Development Corporation of Pittsburgh and Sturgeon-Thornton-Marret Development Company (STM) of Louisville—joined forces to form the Broadway-Brown Partnership. In turn, the partnership sought an operator for the hotel, eventually choosing Hilton.

The hotel was not only restored to its original grandeur, but the guest rooms were doubled in size, reducing the total number from 612 to 296. Theater Square, surrounded by new low-rise buildings with 40,000 square feet of commercial space and set back from the old building line, provides a wid-

BROADWAY RENAISSANCE

Project Type: Redevelopment of three square blocks in the CBD, including the rehabilitation and reopening of the grand Brown Hotel, rehabilitation of an existing office building, construction of new commercial and retail buildings (Phase I), and new market-rate apartments and condominiums (Phase II). Further redevelopment is in the planning stage.

Developer: Phase I: Broadway-Brown Partnership, formed by Cranston Development Corporation, Pittsburgh; and Sturgeon-Thornton-Marret Development Company, Louisville.

Phase II: Caldwell American Investments, Inc., Troy, Michigan.

Construction Supervision: Phase I: Landmarks Design Associates, Pittsburgh.

Phase II: Caldwell American Investments, Inc.

Architecture: Phase I: Landmarks Design Associates.

Phase II: Skidmore, Owings & Merrill, Chicago office.

Financing: Phase I: total project cost—$42.9 million. Financing components were $7.6 million in state economic redevelopment bonds; $5 million in UDAG funds to city of Louisville; $5 million in school bonds; $2 million in local labor pension funds; $1.5 million loan from Kentucky Industrial Finance Authority; $12.2 million in private mortgage loans; $5 million in Community Development Block Grant funds; and $4.6 million in equity investment from the developers, Louisville banks, and CBD-headquartered corporations.

Phase II: total project cost—$27.6 million. Financing components are $17 million in city industrial revenue bonds through Manufacturers Hanover Trust, New York City; $2 million state economic redevelopment bonds; $2.6 million in city equity; $1.9 million city loan; $1 million county loan; $1 million grant from James Graham Brown Foundation, Louisville; and $2.1 million in conventional financing for condominiums. An interim loan of $350,000 was made by Citizens Fidelity Bank, Louisville, to Caldwell American Investments.

Status: Phase I: construction began in 1983; hotel rehabilitation was completed and hotel opened in January 1985; new two-story office buildings buildings in Theater Square were completed and opened in June 1985.

Phase II: construction began October 1986 and is expected to be completed October 1988.

ened space unknown on the mall previously. The facade and lobby of an Art Deco cinema has been preserved and converted to a shop. A fountain, lighted at night, plantings, and ornamental street lamps are also part of the Theater Square design. The parking structure, immediately north of the Brown Hotel, is reached by the new vehicular access to the hotel and also from Third Street. A second-level skywalk connects the garage to the hotel. The narrow end of the garage facing Theater Square has been given a facade to match the other new commercial construction and has been set back to provide a small plaza with tables and chairs.

The Broadway Project Corporation invited proposals from developers nationwide for the second phase's market-rate housing, and in 1983 chose Caldwell American Investments, Inc., Troy, Michigan. Caldwell commissioned the Chicago office of Skidmore, Owings & Merrill to design the project.

It is expected that the first housing units will be ready for occupancy by late 1987. The housing will be constructed in phases. The first will consist of 231 units with a planned total of 550. The second phase will occupy property along Third Street north of Broadway, much of which has been devoted to surface parking for some time. The 550 units will include garden, townhouse, mid-rise and high-rise apartments, and townhouse condominiums.

Eighty distinctively designed units called the Crescent will form the centerpiece of the initial construction. Reminiscent of the curved rows of townhouses in Bath, England (which inspired the design), the Crescent will consist of two semicircular, three-story apartment rows facing each other across Third Street. They will be built atop a 346-car, ground-level garage and will be linked by pedestrian bridges across Third Street and surrounded by landscaping. At the eastern edge above the garage, 22 two-story townhouse condominiums will line a landscaped court-

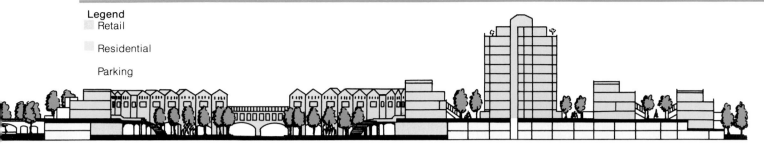

The second phase of the Broadway Renaissance will include mid- and high-rise apartments, condominium garden townhouses, and enclosed parking facilities.

yard and pedestrianway, modeled after Belgravia Court in the Old Louisville neighborhood south of the central business district. Steps and ramps will link the elevated housing level directly to Theater Square.

The first two phases of the Broadway Renaissance will occupy approximately two square blocks of the target area. The third phase, still in the planning stage, will involve the redevelopment of the remaining southern area. The two northern blocks, which require much less planning and redevelopment, are not yet on a scheduled track.

The Broadway Project Corporation has final authority over the plans of developers. Maintenance of completed projects is the responsibility of the owner or operator.

Financing and Development Costs

The financial package for the Broadway redevelopment is the most complex of any of the varied downtown redevelopment projects. The hotel became the headquarters of the Louisville Board of Education shortly after it closed in 1971. The Louisville school system merged with the Jefferson County system in 1975, however, and administrative offices were moved to the latter's headquarters.

The innovative Brown School (located in the Brown Office Building) also moved away from the area. The city of Louisville technically held title to the school, because $5 million in city bonds had been issued to convert the hotel and office buildings to office and school uses. The County Board of Education paid $500,000 in rent annually, which was used to retire the bonds and which the board was obligated to pay even after the buildings were vacated. With that burden, the school board was not inclined to wait for the Broadway Project Corporation to complete a financial package for its project. Indeed, the school board actively sought buyers in 1980 and found some interest among developers who wanted to convert the hotel into apartments, keeping some rooms for hotel use. The corporation bid $4 million for the hotel and office building in November 1980, hoping to lease the structure to avert any other sale and to complete the purchase after other financing had been arranged. Part of this plan called for the city to borrow $1 million against future receipts of federal Community Development Block Grants and to

Site plan for the Crescent, the Broadway Renaissance residential complex.

make this available as part of the purchase price. But the Board of Aldermen, feeling that this procedure would be too risky, refused to ratify the agreement.

In June 1981, the school board sublet the hotel to a developer who proposed to turn it into a life care center for the elderly. When final agreement was reached with the Broadway-Brown Partnership in the fall of 1981, however, the project corporation assumed the lease (which included the office building) from the life care center developer with a $330,000 loan, of which $250,000 came from the city and $80,000 from the county. This represented one year's "rent" to be applied to the city bond issue while federal and state funds were sought to purchase and renovate the property.

Phase I Funding. The state initially agreed to issue $17 million in economic redevelopment bonds, while the city would apply for an $8 million Urban Development Action Grant. This would provide half the estimated $46 million for Phase I, with the rest to be sought from private sources in Louisville. In early 1982, however, the new state administration announced that it would not approve the $17 million in state bonds. The state eventually agreed to provide $7.6 million in bonds and a direct loan of $1.5 million through the Kentucky Industrial Finance Authority. The city received a $5 million UDAG.

Private investment in Phase I included $12.2 million in conventional loans, and $4.6 million in equity from the developers, Louisville banks, and CBD-headquartered companies, with Capital Holding providing $4.5 million of this. Five local labor unions also contributed $2 million in pension funds to the project—making it the first time that unions had participated financially in downtown redevelopment. The Parking Authority of River City approved a $3 million bond issue for the 475-car garage. The total financial package was $42.9 million, excluding the garage. Funding was 48 per-

cent private and 52 percent public (city, 21 percent; state, 20 percent; federal, 11 percent) with most of the latter an obligation of the Broadway-Brown Partnership.

The UDAG provided a five-year interest-free loan, which the developers are to pay back to the city from 50 percent of the cash flow of all elements of Phase I. Because the first draw-down was not made until 1985, repayment will not begin until 1990. The $7.6 million in tax-exempt state economic development bonds is to be paid back at a rate determined by cash flow, but can be deferred until 50 percent of the cash flow is in excess of the minimum payment. The $1.5 million industrial loan is being repaid on a regular schedule over 10 years, with the final payment to be made in 1993.

The public space in Theater Square is owned by the city, which used $5 million in Community Development Block Grant funds to acquire and clear the site (with the Urban Renewal Agency as agent) and to develop the public amenities. The city sold the commercial areas, site of the new construction, to the Broadway-Brown Partnership for $10. The city will also hold technical title to the Brown Hotel until the Broadway-Brown Partnership pays off outstanding bonds from the school renovation of the early 1970s.

Phase II Funding. Funding of $27.6 million for construction of the first 231 units of market-rate housing had been assembled by the end of 1984—or so it was thought. But in January 1985, Louisville lost an anticipated $4.5 million UDAG because it was no longer distressed enough to qualify. Within a few months, however, local corporations and the city provided the funds to bridge this gap. As a limited partner in the development, the city had, for the first time, become involved in a joint venture project in the downtown.

Louisville is providing $2.6 million as equity and $1.9 million as a loan. In addition, the city will issue $17 million in industrial revenue

bonds to be repaid by Caldwell American Investments. Jefferson County is providing a $1 million loan and will hold title to the open spaces in the project, which will be leased to Caldwell American Investments with the payments used to retire the debt. The state has authorized $2 million in economic development bonds to be retired by Caldwell American Investments. Ten CBD-based firms have also guaranteed the purchase of 22 condominiums at $110,000 to $120,000 each, in the event that other purchasers are not found.

Status

The Broadway Renaissance project has already encouraged a substantial amount of other redevelopment in the immediate neighborhood. The 17-story Heyburn Building across Broadway, once drifting in the financial doldrums and auctioned to its mortgage holder, was purchased in 1982 by a local developer aided by a $6 million issue of municipal industrial revenue bonds (IRBs). The once half-empty building had an occupancy rate of over 85 percent by the end of 1986.

As a result of the Broadway Renaissance, the Theatre Building, on the mall north of Theater Square, was renovated in 1985, funded by $2 million in city IRBs. It offers 24,000 square feet of office space and 8,000 square feet of retail space, and leasing is progressing well. Capital Holding has also completed a $2 million renovation of its corporate headquarters, and other established businesses have renovation plans on the drawing boards.

Although assuming the success of the Broadway Renaissance would be premature at this point, the ambience of Fourth and Broadway has improved dramatically and is expected to continue to improve after the shuttle bus service to the Riverfront Project begins operating. At the end of 1986, space in the hotel, in the office building, and in Theater Square was about 75 percent leased. The hotel reported an occupancy rate after its first year of about 50 percent. Special events are often held in Theater Square, and on fine days the benches and fountain area are thronged with people, especially during the noon hour. The prognosis is promising.

WEST MAIN STREET

As a city that grew rapidly in the 19th century, Louisville has a large stock of Victorian architecture and isolated examples of even earlier buildings. Once regarded only as candidates for demolition, these structures have come to be seen in a new light in recent years. The rising cost of new construction, the national interest in preservation of older structures, and tax advantages for rehabilitating older commercial buildings have created a miniboom in the adaptive use of Louisville's older building stock, especially those buildings located in the central business district. The effect of adaptive use has been most dramatic in the West Main Street area of downtown, where a group of older structures extend for several blocks.

History

The city began with Main Street, which became the thoroughfare for commerce. Early visitors invariably commented on the spacious buildings and bustle of activity on the street. Lined with banks, offices, hotels, wholesale houses, insurers, and similar enterprises of a mercantile economy, Main Street reigned supreme as the "headquarters" of the city's decision makers.

Except for an occasional demolition to make way for a parking lot, the city's treasure of old architecture was virtually intact in the early 1960s, especially along West Main Street. The buildings were sound structurally, although they were occupied by low-overhead businesses and presented a rather neglected face to the world.

In the late 1960s, when the Louisville Urban Renewal Agency was seeking a developer to partici-

pate in the Riverfront Project, a well-known New York developer was asked to look at the site. His verdict: "No one's going to invest any money next to this dunghill."

But many Louisvillians had long admired the facades along Main Street (even when it was unfashionable to do so) and the completion of the Riverfront Project turned attention to the thoroughfare when interest in adaptive use was on the rise. The city created a Historic Landmarks and Preservation Districts Commission in 1973, which was soon able to have West Main Street listed on the National Register of Historic Places (as well

as designated a local historic district). Thus, buildings are eligible for tax benefits when renovated. These benefits have become more attractive through time, both at the local and federal levels.

Site Development

Redeveloping West Main Street involved adapting to new uses the buildings along the three and one-half blocks listed on the National Register. There were no utilities to

A typical streetscape on West Main Street.

be relocated, no street patterns to be altered, no earth to be moved, and no zoning to be changed. The major problem for the developer was in meeting federal requirements for renovation to qualify for tax credits. This meant that developers had to restore building exteriors as closely as possible to their original appearance, using original or similar materials. Suddenly, a great demand arose for old photographs, drawings, or architectural plans of West Main Street buildings to use as guides and to demonstrate to the U.S. Department of the Interior that the completed renovation was rooted in historic reality. The first major restoration/renovation occurred in 1972, and activity continues.

Planning and Design

Because each renovation is a separate project, and each is carried out by a different group of developers, no overall plan exists. However, federal rehabilitation guidelines impose some common disciplines that must be followed for buildings to be certified for tax credits. Further, as most of the structures were originally built during the same period and in a similar style, the building stock has a natural unity of design.

Most of the buildings are narrow but deep, typically measuring about 25 feet by 300 feet. Architects, accustomed to designing new structures and using contemporary materials, are challenged by the old buildings, many of whose upper floors were often used as open warehouse space. The greatest difficulty in adapting a building is in providing natural light throughout when the building has windows only at the front and rear. Designers have solved this problem and turned many "shoebox" buildings into quality office space by installing skylights, lightwells, and inner courtyards (in larger structures); by opening up parts of floors; and by carefully placing walls and planning floor layouts. All renovations

include complete replacement of plumbing, heating, and wiring, and the installation of central air conditioning and modern elevators.

The rear windows of these buildings overlook the Ohio River, creating particularly attractive views for offices or conference rooms. Adaptive use was originally aimed at offices, but in 1985 the first housing project was begun. (Three such projects had already been completed on East Main Street.) Adaptive use for housing requires buildings that are wider than and not as deep as standard office buildings. The housing project on West Main contains 20 apartments, some with balconies overlooking the river.

Financing and Development Costs

The designation of West Main Street as a historic preservation district in 1973 provided the needed mechanism with which to rescue the street from its miscellaneous low-level uses. Before, lending institutions had looked askance at committing substantial sums to the area; would-be purchasers and renovators needed to be well endowed with personal resources, even though selling prices were relatively modest. But after a section of West Main Street was listed on the National Register, the availability of a 10 percent federal investment tax credit (ITC) or five-year write-off of renovation costs made investment much more appealing to developers.

Public funding also helped turn the tide. In 1974, the Junior League of Louisville purchased a recently burned-out building shell on West Main Street as its headquarters. The project was aided by a $9,278 grant in Community Development Block Grant funds, one of the earliest CDBG projects in Louisville. In 1975, the city chose to locate the new Museum of History and Science in a large building vacated by a dry goods wholesaler that had moved to a suburban location. Voters had approved a $600,000 bond issue for the muse-

um in 1965, but disagreement about the location had delayed the project. Opening the museum on Main Street in 1977 represented a giant step forward in the thoroughfare's resurgence. Additional funding for the museum came from the local James Graham Brown Foundation ($1.5 million) and from the federal Economic Development Administration ($2.6 million).

National Register status was directly responsible for the first major private renovation on West Main Street. The 65,000-square-foot structure, built in 1856 at 600 West Main Street, was purchased in 1976 for $300,000, and its painstaking renovation was completed in 1979 at a cost of $2.5 million, which included a federal preservation grant of $100,000. The event heralded Main Street's arrival.

The great leap forward came in 1980, however. In that year the Kentucky statutes governing use of industrial revenue bonds were liberalized, making these bonds available for a wide range of commercial construction, including building renovations. Further incentive came in the 1981 federal legislation increasing the maximum investment tax credit to 25 percent, for which every building in the historic district is eligible.

From 1980 through 1985 a total of $37.1 million in industrial revenue bonds (IRBs) was issued for the purchase and renovation of buildings in the three and one-half blocks of West Main. The city issued $24.8 million of this amount, and the county issued $8.8 million. Certified renovation investment was $22.9 million during the same period, indicating purchase costs of about $14.2 million. Because of the individual and uncoordinated nature of the projects, other investment (including that made before 1980) is difficult to determine, but the amount estimated is around $60 million. IRBs have been used to purchase and renovate buildings throughout the CBD, as well as on West Main Street, and some of these buildings qualified for the ITC. IRBs for such purposes—ex-

cluding West Main—have totaled $58.3 million, with $55.5 million from the city and $2.8 million from the county.

Status

Because of a five-year tax moratorium on increasing the value of renovated buildings, local property tax receipts will not begin to reflect the change in property values on West Main Street until early 1987 (when 1986 property tax bills will be issued); after that, values will increase dramatically each year. A more immediate change in property values, however, can be gauged from purchase prices and rental rates.

The first notable renovation occurred in 1972 before tax incentives were available. The four-story building at 600 West Main Street, immediately west of the Riverfront Plaza/Belvedere, was purchased for rehabilitation for $38,000. In 1984, another (larger) unrestored building a block away and two small adjacent structures were sold for $1.25 million. The building at 600 West Main, purchased in 1976 and renovated over a three-year period for $2.8 million, was sold in 1982 for $4 million. Between 1977 and 1985 the cost of unimproved buildings in the district climbed

from $3 or $4 a square foot to around $20 a square foot.

Except for the Museum of Science and History, practically all of the renovated space is devoted to offices, especially those attracting law firms. Rents range from $5 to $13 a square foot, compared with prerenovation rents of $1 or less. The average rent is $10 a square foot, half that of the top rate in the new high rises but higher than rates in most other renovated office space in the rest of the CBD.

With the exception of restaurants, retail development has not yet proved successful. Several art galleries and a bookstore arrived

on the scene prematurely. But as the preservation movement gains momentum—with some $11 million in new projects launched in 1985—and as adaptive use broadens to include market-rate housing, retail development is likely to begin showing up. The project containing 20 apartments, in fact, includes 12,000 square feet of retail space on the ground floor of the renovated building. With parking space at a premium in the area, the Parking Authority of River City—a 514-car, 10-level garage just off Main Street—opened in 1986. The $3.5 million structure, financed by a PARC bond issue, eliminates another of the surface parking lots that was developed in the 1950s.

NEIGHBORHOOD PROJECTS

As Louisville's economic base shifted and one-third of its population moved to what seemed greener pastures beyond the city limits, the impact was felt not only in the central business district but also in many residential areas. Particularly affected were low-income neighborhoods and once-affluent neighborhoods that had long before lost their prestigious aura. Though these neighborhoods, like the downtown, were tougher than many observers believed, they needed help. In the early 1960s, concern about the future of downtown kindled a parallel interest in rescuing older residential areas that had suffered from neglect and changing uses. At the same time, activity in historic preservation was beginning to show the first signs of the strength it would later achieve. In 1961, a group was formed to arouse interest in saving an old and decaying area immediately south of downtown. Composed of civic and community leaders, many of whom grew up in the old neighborhood, the group named the area Old Louisville.

The countermove from the suburbs to the city was also beginning in the 1960s, creating a boon for Old Louisville. Soon the movement back to the city spread to other older neighborhoods, particularly the Highlands and Crescent Hill, and even Butchertown—an area of mixed industrial and residential use containing some of the oldest, most charming, but most neglected housing in the city. Although the move back to the city has never grown to flood proportions, it has had a noticeable effect, which has been reinforced by many young professional newcomers who prefer renovated older housing in the city to life in suburbia. Raising the public's awareness of urban neighborhoods was a first step in the process of gentrification. Residents formed associations to promote the improvement of their neighborhoods. Today, scarcely a Louisville neighborhood exists that does not have such an association.

With help coming from the federal government (particularly in the form of Community Development Block Grants), private corporations, and the neighborhoods themselves, many older residential areas have been able to hold their own; others have improved markedly; and a few have been able to recapture some of their old prestige. The city's Historic Landmarks and Preservation Districts Commission has designated five districts under local ordinances, providing some measure of protection against demolition and unsuitable exterior alterations. Four of these, as well as 17 other districts, are also on the National Register of Historic Places, an unusually large number for a city of Louisville's size and indicative of widespread

RESIDENTIAL HISTORIC DISTRICTS OF LOUISVILLE

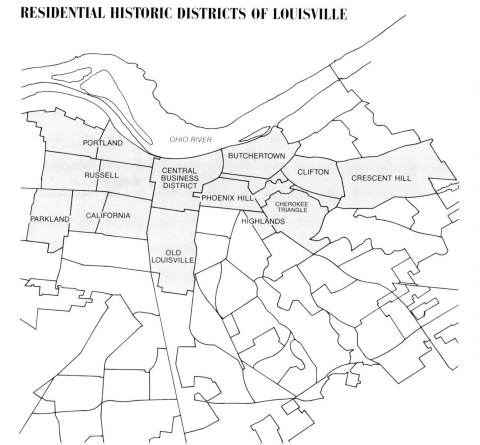

FIGURE 3-5
INVESTMENT TAX CREDIT REHABILITATION PROJECTS IN RESIDENTIAL HISTORIC DISTRICTS[1]

Neighborhood	Completed	In Progress	Proposed
Butchertown	$ 892,456	250,000	$1,032,044
Cherokee Triangle	373,000	346,000	–
Clifton	108,000	–	87,000
Crescent Hill	1,980,000	–	–
Highlands	1,643,152	412,995	587,000
Limerick	296,092	80,000	482,500
Old Louisville	7,550,757	6,573,053	1,368,470
Parkland	–	614,500	–
Portland	20,000	–	–
Phoenix Hill	1,592,800	535,000	100,000
Russell	–	100,000	1,151,400

[1] From the inception of ITC in January 1982 to August 1985.
Source: Louisville Landmarks Commission.

community interest. Established in 1973, the Landmarks Commission has since handled 2,500 applications for renovations under the guidelines set by city ordinance. Use of the investment tax credit and accelerated cost recovery increased the volume of renovations in these districts; by mid-1985, some 985 units had been rehabilitated under the ITC program. An additional incentive is that both Louisville and Jefferson County allow a five-year moratorium on tax increases on rehabilitated buildings that are at least 25 years old.

Below-market-rate construction or permanent financing from the state-sponsored Kentucky Housing Corporation has also aided the process of neighborhood revitalization. The housing corporation, for example, entered into a joint venture with the Brown-Forman Corporation to renovate nine houses and construct 22 new ones in an old and seriously depressed inner-city neighborhood called California. Earlier, Brown-Forman had renovated three houses in the California area under the Adopt-a-House Program initiated by the private non-profit Preservation Alliance. In 1984, the housing corporation initiated its "cluster-loan" program, providing financing for builders to construct clusters of new housing for low-income residents in deteriorating neighborhoods. It made

available $273,000 to a group of builders who in 1985 erected eight new houses in California ranging in price from $32,000 to $46,000. All were sold before the end of the year, financed by 7.5 percent, 30-year mortgages from the housing corporation.

But gentrification is occurring most rapidly in neighborhoods in which older housing was built to top quality standards and is substantially intact, and in which a large pool of contiguous housing is available for renovation.

OLD LOUISVILLE

The Old Louisville neighborhood, lying immediately south of the CBD, stretches approximately two miles from Broadway to the University of Louisville's Belknap Campus. It is about three-quarters of a mile wide, bounded on the east by Interstate 65 and on the west by Sixth Street. Once the home of the city's elite, it is described by architectural historians as containing the largest concentration of Victorian houses in the United States. Some are mansions; others are more modest. The average square footage of the mostly stone and brick houses is about 3,500. In 1962, Old Louisville inaugurated the city's historic preservation movement, now a potent factor in development throughout the city.

History

The northern half of Old Louisville was developed while Louisville was shifting to a manufacturing base during the years following the Civil War; the southern half was developed over a period spanning the 1880s through the early 20th century, when a new managerial class was forming.

Laying claim to the most prestigious address was Third Street, described in the 1890s as "lined with palaces." Rivaling Third Street was St. James Court with its splashing fountain and its tree-lined mall extending between dual carriageways. But as early as the 1920s, when the automobile was creating a suburban explosion, a local magazine declared Third Street "passe."[3] The Depression of the 1930s, during which real estate values plummeted, was not kind to the area. Old Louisville suffered further during World War II, when many of its large houses were partitioned into small sleeping rooms and apartments to house the influx of defense plant employees. The federal government encouraged this trend by making available low-interest loans, and by implying that failure to provide housing for de-

[3] *Journal of the Louisville Board of Trade,* 1927. This journal was the predecessor to the *Louisville* magazine.

An example of the Victorian-style houses in Old Louisville.

fense plant workers in this area (with its excellent public transportation) was unpatriotic. The second suburban explosion after World War II resulted in the departure of most of the remaining well-to-do residents, the rise of the absentee landlord, and the neglect of many of the fine old homes.

Nevertheless, the neighborhood retained many assets: two institutions of higher education, the J.B. Speed Art Museum, the main public library, Memorial Auditorium, and other amenities such as the 17-acre urban oasis, Central Park. It also had a large "alumni" group—business and civic leaders who had been born in Old Louisville and spent their early years there before their families moved to the newly fashionable suburban areas. In 1961, many of these "natives" formed the Old Louisville Association to promote interest in the neighborhood. In 1962, many of these same individuals formed Res-

toration, Inc., to undertake the renovation of housing units and to place them on the market.

Planning and Design

Restoration, Inc., originally planned to buy a group of houses on a short, quiet street on the eastern perimeter of Old Louisville, but premature newspaper announcements caused a shift in location. Fearing real estate speculation in the initial target area, the organization quietly turned its attention to Belgravia Court, a component of the St. James Court complex, where it purchased a group of nine contiguous houses dating from the 1890s. A local interior designer who had demonstrated skill and enthusiasm in this new field was engaged to oversee the design and renovation. The project was to act as a pump-primer to encourage private renovation efforts, which in fact has been the case, although these efforts have proceeded at a somewhat slower pace than the initiators had hoped. The houses were brought up to contemporary

standards by installing new wiring, plumbing, heating plants, and central air conditioning. Interior layouts were revamped and imaginative use of exterior paint highlighted architectural details.

The Louisville Urban Renewal Agency, then the recipient of federal funding, also had plans for Old Louisville, unveiling them in 1964. The agency, accustomed to packaging and clearing large tracts for redevelopment, acquired and cleared land for the expansion of the University of Louisville campus but was less successful at implementing neighborhood renewal. Although low-interest loans were available for housing rehabilitation, the application and contracting process was so complex and time-consuming that only part of the sweeping proposals for remodeling the neighborhood were carried out. The better contractors found the bidding process so cumbersome that generally they avoided urban renewal contracts. The field was left largely to less competent and underfunded contractors, who sometimes abandoned a half finished project when they found that they had bid too low to make a profit. The agency never activated its plans for the bulk of the area. Some property acquired and cleared for a street-widening project was abandoned and remained vacant and on the market in 1986.

In planning for Old Louisville, the agency concluded that heavy automobile traffic, especially on Third and Fourth Streets, had been partly responsible for the neighborhood's decline. To remedy this, the agency proposed that alternate blocks of Third Street, which is very wide, be transformed into pedestrianways to eliminate through-traffic. The city's Bureau of Traffic Engineering demurred, however.

A second proposal, which aroused a storm of protest from residents, called for a traffic bypass along the western edge of the area. This Ninth Street thoroughfare would have demolished many homes, but the greatest danger that residents perceived was

the possibility of an elevated expressway with an interchange being built above the thoroughfare; this would threaten several of the restored houses on Belgravia Court and diminish property values for some distance around. City and state traffic and highway engineers were also cool to the proposal; they had not been consulted and the concept was not in their long-range planning schemes. Finally the mayor, bowing to citizen pressure, killed the proposal in 1969. Many of the houses that would have been demolished have since been renovated.

Management and Maintenance

As the gentrification process gradually made headway, the area's remaining churches began to plan for the future, spearheading the 1969 formation of the Neighborhood Development Corporation. This nonprofit organization serves as a watchdog for such neighborhood concerns as zoning, upgrading of schools, and design of new structures. It has also rehabilitated some of the more modest housing on the area's fringes.

The affiliated Old Louisville Neighborhood Council, an umbrella group representing smaller

neighborhood groups, provides a forum in which to discuss and find solutions for neighborhood problems; it also sponsors events to promote the area and to maintain a sense of unity. Residents support these organizations and also sponsor various fund-raising events, the largest of which is the annual three-day St. James Court Art Fair, which attracts as many as 100,000 visitors from throughout the metropolitan area.

In 1972, much of Old Louisville was placed on the National Register of Historic Places. In 1974, the newly created Louisville Landmarks and Historic Districts Commission selected the southern half of the area as the city's first historic district, which protected structures in the district from unacceptable exterior changes or hasty demolition.

Financing and Development Costs

Restoration, Inc., invested only $150,000, or slightly over $16,000 each for the purchase and renovation of the first nine houses in Old Louisville in 1962. Today, the cost of purchasing and renovating a house is well over $100,000, except in some fringe areas. Revitalizing

the neighborhood has been an ongoing, house-by-house process largely accomplished by individuals. As a result, the total investment—especially during the early years—is almost impossible to calculate.

Under the five-year tax moratorium on increased value of renovated houses, the city reports that the total investment in certified rehabilitation from the beginning of 1980 through 1985 was $7.6 million and is continuing to rise. Almost all of this expenditure is in conventional loans and mortgages issued through Louisville financial institutions. Estimates for such expenditures before 1980 range from $5 million to $7 million.

More recently, investment groups have used industrial revenue bonds to rehabilitate old houses and to construct new units. As of 1986, Old Louisville was the only residential district in the city in which IRBs had been used. (They have also been used for residential development in the CBD.) By the end of 1985, a total of $33.6 million in IRBs and loans from Community Development Block Grant funds had been applied to Old Louisville housing needs.

Status

Although no special tax incentives at either the federal or local levels existed in 1962, the initial work on Belgravia Court tapped a latent community interest, especially among young professionals. The large and elegant space offered by older houses and their low purchase price of $7 to $9 per square foot, plus a boost from the media, triggered the sale of the first nine houses. Soon, individual renovators were purchasing other unrestored houses in both Belgravia Court and the intersecting St. James Court. The seed thus planted began spreading outward to the rest of Old Louisville.

Today, between 75 and 80 percent of the rehabilitation activity in all 21 National Register districts in the city is in Old Louisville. One of the neighborhood's attractions is its proximity to the CBD. Other statistics shed light on the changes in the neighborhood. The decline in population, ordinarily viewed as a cause for alarm, instead reflects the transformation of housing that had been divided into small and unsatisfactory units for a transient population into housing with two or three larger apartments that attracts a much more stable population. Some houses have been returned to single-family units with the owners occupying them. The median income, generally below the city's average in 1950, had risen above the city's average in all tracts except one in 1980. (See Figures 3-6 and 3-7.)

Although tax receipts will not reflect the bulk of the increased assessments until early 1987, a

FIGURE 3-6
OLD LOUISVILLE POPULATION CHANGES BY CENSUS TRACTS

Census Tract	1950	1960	1970	1980
50	6,434	3,149	2,022	1,692
51	6,710	4,575	3,442	2,972
52	6,251	5,409	4,699	3,362
53	3,889	3,086	1,759	1,948

Source: U.S. Census Bureau.

FIGURE 3-7
OLD LOUISVILLE MEDIAN FAMILY INCOME CHANGES BY CENSUS TRACTS[1]

Census Tract	1950	1960	1970	1980
Citywide	$2,723	$5,280	$8,564	$12,274
50	1,763	3,901	6,935	16,000
51	2,419	4,407	6,313	8,041
52	2,632	4,219	6,055	13,671
53	2,724	4,688	6,711	15,121

[1]The greatest changes have occurred in the two southernmost tracts, 52 and 53. The astounding increase in Tract 50 relates to the popularity of the 800 Apartments with many high-income retired persons. Elsewhere, the tract is occupied mainly by public and private institutions. Tract 51 contains a number of public and private high-rise apartments for the elderly.
Source: U.S. Census Bureau.

St. James Court fountain in Old Louisville.

sampling taken by the Landmarks Commission of recently completed projects showed that the $1.5 million assessed value before rehabilitation will be increased to $2.6 million.

Investors are now renovating large projects. A "cluster" project has restored a full block of houses that had been defaced with one-story, frontyard commercial extensions. The $2.9 million rehabilitation was financed by $1.5 million in IRBs, owner equity, and Community Development Block Grant loans. The investment group is currently expanding the project to an adjacent street.

Station House Square represents an example of new housing in Old Louisville. An investment group completed the $4.9 million project in late 1986 on land cleared through urban renewal. A $3.5 million city IRB issue, private financing, and owner equity provided the financing for the 93 apartments and townhouses. Two county IRB issues totaling $27.2 million have assisted construction of church-affiliated, multiple-unit housing for the elderly.

THE HIGHLANDS/CHEROKEE TRIANGLE

On the high ground east of downtown Louisville and Phoenix Hill lies a large area containing several closely related neighborhoods known collectively as the Highlands. At the turn of the century, this area was Old Louisville's only serious competitor as a prestigious location. Although the Highlands suffered less than Old Louisville from negative changes through time, there were enough to cause concern and to prompt action to reverse signs of decline.

History

The Highlands began life shortly after the Civil War, but because of its distance from the central business district and the hard climb it gave horse-drawn vehicles, it developed slowly. Then, in the 1890s, the electric streetcar, providing easy access, and the creation of Cherokee Park, providing a 410-acre sylvan retreat, spurred rapid development. In the following years, the Highlands grew ever more fashionable, and by the 1920s, its tree-lined streets and winding roads were recognized as the most prestigious of Louisville addresses.

Developing over a long time span, the Highlands covers a large area and contains a variety of housing styles ranging from modest cottages and bungalows to grand mansions. Each of the smaller neighborhoods is set apart by geography, age, and quality of housing, and each has its own neighborhood association. Although the Cherokee Triangle neighborhood was the site of the earliest development in the 1870s, most of its housing is roughly equivalent to Old Louisville's residential development of the 1890s.

Being on the fringe of the city, the Highlands had no barrier to outward growth, unlike Old Louisville, which was boxed in by lower-income neighborhoods and the CBD. The Highlands as a whole contains a variety of architectural styles from the 1870s to the 1920s. The area collectively maintained its prestige, especially in the newer areas at the outward ring of growth, because of its varied topography, large lots, the proximity of Cherokee park, and the absence of constraints to expansion. Consequently, the move to suburbia had far less effect on the Highlands overall than on other Louisville neighborhoods. (See Figure 3-8.)

Despite its relatively strong position, the Highlands by the 1960s, faced problems. As some of the long-time residents left the area, their large, single-family homes were converted to efficiency apartments or demolished to make way for apartment buildings that were usually incompatible with the area's architectural character. Bardstown Road, the neighborhood's main artery and its commercial heart, began to grow shabby in spots. Some of the older houses showed marked signs of neglect and some were remodeled inappropriately.

Planning and Design

A survey conducted among residents in 1972 by the Highlands Development Committee (a citizen group formed in response to the negative changes) showed that 43 percent felt the area overall was changing for the worse, 29 percent found no change, and 28 percent said it was changing for the better. But in individual neighborhoods the response differed: only 27 percent of residents felt that their immediate area was changing for the worse.

The difference in response reflected the influx of newcomers committed to the improvement of their particular neighborhoods. The rise of the preservation movement and neighborhood conscious-

Typical street in the Highlands/Cherokee Triangle neighborhood.

ness in the 1970s found fertile ground in the Highlands, which provided a ready-made landing place for younger people interested in urban living and amenities. The Cherokee Triangle, with its older and less expensive housing, was especially favored.

The National Register of Historic Places placed the Highlands on its list in the early 1970s, along with the contiguous Cherokee Triangle. Shortly after, the Triangle was also designated a local historic district. The listings have made the two districts eligible for investment tax credits, with the Triangle also eligible for the five-year tax moratorium on increased property values resulting from housing rehabilitation.

Aside from normal zoning regulations and historic preservation district status, no overall planning scheme has been devised. But because the Louisville Landmarks Commission designated it a historic district, the Cherokee Triangle has been able to halt the indiscriminate razing of older houses and prevent unacceptable exterior alterations.

Management and Maintenance

As in the case of other Louisville neighborhoods, the momentum to solve management and maintenance problems comes from the neighborhood associations, which have close ties with their aldermen. To halt the slow deterioration of the Bardstown Road commercial district, businesses and neighborhood associations have jointly formed a nonprofit group, Bardstown Road

Interior of a condominium at 1400 Willow Terrace in the Cherokee Triangle. The project opened in 1983.

Tomorrow, Inc., which encourages store owners to upgrade retail outlets and offices.

Financing and Development Costs

The amount of private funds invested in the Highlands and Cherokee Triangle historic districts before the investment tax credit went into effect in 1982 cannot be readily determined. But from 1982 through 1985 ITC projects totaled $2.9 million and more were in the pipeline for approval. The total private investment since 1970 is estimated to exceed $7 million, which is less than in Old Louisville because the bulk of the housing had

been maintained in reasonably good condition. Some $355,000 in Community Development Block Grant funds was channeled through Bardstown Road Tomorrow, Inc., to make loans to businesses for renovation during the seven-year period from 1979 through 1985.

Status

Gentrification in the classic sense did not occur in the Highland/Cherokee Triangle area because the neighborhood had lost only part of its population. Rather, a neighborhood wishing to remain strong took action to avert decline. As Figure 3-9 shows, incomes have always been above the Louisville median, but they increased their lead somewhat during the 1970s and indications are that this trend is continuing, reflecting the ongoing influx of young professionals. The slight decline in population reflects the reconversion of many older houses from high-density effi-

FIGURE 3-8
HIGHLANDS/CHEROKEE TRIANGLE POPULATION CHANGES BY CENSUS TRACTS

Census Tract	1950	1960	1970	1980
82	6,006	4,982	5,213	4,405
83	3,577	3,402	3,388	3,158
84	4,662	4,161	3,950	3,434
85	2,476	2,458	2,528	2,227

Source: U.S. Census Bureau.

FIGURE 3-9
HIGHLANDS/CHEROKEE TRIANGLE FAMILY MEDIAN INCOME CHANGES BY CENSUS TRACTS[1]

Census Tract	1950	1960	1970	1980
Citywide	$2,723	$5,280	$ 8,564	$12,274
82	3,516	7,151	10,143	21,458
83	3,764	7,542	10,646	22,287
84	3,472	6,269	9,540	17,695
85	4,100	7,520	12,689	25,246

[1] Census Tract 82 corresponds exactly with the Cherokee Triangle; others correspond fairly well with the Highlands historic district. The process of gentrification is especially evident in the Cherokee Triangle.
Source: U.S. Census Bureau.

ciency apartments to only one or two large apartments, or to a single-family house occupied by the owner. As with other Louisville neighborhoods, the increase in property values will gradually show up in tax receipts as the moratorium on increased assessments begins to expire five years after each renovation.

PHOENIX PLACE

Can market-rate housing be built in the inner city with a public housing project as a neighbor and be successful? Most developers would be dubious, but in Phoenix Place, this approach is working. Redevelopment of the area also offers an example of private initiative teaming with public agencies to transform a distressed neighborhood and persuade professionals to live close to the central business district.

History

Phoenix Hill, just east of the downtown, is what remains of an old and once-stable neighborhood that was partially cleared for public housing in the late 1930s and for the Medical Center in the 1950s. The name is misleading as the topography of the area is quite flat. In the early 19th century, the area was known simply as Uptown as distinguished from Downtown, now the CBD. The name Phoenix Hill was adopted when businesses in the neighborhood slowly began a

campaign in 1976 to turn the area around. The name was appropriated from a brewery and public garden once located on the slope of land just west of the Highlands neighborhood.

Despite the attrition of the years, Phoenix Hill still retains a number of modest brick and frame houses—some dating to the 1840s—that were home to Louisville's mid-19th century German and Irish immigrants. During the early 20th century, the neighborhood slowly began changing character as the prospering residents moved up the hill to newer and more fashionable areas and were replaced by a low-income population. After World War II, the erosion of the

neighborhood accelerated. The population dropped from 16,500 in 1950 to about 5,800 in 1975. During the same period, about 2,100 residences were demolished, largely to make way for the new Medical Center.

The poverty level in the Phoenix Hill residential area was more than double that for the city as a whole, with a 30 percent unemployment rate (including residents in public housing). Many residents were elderly and depended on social security as their only means of support. In 1980, the average family income was about $5,000. An air of gentle decay hovered over a once-vigorous area.

Drawing their strength from other parts of the metropolitan area are, however, a number of established businesses in the neighborhood: a major building contractor, a paint manufacturer, a bank, several small light-manufacturing and processing operations, and one of the city's best-known Italian restaurants. Businesses such as these joined forces in 1976 to form the Phoenix Hill Association to develop a plan for revitalizing the neighborhood.

Renovated and new housing can be found side by side in Phoenix Place.

Planning and Design

The Phoenix Hill Association took its case to city hall and was assured that government would do what it could to help. The Home Builders Association of Louisville agreed to cooperate with the city in erecting 125 housing units for low- to middle-income residents. In 1977, the Louisville and Jefferson County Planning Commission completed a preliminary survey of the neighborhood, but elections that year for mayor and aldermen delayed action.

Finally, in 1979, a $148,000 contract, using Community Development Block Grant funds, was awarded to the Memphis firm of Colloredo Associates to design a

Phoenix Hill site plan. Phoenix Place is the cluster of housing located between Chestnut and Muhammad Ali Boulevard.

PHOENIX PLACE

Project Type:	Center-city, market-rate housing involving a mix of new construction and rehabilitation of existing structures.
Developers:	McCormick, Barton & Associates, Inc., St. Louis; Bright Properties, Inc., Louisville.
Construction Supervision:	Kremer Group Architects, Louisville.
Architecture:	Trivers Associates, St. Louis.
Financing:	Total project cost: $25.3 million. Financing components were $8.3 million in city IRBs; a $9.3 million loan from the city; $6.7 million in conventional mortgage loans through Rowland & Company, St. Louis, mortgage bankers; and $1 million in developers' equity.
Status:	Phase I construction began in 1983; the project opened in 1984.
	Phase II construction began in 1985; the project opened in 1986.

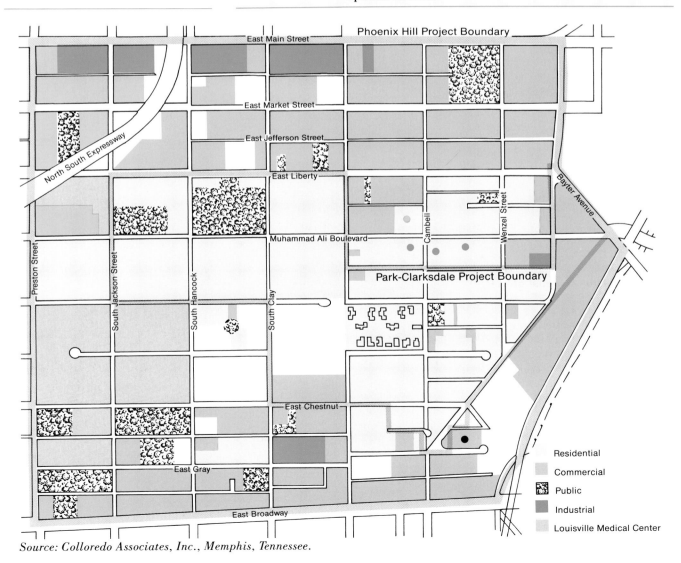

Legend:
- Residential
- Commercial
- Public
- Industrial
- Louisville Medical Center

Source: Colloredo Associates, Inc., Memphis, Tennessee.

"new town" in Phoenix Hill. The plan, completed in early 1980, called for demolition of 204 substandard houses, construction of 280 new housing units, and closing or rerouting certain streets to reserve parts of the new town for pedestrian traffic only. Meanwhile, the beginnings of recession had ended the Home Builders Association's plan to erect new housing with private financing. The Colloredo proposal created sharp debate between neighborhood residents, weary of the slow progress, and public authorities.

With a HUD loan to the city assured, however, the Board of Aldermen approved the plan in April 1983, and shortly afterward the Louisville Urban Renewal Agency, which was to be the agent in acquiring land, also approved it. Aldermanic approval cleared the way to seek developers. The successful bid was made by a partnership between a Louisville developer and a St. Louis developer, who proposed an urban village called Phoenix Place, which would be developed according to the approved plan but would use some of the sound existing housing. The project would include 140 units—of which 114 would be new construction and 26 would be renovated older housing—with a landscaped mall instead of a closed street, a swimming pool, a clubhouse, and other amenities. Each unit would have a fully equipped kitchen and a washer and dryer.

Aiming for middle- and upper-middle-income tenants, the developers set rents ranging from $300

Recreational amenities are part of the Phoenix Place housing development.

to $400 per month for one- and two-bedroom apartments and townhouses. They believed that professionals employed in the Medical Center and the CBD would be drawn to Phoenix Place because of its convenient location. Because Community Development Block Grant funds were involved, 20 percent of the units were reserved for HUD Section 8 subsidies. A group of Louisville developers also entered the scene with a proposal for a more modest project of 46 townhouses near the main development; these would be fully subsidized by Section 8. The Urban Renewal Commission approved both proposals in 1983.

Site Development

Site preparation consisted of demolishing 204 dilapidated or abandoned housing units, relocating utilities to serve the new construction, and closing parts of two streets. City government also brought up to standard other thoroughfares in the area and installed a number of new street lights. The Urban Renewal Agency handled property acquisition and resales to private developers. The only homeowner who objected to selling her house reached a compromise with the developer in which she sold the house but was then permitted to remain as a tenant in the renovated cottage for the remainder of her life. Work began on the initial

phase in the fall of 1983 and was completed one year later; a second phase began in the summer of 1985 and was completed by the summer of 1986.

Financing and Development Costs

A HUD loan to the city for $3.2 million (with repayment from future CDBGs) made possible the initial phase of the project. The loan was used to acquire and clear land, relocate families, repair streets, and improve street lighting. This step paved the way to seek developers. With the completion of the first 140 units, the developers soon decided to add another 140, thus implementing the full Colloredo planning design.

In putting together a package of public and private financing, the city requested $2 million in UDAG funds for the expansion. But in November 1984, the Department of Housing and Urban Development turned down the request for the same reason that the Broadway Renaissance UDAG was denied a few months later: Louisville was no longer distressed enough to qualify.

Rather than see the second phase of the project scuttled, the city agreed to replace the shortfall with $2 million from the $15 million special dividend it received from refinancing the bond debt of the municipally owned water company. For the total 280 housing units in both phases, the city issued $8.3 million in industrial revenue bonds on behalf of the developers, as well as a loan of $9.3 million, of which $7.3 million came from Community Development Block Grant funds and $2 million from the water utility dividend. In addition to repaying the IRBs and the loans, the developers secured $6.7 million in conventional mortgage financing and provided $1 million in equity. Financing for the entire project totaled $25.3 million.

Status

Phoenix Place easily found tenants. Many began moving in even before all the units were completed. Shortly after its formal opening, the project was 100 percent occupied. The tenants are predominantly professionals who work in the Medical Center or in the CBD. Many are single. With that endorsement, the developers decided to carry out the rest of the Colloredo proposal: they developed 102 new and 38 renovated units, almost all of which rented shortly after they were completed in late summer of 1986.

The success of Phoenix Hill triggered other nearby market-rate apartment developments. The latest is the conversion of a three-story, 1881 structure—most recently used as a printing plant—on East Main Street only four blocks from Phoenix Hill. The conversion includes a total of 32 one- and two-bedroom apartments with some units on two levels. Rentals will range from $375 to $500 a month. Other housing developments underway throughout the CBD demonstrate that developers who are participating in public/private partnerships are confident of a resurgence of downtown living.

LESSONS LEARNED

- **Private sector efforts alone are not enough.** Louisville's first efforts at meeting the problems of inner-city decay by relying exclusively on the private sector failed, because such an approach provided no motivation other than philanthropic impulse. Commendable as such an impulse may be, it can work only in special circumstances and in a highly limited context—such as Brown-Forman Corporation's participation in the renovation of housing in its own California neighborhood. A profit motive must also be built in to persuade the private sector to commit large amounts of risk capital to urban rebuilding.

- **Piecemeal efforts do not work.** This lesson was learned in the 1950s. Large projects must be planned and implemented on a large scale—not in separate bits and pieces. Louisville's successful Medical Center became the first such project. The Galleria and the Broadway Renaissance of the 1980s repesent the most recent examples.

- **Public/private partnership is essential.** The Medical Center put city government (which was reluctant at first) into the business of restructuring the built environment. The local private sector had not yet learned that it must do more than simply generate plans for the public sector to implement; it must also actively participate. In steering the Riverfront Project through a morass of financial problems, Louisville's private sector laid the groundwork for public/private cooperation. Such an arrangement becomes, in fact, a business partnership from which each party hopes to benefit: the private sector can benefit through a reasonable return on its investment; the government can benefit

through increased tax revenues. Both hope that current redevelopment will generate future development.

- **CEOs must participate.** If the public/private partnership is to work most effectively, chief executive officers must participate in planning and strategy. Projects like the Galleria or the Broadway Renaissance could never have gone beyond the hopeful stage if CEOs and other executives, as well as top elected officials of both local and state governments, had not been involved. Only at these levels can commitments be made that will assure the successful implementation of large-scale projects.

- **A development stratagem must be prepared.** One of the basic faults of the urban renewal approach in Louisville has been that it has been geared principally to demolition, often in less-than-desirable locations, with no clear idea of what was to replace the buildings destroyed. Not all cleared land was put to the best use, and some of it had to wait until the 1980s to find new uses.

- **Good icing does not guarantee a good cake.** The urban renewal approach often proved wrong because the market was not always considered. The Fourth Avenue Mall failed to attract more shoppers to the CBD's main shopping thoroughfare. Trees and benches alone could not solve the problem; the project needed accessible parking and major improvements in the quality of shopping.

- **The question of "enough" office space is an open issue.** Louisville learned that, contrary to what many said, expanding the supply of office space in the CBD did not result in a permanent surplus. The availability of quality office space in the downtown is often the crucial factor in attracting firms from elsewhere, or in retaining firms, particularly those that need to expand.

- **The future.** The final results of Louisville's public/private redevelopment of the CBD and its anticipated residential renaissance will not be known for another five to 10 years. In that sense, redevelopment in the city is an ongoing experiment. But the increase in downtown employment and 30-day shopper figures, the 100 percent occupancy rate in Phoenix Place, the massive amounts of private investment in housing renovation in older residential areas, and other positive developments indicate that the city is going in the right direction.

PITTSBURGH

PITTSBURGH
A COMMENTARY

D uring my 17 years as a transplanted Pittsburgher, the city has undergone dramatic changes. A bit of pride creeps into my occasional "tour guide" presentation to out-of-towners as I catalog the explosion of commercial, retail, residential, and cultural projects, some of which I worked on as an urban planner and later as a real estate lawyer.

With justification, the remarkably successful 40-year public/private partnership that has been the driving force behind Pittsburgh's phoenixlike revival has been elevated to almost mythological status along with the industrial giants who conceived and engineered Pittsburgh's first explosion of growth at the turn of the century.

Squirrel Hill continues to be a choice yet affordable residential area that is easily accessible to downtown.

Andrew Bacque/Courtesy Pittsburgh Department of City Planning

Yet, for all the manifest success of Pittsburgh's "renaissance," what remains to be done by the public/private partnership is formidable, and the markers of success not as obvious as the glass, stone, and steel monuments of the last 40 years.

Like many other northeast and "rustbelt" cities, Pittsburgh has hooked its vision of the future to a high-tech, information-based, research and development economy and the large supporting service sector generated by that economy. But is there enough high-tech and R&D out there to justify these visions of the future? If not, and if Pittsburgh is going to compete strongly with other areas to attract high-tech firms, what must be done to capture these scarce economic jewels? Can the city realistically retrain a large workforce that was trained in the skills needed for disappearing industries? How serious an impediment to development is Pittsburgh's aging infrastructure, and what is the strategy for its replacement? What tax and financial incentives for development can be created without mortgaging the long term ahead for short-term "fixes"?

With all of its promise for the future, the hard reality of Pittsburgh's present is that its population has declined over the last three decades by more than one-third, creating very difficult public/private policy choices. Does the public sector unselectively support all proposed private development activity? Or does a static population and a limited economic demand require a strategy that actually discourages some development projects that might impair the economic viability of established development in critical locations like the central business district? Should scarce public resources for neighborhood revitalization be directed primarily to neighborhoods experiencing the worst deterioration and population loss, or should they be directed to neighborhoods that are sound enough physically, economically, and socially to make their revitalization through public/private efforts reasonably feasible?

Unfortunately, one of the major keys to Pittsburgh's future may lie in the political process of many suburban municipalities that surround the city. (There are 129 municipalities, in addition to Pittsburgh, in Allegheny County alone.) Although it is not unusual for a major city at the center of a metropolitan area to offer the cultural, recreational, medical, educational, and other institutional resources for the metropolitan area, Pittsburgh suffers from the legal inability to shift at least some of the cost of sustaining those metropolitan resources to the residents of the other municipalities that use and enjoy them. In addition, Pittsburgh suffers indirectly from the general reduction of resources and taxes resulting from the inefficiencies of a fragmented, governmental structure.

Several other lingering but important issues (and opportunities) remain. Can Pittsburgh generate the additional downtown residential development that may be necessary to sustain and extend the vitality of its existing and proposed downtown retail and entertainment sectors? Even with its compact and relatively crime-free central business district, the city has had difficulty generating in-town living, perhaps, ironically, because of the high quality and convenient transportation of many of its traditional residential neighborhoods.

Pittsburgh has also been somewhat slow to accommodate the new housing markets created by shifting demographic groups ranging from yuppies to empty nesters, and has unnecessarily conceded those markets to the suburbs. In this new world of smaller and often childless families, Pittsburgh's old but often elegant housing stock offers significant opportunities for adaptive use if the formula can be found to use these resources without adversely affecting the traditional single-family neighborhoods in which they are located. Pittsburgh's riverfronts—where smokestack industries now stand idly—also offer rich unmined resources that could provide new living environments and commercial opportunities.

Obviously, there are many problems yet to be solved and many opportunities yet to be taken advantage of. But those of us involved in Pittsburgh's development maintain a strong and realistically based belief that Pittsburgh, through a combination of good leadership and good fortune, has the right mix of economic, social, and physical elements to build a vital and exciting future.

Joel P. Aaronson is a partner with the law firm of Reed Smith Shaw & McClay in Pittsburgh, Pennsylvania.

Townhouses in Manchester area of Pittsburgh—one of the many affordable housing choices available near the downtown.

BACKGROUND AND CONTEXT

PITTSBURGH PRESENT

Located at the confluence of the Monongahela and the Allegheny rivers, which join to form the Ohio River, Pittsburgh is set amid rugged hills and river valleys, its land rich in oil, gas, and other natural resources. The city itself ranks third in the nation as a major corporate headquarters center and second in the control of invested capital. Giving testimony to this is the skyline of the Golden Triangle, heart of Pittsburgh's downtown, which is made up of corporate headquarter towers of giants such as PPG Industries, U.S. Steel, Mellon Bank, Westinghouse, and ALCOA.

The city is in the midst of a building boom that began in 1977 and that has added 6.5 million square feet of new office space to the downtown inventory since 1980, and has brought a $482 million public investment in the neighborhoods. And growth continues.

All this is capped by Pittsburgh's number one ranking in Rand McNally's 1985 *Places Rated Almanac* as the best place in which to live. Not bad for a city that was once known as, "hell with the lid off," and about which Frank Lloyd Wright advised, "Abandon it." During those years, Pittsburgh's steel furnaces were belching out fire and smoke and grit and earning it the title, "Hearth of the Nation," and its reputation as a smokey city.

Pittsburgh's transformation from a tired, dark smokestack community to a vibrant urban center began some four decades ago. Spearheaded by industrialist financier Richard King Mellon through the Allegheny Conference on Community Development, and by Mayor David L. Lawrence, public and private interests combined with public and private capital to initiate a rebirth marked by extraordinary energy and leadership. It was a bootstrap effort. Known as the Pittsburgh Renaissance, it began with the imposition of smoke and flood controls and the rebuilding of the downtown. Half a billion dollars and 20 years later, Pittsburgh boasted clear air, a skyline punctuated by new corporate skyscrapers, a waterfront park, and a midtown square. Accompanying these changes were increased tax revenues, new private investment, new instruments of government, and strengthened public/private cooperation. The city's airport was established as an international hub, and new expressways provided links to the Pennsylvania Turnpike. Growth occurred beyond downtown to provide housing and spur economic development. One-fourth of Pittsburgh's downtown was rebuilt in 10

The city's transition from heavy industry to corporate and service employment is reflected in the dramatic downtown skyline. The tallest building is the U.S. Steel Building, followed by One Mellon Bank Center, PPG headquarters, and One Oxford Centre. Gateway Center and Point State Park are in the foreground.

Bill Exler

years, and since 1957, the amount of office space has doubled, with a current inventory of 23.5 million square feet.

After a hiatus lasting from 1970 to 1977, the pace of construction again accelerated in the 1980s, a period that Mayor Richard S. Caliguiri called Renaissance II. An additional 2.5 million square feet of office space is projected in the next two years, most of which should be occupied within 36 months—if current absorption rates of 500,000 to 600,000 square feet a year continue. Rental rates have risen steadily, and, despite a recent dip, occupancy rates hover around 90 percent.

Helped by office growth and the compact size of the Golden Triangle—less than one square mile—the city has maintained its vitality as a retail center. With about 4.9 million square feet of retail space, the downtown stores of department store chains continue to capture the highest volume of sales. In recent years, almost 90 percent of the office space constructed in the region has been in the central business district, pointing to the desirability of downtown and leading to an increase in office-related jobs. More than 130,000 people work downtown, a number that is expected to grow significantly.

Overall, recent and planned construction will result in a net increase of 9.1 million square feet of new office and commercial space; a net increase of 32,000 employees by 1987, and a new tax-generated figure of $14,436,769 net per year.

New development has been propelled by pent-up demand for space (occupancy rates hit 99 percent in 1980); the explosive rate of growth of the banking industry; the expansion of corporate-based headquarters; and the growth of service-oriented companies. It has been abetted by a cooperative city administration; increased public services and amenities; new transportation facilities; and the opening of new markets, notably conventions and tourism. In partnership, the public and private sectors

have made downtown and Renaissance II a solid success.

This growth would not have been possible without the physical transformation brought by Renaissance I. It is being fueled by changes in the economy and sustained by traditions and qualities from Pittsburgh's past.

While the Golden Triangle was being physically transformed, population and employment figures were undergoing drastic changes as well. Since World War II, the city's population had declined rapidly from a high of over 700,000 in 1950 to 424,000 in 1980. The metropolitan area population is currently about 2.4 million.

In 1955, nearly one-half of the region's workforce was employed in manufacturing. Today that number is down to one in five, and the University of Pittsburgh, not the steel industry, is the city's largest employer.

The economy of the Pittsburgh region is shifting from one that depends on a specialized industrial base to one that is more balanced and diversified—from industry and heavy manufacturing to services and advanced technology. Through concerted efforts, Pittsburgh has evolved into the third largest research and development center in the country, with about 170 R&D laboratories in the region and 20,000 employees spending more than $500 million annually.

That the high-technology industry now provides 20 percent of the manufacturing jobs in the region is due partly to a $100 million federal grant for the establishment of a national software engineering institute, to a recent $40 million grant to become one of five supercomputer sites in the country, and to the location of a biomedical research center in the area. As these new computer and research entities become established and expand, the number of employees should continue to increase.

The most dramatic physical manifestation of the shift from steel and heavy industry to services and high technology is taking

place on the 51-acre site of a former J&L Steel Plant less than one mile from the Golden Triangle. The Urban Redevelopment Authority (URA) and the Regional Industrial Development Corporation (RIDC) are dismantling the mill and will redevelop the site as the Pittsburgh Technology Center—with emphasis on robotics, biomedical technology, computer software and hardware, and related commercial research and development. The project will receive financial support from the commonwealth of Pennsylvania, while Carnegie Mellon University and the University of Pittsburgh will help promote development.

Meanwhile, Pittsburgh continues to be a center for international headquarters and finance. Many of the 15 Fortune 500 Pittsburgh-based companies grew out of the area's industrial past. Other companies are being actively and successfully pursued. Over the past 10 years, 255 new firms have moved to the area, and at last count, 92 foreign-based companies—accounting for some 55,000 jobs—have located their U.S. headquarters in the Pittsburgh area.

Some examples of headquarter expansion downtown are: the PPG Industries World Headquarters Building(s) consisting of six units on five acres of ground; One Mellon Bank Center, a 54-story building containing 1.5 million square feet of space; the CNG Tower; Federated Investors Tower; and a new building under construction that will become the new headquarters of the First Federal Savings and Loan Association. The ability to secure anchor tenants from Pittsburgh's corporate community before construction begins helps to sustain the ongoing pace of new building.

These projects attest to the rapid growth in banking and service organizations. Seven years ago, Mellon Bank occupied 800,000 square feet in downtown. Today, it has expanded into almost 3 million square feet. Similar growth is expected in other banking institutions.

From steel and heavy industry . . .

. . . to services and high technology.

Downtown office space development has helped generate gains in retail sales and growth, and in an effort to avoid single-purpose office buildings set off by empty plazas and to keep street level shopping in good health, the city has adopted a policy of encouraging large new office developments to incorporate substantial components of retail space.

Reinforced by zoning incentives and other public assistance, downtown cultural and convention facilities are expanding in at least two significant projects and processes: one is the Pittsburgh Trust for Cultural Resources/CNG Tower/Benedum Center for the Performing Arts and the other is Liberty Center, the convention center office and hotel project (described later). Add to this the $13 million reconstruction of Grant Street, new parks and street furniture, and $60 million in the city's capital budget to upgrade public services and amenities in the Golden Triangle, and the downtown's magnetism for development increases considerably.

Transportation improvements and the Golden Triangle's location at the hub of a regional transportation network reinforce the drawing power of the central business district. Over $600 million has been invested in transportation improvements in the last decade: a downtown expressway loop of interstate systems is near completion. Light Rail Transit opened in 1985, replacing trolleys on downtown streets; and the East Busway, which runs on old railway rights-of-way, is helping commuters go to and from downtown rapidly. Downtown garage spaces are being refurbished, new spaces are being added, and shuttle services to outlying parking areas are augmenting downtown parking facilities.

In addition, civic/business leaders and local government officials have worked to create a favorable setting for office development by improving the air quality; cleaning the rivers; using urban renewal to clear land and make sites available; and providing open spaces, good public transportation, highways, and parking.

These and other factors have spurred development focusing on the central business district, which has become the city's economic and social core and which is estimated to have involved more than $2 billion in public and private investments over the last decade. To understand Pittsburgh's revitalization, how it happened, and why it works, one must examine the history of the city, its growth, and its people.

PITTSBURGH PAST

Like most good real estate, Pittsburgh is well located. In 1753, George Washington stood at the point where the three rivers meet and described it as, "extremely well suited for a fort." The French subsequently built Fort Duquesne there, which the English took over in 1758 and renamed Pittsburgh, in honor of William Pitt. Fort Pitt became a United States fort in 1777, and a plan for the downtown area was laid out in 1784.

In its early years, Pittsburgh was primarily a mercantile economy. Situated at the forks of the Ohio at the western foot of the Alleghenys, it became the gateway to the West and thrived by selling food and goods to thousands of migrating settlers. The same rivers that took settlers west also gave Pittsburghers access to iron ore via the Great Lakes and made it the vital inland port that it remains today. Coal was abundant in the nearby hills (the Pittsburgh coal seam is the world's richest), which was inducement for the Pennsylvania Railroad to build its line through the town in 1852 to be soon followed by more than a dozen other rail lines. By the late 19th century, Pittsburgh's economy was based on industry rather than on trade. Known as the "Forge of the Universe" the city was producing half the glass, half the iron, and much of the oil in the United States. At the turn of the 20th century, Pittsburgh was the nation's leading producer of iron and steel and had become the home of manufacturing giants such as Carnegie, U.S. Steel, Frick, ALCOA, Westinghouse, and Pittsburgh Plate Glass (PPG). Its population had risen to 321,000 as thousands of immigrants poured in to work in the steel mills and in other heavy industry.

When Andrew Carnegie sold his steelmaking operations to U.S. Steel in 1901, the transaction was said to have made instant millionaires of 89 of his top managers. And U.S. Steel became the nation's first billion-dollar corporation. Mellon Bank, Koppers, Carborundum, and Gulf Oil were gaining notoriety and wealth at about the same time, as was H.J. Heinz, who began centralizing food processing operations and revolutionizing agriculture.

With all this activity, thick smoke was rising from furnaces and foundries, steamboats and railroads, all fueled by Pittsburgh's soft coal, and the city was settling under a sooty haze that often made morning seem like evening. Street lights burned all day.

Civic leaders began to express concern about the environment, and in 1910, Frederick Law Olmsted conducted an environmental study for the Pittsburgh Civic Commission. Published in 1911 and entitled *Improvements Necessary to Meet the City's Present and Future Needs*, the report urged smoke and flood controls, renewal of housing, improved transportation facilities, and cleanup of the rivers. It spurred the formation of the City Planning Commission in 1911, the Bureau of Smoke Regulation in 1914, and the Pittsburgh Regional Planning Association (PRPA) in 1918. Although the report's recommendations would not be implemented for another 40 years, the stage was set for the involvement of the community's industrialists and business leaders, thus establishing the hallmark of Pittsburgh's future success in urban reconstruction.

Two world wars and eight years of depression during the 1930s stalled any serious rebuilding efforts; the Pittsburgh renaissance would not begin in earnest until the 1940s. When the private sector, led by Richard King Mellon, organized the Allegheny Conference on Community Development in 1943, and joined forces with organized labor and city hall, led by Mayor David L. Lawrence, Renaissance I was launched. Together, the two sectors began to clean up the environment and to rehabilitate the city. The redevelopment of the Golden Triangle initiated the rehabilitation.

Liberty Center under construction.

REDEVELOPMENT STRATEGY AND MECHANISMS

Pittsburgh's redevelopment strategy was born out of necessity. The city's leadership, both public and private, faced complex urban issues head-on and took advantage of government programs and economic leverage to carry out essential improvement programs. This private/public partnership and trust, established early in the Pittsburgh effort, helped Pittsburgh's rebuilding program to succeed. The financial capacity of the corporate community was solidly melded with the political astuteness of elected officials to bring about civic improvement and change.

The second factor that helped the city's revitalization effort to succeed was that the focus was not on building, but on legislation—specifically on smoke and flood control. Pittsburgh cleared its skies and rescued its downtown from periodic floods, which, in 1936, had covered parts of the Golden Triangle with 15 feet of water.

Pittsburgh's renewal efforts have been described as having three stages—Renaissance I, spanning the post–World War II effort to 1969; the interlude or "leveling-off" period between 1970 and 1977; and Renaissance II, covering the current rebuilding and renewal activities.[1] Although some contend that Pittsburgh's rebirth and renewal have been one continuous process beginning with the postwar efforts, there are certain trends, both na-

tional and local, that give each stage some distinctive characteristics worth noting.

RENAISSANCE I

After World War II, Pittsburgh was decaying under sooty skies and repeated floods; housing was inadequate; and downtown property values were dropping at the rate of $10 million a year. Even though the city was still home to more than 100 companies, business leaders feared that it would lose population and major corporations unless it underwent some drastic improvements. In 1946, enlisting the counsel of knowledgeable and dedicated professionals, gaining support from public officials and organized labor, and using considerable personal clout, the corporate community, through the Allegheny Conference, developed a set of legislative proposals that enabled them to:
• extend smoke control over counties;
• extend planning controls over county subdivisions;
• create the Pittsburgh Parking Authority;
• expedite the Penn-Lincoln Parkway; and
• establish a Department of Parks and Recreation.

Earlier, the state had approved a proposal to create a park at the Ohio River forks, a project that the Allegheny Conference was to shepherd. Spearheaded by another recommendation from the Allegheny Conference, the first Urban Redevelopment Authority (URA) in Pennsylvania was established in Pittsburgh in 1946 to help revitalize the area abutting the new park. The Redevelopment Authority initiated the development of Gateway Center—the first downtown renewal project in the country—predating by three years the federal

---

[1] Stefan Lorant, *Pittsburgh: The Story of an American City,* 3d ed. (Lenox, Massachusetts: Authors Edition, Inc., 1980), p. 449. Also see R. Scott Fosler and Renee Berger, eds., *Public-Private Partnership in American Cities: Seven Case Studies* (Lexington, Massachusetts: D.C. Heath & Company, 1982), pp. 59–127.

Housing Act of 1949, which inaugurated nationwide Title I urban renewal. These actions were all achieved through a strong public/private partnership under the leadership of Mayor David L. Lawrence, other public officials, and several prominent corporate businessmen.[2]

The year 1946 also saw Allegheny County break ground to develop a $530 million airport for greater Pittsburgh and the state break ground for the Penn-Lincoln Parkway—the first nontoll, limited-access freeway in Pennsylvania.

By 1966, 20 years after its inception, the URA was involved in 20 different projects spread over 1,608 acres of city land—about 600 of which were cleared—and accounted for more new construction and related community improvement than the city as a whole had experienced in any previous 50-year period of its two centuries of development. Private investment of over $500 million and public funds of about $155 million were expended on projects ranging from housing to highways, from corporate offices to Boy Scout headquarters. A colossal civic arena with a retractable dome, an in-town shopping mall, industrial site expansion, parks, neighborhood facilities, streets and expressways, bridges, tunnels, and subway sites—all were part of the renewal program. Downtown sparkled with new skyscrapers, and Pittsburghers enjoyed a 36-acre park and numerous downtown plazas and open spaces, where not one blade of grass had existed before 1950. Ample parking was available and the waterfront was being reclaimed from industrial rails for parks, playgrounds, and recreational development.

---

[2] City Councilman William Stewart and the mayor were the two Democrats on URA's five-member board. The three Republicans were Arthur Van Buskirk, representing Richard King Mellon; Edgar Kaufmann, owner of the downtown department store; and Lester Perry, retiring head of Carnegie-Illinois Steel Corporation.

Downtown had added enough buildings to more than meet the demand by the late 1960s.

Renaissance I peaked in 1968, at about the time that the U.S. Steel Building was under construction and plans were being completed for the Three Rivers Sports Stadium across the river from the Point. The building boom leveled off. The passion and enthusiasm for the "headache" ball had subsided; indeed, across the nation, the romance with the bulldozer had ended.

INTERLUDE

The late 1960s were marked with concerns prompted by the civil rights movement, a change in federal programs, and a concurrent change in national public attitudes. Locally, Pittsburgh began to focus on neighborhood needs; the Allegheny Conference on Community Development turned its attention to social programs; and a new mayor was elected who chose to turn his back on the establishment. Downtown development leveled off.

In January 1968, well before the assassination of Martin Luther King and the subsequent city riots, the Allegheny Conference had established an agenda of social programs that addressed the problems of the urban poor. Interestingly, the major players were the same as those 20 years before—involving seasoned leaders from the Allegheny Conference and from the Pittsburgh Urban Redevelopment Authority. With cities facing forthcoming riots and fiscal crises, the order of the day was to relieve racial tension and urge fiscal restraints.

Federal rebuilding programs shifted from large commercial projects requiring land clearance to more cautious, incremental development, rehabilitation, and citizen-oriented projects. Finally, in 1973, the federal government put a moratorium on all housing and development funds and programs, and in 1974, the nation went through an economic recession. In Pittsburgh,

the U.S. Steel Building came on the market with over 2 million square feet of space; the supply of high-grade space was beginning to get well ahead of demand.

City hall was reformulating urban renewal by deflecting funds from large-scale projects, especially those downtown, and by tightening its budget and reducing its payroll. More significantly, because of the anti-establishment attitude of the new administration, the trust that had been cultivated between business leaders and city hall was eroding.

In spite of these changes, the 1970s was characterized by important additions to the city's physical vitality and growth. Although many of the more dramatic projects resulted from the completion of development begun during the previous decade—the U.S. Steel Building (1970), the Three Rivers Stadium (1970), the Westinghouse Building (1970), the Pittsburgh National Bank (PNB) (1972) and Equibank (1975) buildings, One Oliver Plaza (1968), and the Fountain at the Point (1974)—other projects and activities were occurring that added a new dimension to the city's growth. The convention center was begun during this period; for the first time, serious attention was being paid to tourism as an industry in Pittsburgh. A consensus was reached and work was started on the city's subway; a Light Rail Transit system was to replace the downtown trolleys.

In addition, a new kind of development activity was emerging—retrofitting or adaptive use, which, in effect, was rehabilitation on a grand scale. Also, perhaps because federal largesse had subsided, the ongoing contributions and activities of private foundations for the improvement of the city became more visible.

Illustrating both of these activities was the Howard Heinz Endowment's acquisition and conversion of Heinz Hall—an old downtown movie palace—to Pittsburgh's Performing Arts Center, home of the city's symphony, opera, and ballet.

The Scaife Gallery, built with funds from the Scaife family, opened in 1974 as part of the Carnegie Museum of Art in Oakland. An office and warehouse building area, named First Side, experienced a burst of rehabilitation activity. Incentives for these historic restorations were the revitalized downtown core; the vogue for rehabilitation; and federal tax laws that made the refurbishing of historic landmark buildings financially feasible and desirable.

Local citizens' groups grew stronger and became active in planning and developing new physical improvements, thus broadening the base of involvement. More participants, more planning, and more decision makers had joined the development process.

Pittsburgh's skyline as seen from Allegheny Landing Sculpture Park.

RENAISSANCE II

In 1977, Richard S. Caliguiri was elected mayor, pledging alliance with the business community; office occupancy downtown hit 99 percent in 1980 indicating a need for new office space; the overall economy was improving; and Urban Development Action Grants (UDAGs) became available.

Renaissance II was propelled by other factors. Several corporations—PPG Industries, Dravo Corporation, Mellon Bank, and Duquesne Light—were planning significant headquarter expansions. Their decision to remain in downtown Pittsburgh—some as tenants and others as developers and building owners—had a significant impact on the image and economy of the city. Three corporate headquarters buildings have resulted, each with more than 1 million square feet of space— PPG Place, One Mellon Bank Center, and One Oxford Centre.

Other Renaissance II projects include some 14 major developments involving more than $2 billion in public and private investments, reflecting once more the public/private cooperation that characterized Pittsburgh in Renaissance I. Corporations, developers, public agen-

cies, civic organizations, foundations, and citizens are all players in varying degrees, working together to bring about a new wave of large-scale construction in downtown.

The shifting economy—from heavy manufacturing to service-related and high-tech industries— has determined the need for and kinds of space required. The new working population has demanded and has received new downtown amenities, such as retail outlets, food establishments, open spaces, and cultural facilities.

Growth has also meant the expansion of downtown, and major commercial development is now emerging across the rivers from the Golden Triangle. As federal and other public rebuilding programs and funds dwindle, new uses of public and private dollars are emerging. Programs such as UDAG are helping to structure new kinds of projects; and new financial mechanisms, tax shelters, and historic preservation tax credits are influencing projects chosen for development. Shrinking public dollars have encouraged the use of leveraging by public agencies— equity participation by the Urban Redevelopment Authority; zoning incentives; new standards and requirements for street furniture; and development criteria imposed by the City Planning Commission.

Clyde Hare

*Land use plan for the Pittsburgh
central business district.*

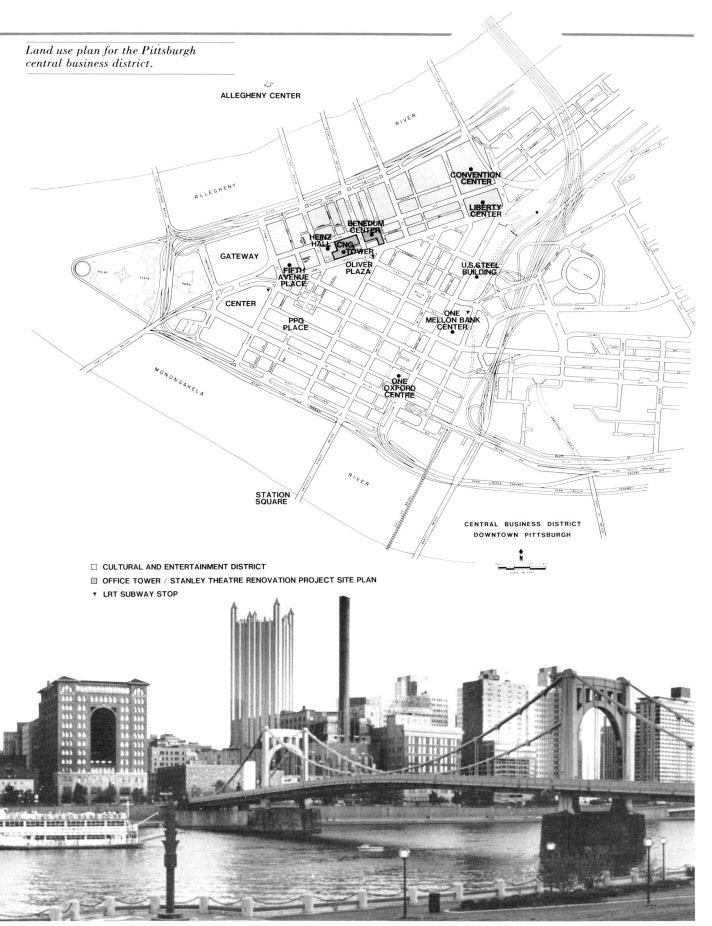

ALLEGHENY CENTER

RIVER

ALLEGHENY

CONVENTION
CENTER

LIBERTY
CENTER

GATEWAY

HEINZ
HALL

BENEDUM
CENTER

CNG
TOWER

U.S. STEEL
BUILDING

FIFTH
AVENUE
PLACE

OLIVER
PLAZA

CENTER

PPG
PLACE

ONE
MELLON BANK
CENTER

MONONGAHELA

ONE
OXFORD
CENTRE

STATION
SQUARE

RIVER

CENTRAL BUSINESS DISTRICT
DOWNTOWN PITTSBURGH

N

SCALE IN FEET

☐ CULTURAL AND ENTERTAINMENT DISTRICT

▦ OFFICE TOWER / STANLEY THEATRE RENOVATION PROJECT SITE PLAN

▼ LRT SUBWAY STOP

SPECIAL QUALITIES—SUMMARY

The seeds that marked the Pittsburgh program and assured its success over the years were sown in those early years beginning Renaissance I. The following actions contributed to the strength of the program.

- Private/public cooperation and mutual trust were firmly established, with the public sector contributing political expertise and the private sector contributing business acumen.
- The organizational framework for the formal creation of quasi-public and public agencies was established. The Parking Authority, the Urban Redevelopment Authority, and the City Planning Commission, among others, were reinforced by the Allegheny Conference. This framework acted as a catalyst for private participation, with organizations like the Pittsburgh Regional Planning Association (PRPA) and the Pennsylvania Economy League giving background planning and research support.
- Foundations participated as passive and active partners, making possible parks, museums, cultural facilities, and other improvements.
- Corporations committed to remaining in Pittsburgh and specifically, in downtown, became tenants and developers. They supported the Gateway Center project by promising to lease space in buildings yet to be constructed; U.S. Steel and Mellon built a new corporate headquarters building, as did ALCOA. These actions set the trend for corporations to follow in the second wave of rebuilding that occurred more than 25 years later.
- Pittsburgh had its Urban Redevelopment Authority in place when the federal Housing Act of 1949 was passed and federal urban renewal funds became available. The city has been benefiting from public funding, where available, ever since.

PITTSBURGH'S DEVELOPMENT ORGANIZATIONS

THE URBAN REDEVELOPMENT AUTHORITY OF PITTSBURGH (URA)

The Urban Redevelopment Authority (URA) of Pittsburgh is responsible for growth and development in the city. Created in 1946 to fight urban blight through redevelopment activities, URA now focuses on urban renewal, housing, and economic development. Through grants, technical assistance, complex and inventive financial packaging, it provides citywide housing and economic development programs. To eliminate blight in redevelopment areas, the Authority also develops and implements plans involving the acquisition and disposition of real estate in the city.

URA carries out its work through four major departments:
- The Department of Housing is responsible for the operations of all housing programs, the coordination of housing development activities, and the development of housing policy for the city.
- The Department of Economic Development develops and implements programs aimed at business and job opportunities in the city; it also implements the city's economic development strategy.
- The Department of Real Estate is responsible for handling all URA-involved land transfers and for implementing complex disposition contracts.
- The Department of Planning and Engineering is responsible for the detailed planning and engineering of citywide land renewal projects.

THE DEPARTMENT OF CITY PLANNING (DCP)

The Department of City Planning staffs the City Planning Commission, established by an act of the state legislature in 1911. The main function of the DCP is to recommend to the mayor and the city council how resources should be allocated, and to promote the orderly development and redevelopment of the city. The DCP performs these duties through four divisions:
- Community Planning and Capital Budget coordinates general and neighborhood planning, and prepares the capital budget and six-year development program.
- Land Use Control administers the zoning ordinance and subdivision regulations.
- The Community Development and Planning Administration administers the Community Development Block Grant program.
- Comprehensive Planning, Development, and Research prepares plans, coordinates all functional planning and major project reviews, and provides special planning services to the DCP divisions and city departments.

ALLEGHENY CONFERENCE ON COMMUNITY DEVELOPMENT (ACCD)

The Allegheny Conference on Community Development, a nonprofit corporation, was created in 1943 for purposes of research, planning, education, and support of programs to improve the Pittsburgh region. Its executive committee, the policy setting group, is composed of chief executives of Pittsburgh's major corporations.

Since its inception, the Conference has been instrumental in developing programs that contributed to the dynamic changes occurring in Pittsburgh and surrounding areas since World War II. Most notable of these have been the elimination of smoke and pollution from the air, the construction of flood control dams on the upper tributaries of Pittsburgh's three rivers, the development of a number of significant buildings, improved transportation, and the addition of open spaces.

Current programs include a series of initiatives to improve the region's economy, aid to public education, contributions toward the reduction in the rise of health care costs, and continuation of planning and development.

PENN'S SOUTHWEST ASSOCIATION

The Allegheny Conference on Community Development set up Penn's Southwest Association in 1972 as a result of a study on the Pittsburgh regional economy. The Association's purpose is to improve the economic vitality of the nine-county region of southwestern Pennsylvania. An action-oriented organization, the Association maintains an ongoing marketing program to attract job-creating businesses to the region and to retain those already there. Its offices in Germany and Japan play a key role in the strategy to market the region to foreign companies.

In 1985 alone, the Association reported 29 new companies in the region; 1,482 new jobs; a $33.3 million payroll; and 848,922 square feet of space occupied by new businesses.

Founded primarily through contributions and grants, Penn's Southwest Association is a tax-exempt nonprofit organization under Section 501(c)(3) of the Internal Revenue Code of 1954, as amended.

REGIONAL INDUSTRIAL DEVELOPMENT CORPORATION OF SOUTHWESTERN PENNSYLVANIA (RIDC)

To combat the loss of industrial jobs in the Pittsburgh region due to automation, the Allegheny Conference created in 1955 the Regional Industrial Development Corporation of Southwestern Pennsylvania. The assignment of the RIDC has been to develop programs that help diversify the Pittsburgh region's economy and that expand job opportunities. A nonprofit, privately financed corporation, RIDC is empowered to engage in many types of activities—the construction of facilities; the buying, selling, and financing of buildings; and the development of industrial parks.

Since 1962, RIDC has created in the nine-county region three industrial parks including 134 buildings with planned employment for 15,000 people. RIDC's infrastructure investments in the three parks to date approximate $25 million. These investments have helped attract private investments in land, buildings, and equipment exceeding $250 million, substantially broadening the tax bases of the communities in which the industrial parks are located.

RIDC is currently focusing attention on recycling vacant inner-city industrial sites and establishing incubator facilities for new product development. It assists businesses in site selection, facility design, and construction; it also helps obtain conventional financing and low-cost financing from federal, state, and local incentive development programs like the Pennsylvania Industrial Development Authority and the industrial revenue bond and mortgage program. In addition, RIDC is the grantee/operator of two foreign trade zones in the Pittsburgh area.

RIDC is a nonprofit community-sponsored agency that is financially supported by the public and private leadership of the community who are represented on its board of directors. At present, income from real estate and other investments contributes to the annual operating budget.

- Quality leadership from both government and business marked the redevelopment program. From the beginning, renewal and redevelopment programs were run with a high degree of both altruism and professionalism. Set up as a separate authority, URA was not subject to political whims or elections. URA's board members were Pittsburgh's leading businessmen and politicians. By any measure, the record of accomplishment was extraordinary.
- While decisions are now made by a broader group of participants—referred to as collective leadership—the quality and integrity of this leadership remains a hallmark of the Pittsburgh effort.

One Mellon Bank Center illustrates the strength of the downtown.

John Rahaim

CASE STUDIES

The case studies selected illustrate the lessons learned and the unique features of urban design and development techniques that have emerged from Pittsburgh's experience.

- **Point State Park/Gateway Center.** Gateway Center is a 23-acre, mixed-use development, privately financed and developed in the heart of downtown in conjunction with the 36-acre public Point State Park. The project is the nation's first commercial redevelopment project—using eminent domain for private reuse purposes. Inaugurating Pittsburgh's rebuilding program, as well as the reclamation of the city's riverfronts as park and waterfront areas, this project illustrates the formation and strong influence of public/private partnership in city rebuilding and the reinforcement of private development (Gateway Center) by public amenities (Point State Park).

- **Allegheny Center.** A predominantly residential mixed-use project on 79 acres near downtown, this federally assisted project was undertaken to revitalize a deteriorated neighborhood by bringing new housing and commercial and recreational facilities to the area. Designed and built in the 1960s as a showpiece "state-of-the-art" development, it accommodates the needs of residents and others while enhancing in-town living. Billed as a "city within a city," it exemplifies successful private redevelopment of publicly cleared land and subsequent spin-off activities.

- **Pittsburgh Trust for Cultural Resources/CNG Tower/Benedum Center for the Performing Arts.** The CNG Tower and Benedum Center for the Performing Arts illustrate the use of the arts as a generator for economic development. An innovative public/private venture was responsible for developing this new downtown cultural and entertainment district. The project includes the construction of a new 32-story corporate headquarters and the expansion and adaptive use of an old theater as a new performing arts center. The development is also significant in having made use of such economic development tools as air rights transfers, zoning incentives, private funds, and UDAG leverage.

- **The Steel Plaza/One Mellon Bank Center.** Combining the expansion of corporate headquarters with the development of the LRT system, this project involves a complex agreement—between three public agencies and a private corporation—that includes land and lease swaps of surface and subsurface properties. It illustrates the use of public design and performance criteria to channel private dollars into public improvements—sidewalks, open spaces, and others.

- **Liberty Center/Convention Hotel and Office Building.** The Redevelopment Authority was the motivator, packager, deal maker and part-investor of this hotel/office complex adjacent to the convention center. The objective was to expand the tourism market and thus encourage new growth areas.

Overall, the case studies illustrate:
- the evolution of the public agency role from one that reacts to one that acts;
- the emergence of design controls;
- a broadened definition of public/private partnership that includes a wider spectrum of participants;
- solutions to hard market realities such as the withdrawal of federal public assistance; and
- the importance of using amenities to improve the quality of urban life and the quality of development.

POINT STATE PARK/ GATEWAY CENTER

In many ways, this 59-acre project at the juncture of the city's three rivers represents the heart of Pittsburgh. It consists of two separate but related developments: Point State Park, publicly financed and owned by the state, occupying 36 acres at the tip of Pittsburgh's Golden Triangle; and Gateway Center, a $150 million privately financed commercial project on a 23-acre urban redevelopment site contiguous to the park. The project was conceived and made possible when the state acquired 36 acres adjoining Gateway for the new Point State Park.[3]

Gateway contains eight newly built office towers,[4] a Hilton Hotel, a luxury apartment building, and four underground parking garages in a landscaped setting. Using its powers of eminent domain, the Urban Redevelopment Authority acquired and cleared the 23-acre, defunct industrial site for the developer—the Equitable Life Assurance Society of the United States. Begun in 1950, Gateway was the first downtown redevelopment project in the country and launched Pittsburgh's extensive renewal program.

When Gateway Center was completed in 1974, it was estimated that almost 25,000 people were working in an area where only 4,000 jobs had existed before 1949, and that assessed values of real estate had soared from $8.3 million

[3] Robert C. Alberts, *The Shaping of the Point: Pittsburgh's Renaissance Park* (Pittsburgh: University of Pittsburgh Press, 1980).
[4] An existing structure in the area, the Pittsburgh Press Building, was refurbished and is still standing.

Downtown Pittsburgh is concentrated in the Golden Triangle, where the Allegheny and Monongahela Rivers meet to form the Ohio River. Point State Park and Gateway Center are located at the apex.

POINT STATE PARK

Project Type:	A 36-acre state park built at the tip of Pittsburgh's Golden Triangle at the headwaters of the Ohio.
Developers:	Commonwealth of Pennsylvania, State Department of Forests and Waters, and State Highway Department.
Construction Supervision:	Allegheny Conference on Community Development, a private citizen's group.
Architecture:	Ralph E. Griswold, landscape architect; Donald M. McNeil, traffic consultant; George S. Richardson, consulting engineer; Charles Stotz, architect.
Financing:	State funding of $17 million, excluding major highway connections, plus some private assistance.
Status:	Park plan approved, 1945; demolition began, 1950; park and fountain dedicated, 1974.

before renewal to more than $47 million. A city investment of less than $650,000 had generated over $150 million of private investments in an area where no major new construction had occurred in 20 years, and assessed property values were dropping at the rate of $10 million a year. Gateway Center also poured over 2 million square feet of prime office space into a downtown office market that was experiencing 99 percent occupancy. Its landscaped plazas and the new Point State Park replaced what had been dilapidated and abandoned industrial sites. With the development of Point State Park and Gateway Center, almost one-fourth of Pittsburgh's downtown core was entirely rebuilt.

Point State Park—aptly named—begins at the apex of the Golden Triangle, where the Monongahela and Allegheny Rivers join to form the Ohio, and was designed in 1945 as uncluttered open space with a clear view west. A fountain, one of the largest manmade geysers in the world, rises 150 feet at the tip of the Point, focusing attention on the rivers and the significant role they play in Pittsburgh's growth and development.

During the three decades of its construction, the project required the demolition of two existing bridges; the preservation of a blockhouse built in 1754 to repel Indian attack, and some restoration of forts; and the construction of two new bridges, a highway interchange, wharfs, landscaping, a museum, and the fountain.

Together, these two developments transformed the Point at the forks of the Ohio from a sooty, blighted area into a majestic park and vital commercial core; reclaimed the waterfront for use by the city's residents; and forged public/private cooperation to bring about a renewed downtown. The project offers a major example of private development (Gateway Center) being contingent on public improvements (smoke and flood control) and on the provision of amenities (Point Park).

Financing

Point State Park. Point State Park was built with public funds and some private assistance. The cost to the state was about $17 million, which was used primarily to acquire the 36 acres of land and to make improvements—excluding major highway connections—such as the construction of bridges, a highway interchange, wharfs, landscaping, the fountain, and the restoration of forts. At the dedication ceremony, eight state officials were present, representing departments that helped in the creation of the park.

The initial announcement by the governor that the state could finance major improvements in Pittsburgh, including developing a park, was made in October 1945. At the time, David L. Lawrence was a candidate for mayor on the Democratic Party ticket, and the story goes that this announcement made by a Republican administration so close to the election was designed to embarrass and defeat him. Instead, Lawrence welcomed the news and pledged to support the program if elected. He was good to his word for 20 years, including his entire four-term, 13-year tenure as mayor and his four years as governor. He cooperated with the business community to bring about Pittsburgh's rebirth, initiating the now legendary public/private relationship that he and Richard King Mellon came to symbolize.

State funding was preceded by lobbying from Pittsburgh's business community and a great deal of planning and research. Civic agencies and leaders in Pittsburgh commissioned numerous studies; the Pittsburgh Regional Planning Association spent over $1 million between 1918 and 1945 for studies of the Point and its traffic problems. But despite these studies—even that of Frank Lloyd Wright who designed a monumental scheme in 1947—the Point remained a blighted area subject to floods and covered with unsightly structures and

railroad terminals that blocked access to the waterfront.

In 1945, the Regional Planning Association presented a final plan for the park to the governor who approved it and committed $4 million to its implementation. Because the plan required concerted action by numerous interested agencies, both public and private, to make it a reality, the governor and the Secretary of the Department of Forests and Waters asked the Allegheny Conference to represent the state in coordinating and guiding the project. More than a dozen public and private agencies were involved; the project also received financial support in the form of gifts from foundations and private individuals.

Gateway Center. Gateway Center is a commercial mixed-use redevelopment project. Privately financed, it was conceived and directed by corporate leaders in partnership with a public agency.

The major developer, The Equitable Life Assurance Society of the United States, paid the Pittsburgh Urban Redevelopment Authority $50,000 a year for a total of $1 million over 20 years for eminent domain "services." The URA condemned, acquired, and cleared the 23-acre site for Equitable, and the city rebuilt the streets in the project area.

Over $150 million of private capital—compared with less than $650,000 in city funds—was invested in the development of 10 major new structures, ranging in size from 12 to 27 stories, and in related facilities.

At the time the buildings were proposed, rents were projected to be 20 to 100 percent higher than in existing buildings from which Equitable expected to lure its major tenants. Before construction began, the developer required binding commitments from tenants for at least one-half of the office space in the first three buildings. The Urban Redevelopment Authority promised to buy the Jones and Laughlin office building to induce the company to lease space in

Gateway Center with Fifth Avenue Place—Pittsburgh's newest office building—under construction in the background.

Gateway Center. The chairman of the Allegheny Conference Point Park Committee asked Pittsburgh corporations as acts of "civic responsibility" to sign leases in the proposed office buildings. As a result, nine companies, including Westinghouse Electric, Westinghouse Air Brake, Pittsburgh Plate Glass, Jones and Laughlin Steel, Peoples Natural Gas, and Mellon Bank, signed statements of intent to enter into 20-year leases.

These commitments and the fact that downtown office space was 99 percent occupied in 1946 helped move the developers along. In 1950, ground for the first buildings was broken, and in 1952, the first tenants moved in, assuring the city that these corporations would keep their headquarters in Pittsburgh.

The risks were enormous. The URA was committed to buying and clearing land for reuse under a law that could be overturned. Companies committed themselves to taking unseen space in an area that was still subject to flooding, in buildings yet to be built, and at rents yet to be determined. In October 1950, when Gateway was half

GATEWAY CENTER

Project Type: Commercial/residential—consisting of 10 towers in a landscaped setting on 23 acres of downtown land adjacent to the 36-acre Point State Park. The project is the first publicly assisted, privately financed downtown redevelopment in the United States.

Primary Developer: The Equitable Life Assurance Society of the United States.

Landscape Architecture: Clarke, Rapuano and Holleran, New York; Simonds and Simonds, Pittsburgh.

Architecture/ Planning: Gateway 1, 2, and 3: Eggers and Higgens, New York (1950–1953).

Gateway 4: Harrison and Abromowitz, New York (1960).

IBM Building (tower 5): Curtis and Davis, New York and New Orleans, (1963). (Sold in 1973 and became United Steelworkers Building.)

Westinghouse Building (tower 6): Harrison and Abromowitz, New York (1970).

Hilton Hotel: William B. Tabler, New York (1959). Built by Hilton.

Gateway Towers Apartments: Emery Roth & Sons, New York (1964). Built by Tishman Realty.

State Office Building: Altenhof & Bown, Pittsburgh Architects (1957).

Bell Telephone Company Building: Press C. & William C. Dowler for Bell Telephone Company (1958).

cleared, the U.S. Supreme Court finally dismissed the appeal of property owners to invalidate the redevelopment contract. It took prudent legal judgment and courage from all parties to face the risks involved in this venture, and none could have done it without the other.

To enable it to begin operations, the URA sold a $150,000 bond issue in March 1948 to civic-minded citizens (three "friendly" foundations). This was the first long-term urban redevelopment authority debt ever issued in the United States.

Ownership/Management

The state still owns Point State Park, whose 36 acres it had purchased and developed. The city, under contract to the state, maintains the park.

The Blockhouse is owned by the Daughters of the American Revolution (DAR) under the auspices of the Fort Pitt Society, which also maintains it. The Blockhouse caretaker was relocated to an office in the park's museum, thus allowing the caretaker's lodge to be acquired and demolished. This arrangement was reached after many years of

fierce negotiations between the developers and DAR, who managed to salvage the Blockhouse for 50 years even when it was nearly annihilated by industrial blight.

Gateway Center is predominantly controlled by The Equitable Life Assurance Society, which built and managed six of the office towers in the project. Equitable constructed three cruciform, stainless-steel-clad office towers—known as Gateway 1, 2, 3—between 1950 and 1953. These were followed by Gateway 4 in 1960; the IBM Building (now owned by the United Steelworkers) in 1963; and the Westinghouse Building in 1970. Equitable Life manages these buildings through a wholly owned subsidiary, Equitable Real Estate Investment Management, Inc. Equitable originally sold land for the development of a state office building in 1957 and the Bell Telephone Building in 1958.

Equitable still owns Gateway 1, 2, and 3; partially owns 4; sold the IBM Building to the United Steelworkers in 1973; and sold the Westinghouse Building to its major tenant in 1984. The Hilton Chain designed, built, and manages the 24-story Hilton Hotel on land owned by Equitable, which held the original mortgage. Gateway Towers was built in 1964 on Equitable land by Tishman Realty as a 311-unit luxury apartment completed.

In addition to managing the six office buildings it developed, Equitable, through its subsidiary, owns two large landscaped plazas, a pedestrian bridge over a public right-of-way, and four underground garages. It also maintains two plazas adjacent to the buildings it sold to the United Steelworkers and to Westinghouse. Overall, buildings cover less than 40 percent of the site and sit amid a parklike setting.

Clyde Hare

Beginning in 1950, eight new office buildings, a Hilton Hotel, and apartments were built in a landscaped setting to form Gateway Center.

Development Process

Because Gateway Center was the nation's first downtown redevelopment project, the development process involved a great deal of trial and error in devising new approaches. A new concept was being tried that was to change the face of cities across the country—the use of public powers for slum clearance, and, secondarily, for private development. That the project was developed without federal funds made it an anachronism during the 1950s and 1960s when the federal government was giving grants and loans for large-scale projects.

When Pennsylvania passed its Urban Redevelopment Act on May 24, 1945, giving municipal government the right of eminent domain for private reuse, it predated by several years the federal urban renewal program spelled out in Title I of the Housing Act of 1949. When Pittsburgh formed the Urban Redevelopment Authority as an essential instrument for rebuilding the city in 1946, it was the first city to take advantage of the enormous powers transferred to it under the state law. It was able to acquire properties in blighted areas through the use of eminent domain, and turn them over to private parties for private reuse. It meant that, unlike disposition to a public body, private capital could be used to redevelop blighted land; that the land would remain on the tax rolls (public projects paid no taxes); and that large tracts of land could be assembled under single ownership. The latter fact also enabled the creation of large landscaped areas in a project. Although this process is taken for granted today, the constitutionality of the Urban Redevelopment Act had to be tested then.

The lack of federal funds placed Pittsburgh in the position that many authorities, cities, and developers currently find themselves. It had the power; it had the site; but it had no administrative or implementation funds for a project. Therefore, it had to devise ways to construct Gateway Center, which became a national and even international case study. It was at this time that public and private entities first joined efforts, leading to the overall success of Pittsburgh's rebuilding program. Indeed, one of the most spectacular private developments in Pittsburgh's Renaissance II program, the PPG headquarters project, followed the model of private renewal—using the Urban Redevelopment Authority to help develop a six-building, 1.5 million-square-foot corporate complex on a blighted five-acre downtown site. PPG place followed Gateway by 35 years.

Legal Issues

With this precedent-setting project, several legal issues arose. Some concerned legislative proposals; others concerned tests of constitutionality of new state and local laws and processes.

- Smoke and flood controls, which had been enacted earlier, were enforced during this period. In addition, the state legislature passed the "Pittsburgh Package" of bills. Among other things, this package helped extend smoke control legislation over county lines and railroads, and enabled the creation of a public parking authority and a city Department of Parks and Recreation.
- The state legislature amended the Insurance Company Law to allow insurance companies to invest in Pennsylvania real estate. This amendment was upheld in the State Supreme Court in 1947.
- The use of eminent domain for private reuse—in effect, the Pennsylvania Redevelopment Act of 1945—was challenged and upheld in the State Supreme Court in 1947 and again in 1950 and in the U.S Supreme Court in 1950.

Without these legislative measures, Pittsburgh's redevelopment program—with the Point State Park/Gateway Center at the forefront—could not have moved ahead.

Status

Apart from the methodology used—which is of considerable interest because of its conceptual ingenuity and the current concern with public/private partnerships—the combined Point State Park/ Gateway Center development had a profound effect on the city and its people. It became the symbol of rebirth and vitality, and while the project took some 20 years to complete, it seemed that almost overnight Pittsburgh had been transformed into a city of sunny skies, attractive waterfronts, spacious parks, and first-class offices.

Point State Park. Point State Park is a monument to the city's past and a symbol of its resurgence. The Fort Pitt Museum has over 100,000 visitors a year. The park itself is fully used, providing a giant playground as well as a site for festivals, touch football, music, fairs, and fun. The annual Three Rivers Arts Festival, classical and popular concerts, regattas, and Fourth of July and other celebrations are regularly held there. Without the park, Gateway Center would not have been built.

Gateway Center. Still owned and operated by Hilton, the Hilton Hotel is the largest luxury hotel in Pittsburgh with 754 rooms in 24 stories. It is completing an $8 million renovation project and has seen a 10 percent growth in earnings since 1985. Gateway Towers has been converted to condominium apartments and all units have been sold.

In 1985, Equitable finished a $25 million modernization of its four Gateway buildings and garages to keep them competitive with the new office towers that have been built since the project came on the market 30 years ago.

For many years, occupancy of Equitable's four buildings was running at 100 percent until PPG, formerly a major tenant, moved into its own new headquarters building in January 1984. Recent occupancy was at 83 percent in all four buildings, but managers hope soon to increase that figure to 90 percent. Rents run $18 to $20 a square foot—compared with Oliver Realty's reported weighted average rent of $26 for new CBD construction at the end of 1985. The high office-occupancy rates have been sustained despite the addition of nearly 10 million square feet of downtown space since the completion of Gateway.

Pittsburgh has followed the trend in corporate buildings designed around specific program requirements and high technology, together with a strong emphasis on architectural quality and design. The project buildings were built on speculation before the advent of the high-tech craze in office equipment and needs that dictate the shape of office buildings today. Although the cruciform buildings have been criticized for their lack

of architectural merit, they will probably continue to lease well because of their location, their modernization, their maintenance and management, the growth of Pittsburgh's service industry, the creation of small new industries, and the influx of new firms demanding quality office space. Given the current absorption rate of 500,000 to 600,000 square feet per year and the project's prime location, demand is expected to remain high.

Summary

Point State Park/Gateway Center gave the city back its rivers and marked the beginning of spin-off developments and projects that in the 1980s numbered more than 50, with substantial private investment spurring over $2 billion in growth and rehabilitation. More importantly, it gave the citizens of Pittsburgh visible proof that their city is special.

ALLEGHENY CENTER[5]

Only a 10-minute walk from the Golden Triangle and surrounded on three sides by 100 acres of city parks, this 79-acre, mixed-use project was begun in the early 1960s as a redevelopment showpiece that would enhance inner-city living. The plan was to clear a blighted area, retaining several structures of historic and architectural merit; and to provide a range of housing types for an economically mixed population, as well as a traffic-free pedestrian mall, an enclosed shopping center, a 2,850-car garage, a public square, and office buildings. The project was to incorporate the latest and best urban design concepts and was billed by the developer as "a $60 million city within a city."

[5] See also ULI Project Reference File, Volume 1, Number 20, *Allegheny Center (Mall and Office Buildings)*; and Number 19, *Allegheny Center (Residential)*; October–December 1971.

The Carnegie Library, Buhl Planetarium, new apartment buildings, an office building, and a public square are some of the features of Allegheny Center.

Clyde Hare

Allegheny Center today is an attractive, vibrant development that, running true to plan, provides a residential, commercial, and cultural environment in open, landscaped surroundings on Pittsburgh's North Side, within easy walking distance from the heart of downtown. Aside from providing housing and jobs for a cross section of Pittsburgh's population, it has revitalized the economy through a rebuilt commercial core and is acting as a catalyst to improve surrounding parks and residential neighborhoods.

Financing

Allegheny Center was conceived and executed as a federally aided urban renewal project under Title I of the Housing Act of 1949 as amended. The estimated amount required for project improvements was reserved (earmarked) in the initial urban renewal application to the federal government for project approval. Funding for the project, initially estimated at $90 million, came from public as well as private sources.

The Urban Redevelopment Authority used $24.07 million of public funds to cover the early costs of property acquisition, demolition of structures, relocation of families and businesses, and site preparation within the blighted project area. The cleared site was then sold to a private investor who developed the property in accordance with a city- and citizen-approved reuse plan. The difference between the site preparation costs to the URA and the sale of the cleared land was calculated at $24 million, two-thirds of which went to the federal government and one-third of which was split between the state and city.

This $24 million public investment generated approximately three times the amount of private investment. Initially, the developer, Allegheny Center, Inc., a majority interest of which was held by ALCOA, purchased 37 acres for $4.2 million and planned to develop

ALLEGHENY CENTER

Project Type: A federally assisted, urban renewal, mixed-use project on 79 acres of land near downtown.

Developer/ Owner: ALCOA Properties, Inc., and Oliver Tyrone Corporation, Pittsburgh. Project was sold in 1981 to Allegheny Center Associates, a limited partnership.

Architecture/ Planning: Allegheny Center: Deeter Ritchey Sipple, Pittsburgh.

Public Square: William N. Breger, Architect, New York (winner of International Design Competition, 1964).

Features: A 13-acre, in-city shopping mall, including a 2,800-car garage, office buildings, apartment towers and townhouses, and a public square bordered by landmark buildings on a 79-acre site.

Financing: $90 million project: $24 million through federal Title I Urban Renewal Grant; $66 million from private developer investment.

Status: Project certified December 1959; clearance began October 1962; initial occupancy of first phase, 1964; project closed out, 1978.

a $60 million commercial center. More than 1,000 new privately financed housing units in four apartment buildings and townhouses, three office towers, pedestrian malls, a 750,000-square-foot, enclosed tri-level shopping mall were privately developed.

Under the federal urban renewal program, the city was allowed to pay for its one-sixth share of the project cost with non-cash-grants-in-aid in lieu of cash; that is, the city could provide for a new community facility and count the cost of that towards its local share.

Part of the redevelopment plan for Allegheny Center involved a 2,850-car parking garage under the shopping mall. To provide the sorely needed parking space at less cost to the project, and to reduce the city's required cash contribution, the URA and the developer worked out a mechanism by which the garage could be financed through the issuance of tax-exempt bonds. A nonprofit corporation was

created that would own the garage space—and issue the bonds.[6]

Because the cost of building the parking facility was greater than the city's one-sixth share of the project, the Pittsburgh Redevelopment Authority had adequate non-cash credits for other renewal projects and activities, as well as for Allegheny Center.

The city contributed an early planning advance of $112,500 to conduct studies in response to citizens' requests for assistance in 1959 before federal money was made available to URA. Allegheny Public Square was built by the Redevelopment Authority on land that

---

[6] The bonds were issued based on the volume of space—the length, width, and depth of the area sandwiched between the privately owned land below the garage and developed structure over the garage, *minus* the supporting beams and columns for the private structure that ran through the parking area.

127

had been deeded to public use in the late 1700s.

Housing subsidies were provided through federal Section 236 funds to diversify tenant income groups. This interest-reduction subsidy was used to finance the construction of 136 units in 1972 on the east side of the Allegheny Center development.

Ownership/Management

ALCOA Properties, Inc., the primary developer, built and managed Allegheny Center until 1981, when it sold the development to Allegheny Center Associates, a limited partnership. Included in the transfer were four apartment buildings containing 810 dwelling units; two office buildings with a total of 340,000 square feet of rentable space; pedestrian plazas; and a 13-acre shopping mall complex.

The parking garage, operated on a lease basis, is still owned by the City of Pittsburgh North Side Parking Corporation, a nonprofit entity that was created for this purpose. The IBM office building tower is owned and managed by its major occupant. Allegheny Public Square and Fountain, which was built by the Redevelopment Authority, is owned and maintained by the city. The townhouses have all been sold and are owner-occupied.

Development Process

Allegheny Center, surrounded on three sides by the 100-acre North Side Commons Park, had previously been the business core of North Side Pittsburgh, but by the early 1950s, had become the site of numerous rooming houses, tired and vacant commercial buildings, and general decay.

Alarmed by the rapid decline in the late 1940s and early 1950s of the center of Pittsburgh's North Side, residents and business leaders asked the city and civic agencies for help. As a result, in 1954, the Pittsburgh Regional Planning Association (PRPA) conducted a planning study that proposed new

uses for 800 acres of Pittsburgh's North Side, and recommended that Allegheny Center be the centerpiece of area revitalization.

The closing of the Boggs and Buhl department store in 1958 further signaled economic deterioration in the area. The vacant structure, located on a key site, reverted to the Buhl Foundation. In an effort to divest itself of the building, the head of the foundation offered the property to the URA, which demolished it and provided the Buhl Foundation with a note for the value of the property as the only compensation.

Payment was to be made if and when the area became a redevelopment project supported by public funds. If the project did not materialize, the cleared property would revert to Buhl, and the note forgiven. This gave impetus to the project, and also reflected the kind of trust that existed between the business community and the city at the time.

To speed up the renewal process, the North Side citizens' group appealed to the city administration for a planning grant to begin studies without waiting for federal project approval and funding. The mayor agreed to a $112,500 planning advance, and the URA hired a local architectural and planning team that worked with the local citizens' groups and residents to prepare a plan for the 79-acre area. Before development, the area had a checkerboard pattern with streets surrounding a small public square and park. The Buhl Planetarium, the Carnegie Library and meeting hall, a public market, and the Old Post Office Building were features in the deteriorated neighborhood. The planners proposed to close the streets through the area to increase the size of the park.

Traffic would be rerouted through a circular road around a pedestrian mall area; proposed were a commercial core containing a three-level enclosed shopping mall over a parking garage and high-rise apartment towers and luxury townhouses surrounding a

public square and fountain. Three of the four historic structures were to be retained, but the public market had to be demolished. At the time, the economic viability of the market could not be proved and the city could no longer afford to maintain it. This area was being considered for renewal in late 1959–1960 before programs and funds were available for historic preservation and rehabilitation that could have prevented the loss of the structure.

The URA proceeded with required City Planning Commission and City Council approvals and prepared the urban renewal grant application to begin execution of the locally approved plan. It received approval of the project plan and federal funds for site acquisition, demolition, and site preparation work in 1961, and by October of that year, the acquisition of 406 parcels had begun.

With the grant approval covering the whole project, the entire 79-acre area could be treated as a single entity in terms of traffic patterns, street and utility improvements, and required community facilities. The federal funds needed to carry out all these planned improvements by the Redevelopment Authority were either on hand, or reserved by the federal government for this specific project.

Construction began on the commercial center in spring 1964, and construction of the award-winning design (resulting from an international competition) for the Allegheny Public Square and Fountain began in the fall of that year. By 1966, URA had nearly completed acquisition, demolition, and site preparation work; occupancy of the first phase, a 13-acre in-city shopping mall with parking garage, had begun; and construction had started on an adjacent office building and two high-rise apartment towers and townhouses, using conventional financing. Allegheny Public Square, bordered by two remaining landmark buildings—the Buhl Planetarium and the Carnegie Library—was completed in 1968.

While the assassination of Martin Luther King, Jr., and subsequent riots in 1968 softened the market for high-priced townhouses, the redevelopment plan remained largely intact. After five townhouses were built in 1968, designs were altered to lower the prices, and the number planned was reduced. The units were finally sold in 1971. ALCOA built 50 of the proposed 216 townhouses. Between 1970 and 1973, it built two additional high-rise towers containing over 400 units; these, as well as the townhouses, were built with conventional financing. The city held a competition for low- and moderate-income housing on the parcel east of Allegheny Center and, in 1972, 136 dwelling units were built, using FHA 236 subsidies, by Pittsburgh-based National Development Corporation.

In 1974, work began on an IBM office building (completed in January 1977) and a parking garage on a site that had been proposed for residential use. One large parcel remains vacant, but by 1978 the project was reported closed out and fully occupied—almost 20 years after the City Planning Commission had certified the development of the area.

Status

The project area has become an attractive, well-maintained, traffic-free, parklike yet urban environment. The cultural, retail, office, and residential mix provide for a lively, well-used environment.

The historic landmark buildings—the Buhl Planetarium, the Carnegie Library (on city land), and the Old Post Office Building—have been refurbished and are in use as educational, cultural facilities. Part of the Carnegie Library houses the Pittsburgh Public Theater. The Buhl Planetarium is still functioning and the Old Post Office Building contains a children's museum.

The new Allegheny Center owners have spent considerable sums of money on improvements to

Clyde Hare

the buildings that they own and on landscaping the open space and pedestrian plazas on and around their property. Occupancy in apartments is over 90 percent with an 85 to 90 percent occupancy range in the nonresidential spaces.

Monthly rents for market housing range from $353 to $744 for studios and one- and two-bedroom units. Office space, which has an occupancy rate of almost 90 percent, is leased at $16 to $18 per square foot in two buildings with 340,000 rentable square feet. Sears and Zayres anchor the shopping mall, which also contains a Woolworth's and about 70 smaller retail establishments and services such as dental and optical facilities, banks, cleaners, and others. In 1983, a food court was built in the mall, which includes several spaces that can be expanded and diversified as different tenants locate there. The main level of the mall is fully occupied. With an overall occupancy of 85 to 90 percent for 643,471 square feet, management reports retail sales of more than $50 million a year.

An aerial view of Allegheny Center with the barrel-vaulted roof of the 13-acre enclosed shopping mall and parking garage at the upper right. Designed as a "city within a city," Allegheny Center was built in the 1960s just north of Pittsburgh's downtown.

In short, citizens wanted the project; the city supported the effort; the Title I urban renewal process made it possible; the URA had established a track record of sound achievements, along with playing fair; creative financing was available; real estate ventures were considered good investments for corporations; and both the private and public sector participants were "pros" in an ongoing process that involved a structured system of federal regulations and networking.

Because of social changes and economic reversals caused by civil unrest from 1968 to 1969, the project did not experience the immediate financial success expected. But it did begin the revitalization of the North Side. This $24 million public investment generated approximate-

ly three times the amount of private investment (more than $65 million) in the project and prompted new investment in an area that had been in rapid decline economically and physically. Five years after development of the project began, Allegheny Center became the springboard for a $275 million renaissance throughout the North Side. In the project area alone, estimated tax assessments more than tripled, going from $9.25 million to more than $31 million.

As an example of urban design, Allegheny Center is still valid and functioning. Many consider it the best designed urban renewal project in Pittsburgh. But it may be among the last of the big bold projects on the city's redevelopment agenda.

PITTSBURGH TRUST FOR CULTURAL RESOURCES/CNG TOWER/BENEDUM CENTER FOR THE PERFORMING ARTS[7]

The CNG office tower complex and the Benedum Center for the Performing Arts are part of a mixed-use downtown development underway that includes an innovative developer entity called the Pittsburgh Trust for Cultural Resources (Cultural Trust). The following describes how the project package was put together.

In essence, the construction of the $115-million, 32-story CNG national headquarters building on a 1.5-acre parcel of foundation-owned land will help finance the $38 million historical restoration and expansion of a 60-year old theater as a center for the performing arts.

[7] See also Harold R. Snedcoff, "Pittsburgh Downtown Cultural District," *Cultural Facilities in Mixed-Use Development* (Washington, D.C.: ULI–the Urban Land Institute, 1985), p. 216.

Model of CNG Tower, a 32-story office building being constructed adjacent to Heinz Hall and Heinz Hall Plaza.

The developer of the CNG building—the Lincoln Property Company (LPC)—has purchased the air rights of the surrounding low-rise cultural facilities (Heinz Hall, Heinz Hall Plaza, and Benedum Center). These purchase funds, together with zoning incentives and income from real estate development, will go to the Cultural Trust—a nonprofit corporation created to manage and promote the redevelopment of the cultural facilities—to help defray the costs of rehabilitating the historic structures and of upgrading the downtown area adjacent to the office site.

In the process, the office developers will have doubled the development potential of the office site. The renovated theater and the surrounding cultural sites will be safe from future development because their potential for higher density use will be transferred to the office building site.

Scheduled for completion in 1987, this development is expected to attract additional commercial, entertainment, and residential investment in an area newly designated as a cultural district.

The CNG office tower building will be located adjacent to Heinz Plaza, a privately owned park open to the public, and to Heinz Hall, home of the Pittsburgh Symphony Orchestra and other performing arts. The Stanley Theatre across the street from the office site is being renovated to provide a home for the Pittsburgh Ballet Company, the Pittsburgh Opera Company, the Civic Light Opera Company, and the Pittsburgh Dance Council, as well as a facility for touring theatrical productions. Upon completion, the theater will be known as the Benedum Center for the Performing Arts, which, together with Heinz Hall, will form the nucleus of the new arts and cultural district in Pittsburgh's Golden Triangle, extending from Gateway Center to the convention center.

Driven by the expansion of Pittsburgh's corporate office and service sector and by the increased de-

PITTSBURGH TRUST FOR CULTURAL RESOURCES/ CNG TOWER/BENEDUM CENTER FOR THE PERFORMING ARTS

Project Type: Construction of a 32-story, 650,000-square-foot office tower, combined with the renovation and expansion of an old theater as a new center for the performing arts.

Developers: CNG Tower: Lincoln Property Company, Dallas.

Benedum Center for the Performing Arts: Pittsburgh Trust for Cultural Resources (Cultural Trust).

General Contractor: Mellon Stuart Company.

Leasing Agency: Cushman & Wakefield, Inc.

Architecture/ Planning: CNG Tower: Kohn Pedersen Fox Associates, New York.

Stanley Theatre renovation: MacLachan, Cornelius & Filoni, Pittsburgh.

Project Planning and Urban Design: Buckhurst, Fish, Hutton, & Katz, New York.

Real Estate and Development Finance: William G. Conway, W.G. Conway and Company, New York.

Theatrical: Robert P. Brannigan, Brannigan-Lorelli, Associates, Inc., New York.

Legal: Donald H. Elliot, Webster & Sheffield, New York.

Financing: Combined project cost of $150 million will come from: private developer and charitable contribution funds; UDAG loans; and bonds issued by the Auditorium Authority of Pittsburgh and Allegheny County. Sale of unused theater air rights to office developer will help finance rehabilitation of performing arts center.

Status: Project will open August 1987.

mand for cultural and entertainment facilities, this complex will represent the first project on the city's agenda to use the arts as a generator for new economic development.

Financing

Development costs for the first phase are estimated at nearly $150 million, to be derived from both public and private sources. An

Urban Development Action Grant and local city and county bond funds will cover about one-sixth, or $24.5 million, of the cost. The balance will come from philanthropic contributions and developer investment.

As conceived, the economic feasibility of each part of this commercial/cultural development will depend on the other, and consequently the financing package will reflect the interrelationship of interested participants and funding mechanisms. The various sources and proposed uses of the $150 million investment follow.

Private Funds. Private funds totaling more than $127 million will come from two sources: philanthropic contributions and private developer investment.
• Private philanthropic organizations have contributed or pledged $12 million to the project. Ini-

tially, the Howard Heinz Endowment provided the venture capital needed for feasibility studies and for land and building acquisition, and guaranteed the remaining $12 million needed from the private sector.

In September 1984, following the lead of the Heinz Endowment, the Claude Worthington Benedum Foundation announced a $5 million contribution toward the Stanley Theatre renovation, and the rehabilitation project was renamed the Benedum Center for the Performing Arts.

Also making substantial contributions were the Pittsburgh Foundation, the Vira I. Heinz Fund of the Pittsburgh Foundation, and miscellaneous other philanthropic organizations. These contributions are held and managed by the Cultural Trust.
• As the private developer, the Lincoln Property Company of Dallas has secured the nearly $115 million (through the sale of a first mortgage bond issue) required to realize the first phase of the two-tower corporate office complex. The 650,000-square-foot tower currently under construction will be the headquarters for Allegheny International (AI), a Pittsburgh-based Fortune 500 company, and the Consolidated Natural Gas Company (CNG). AI's commitment to be the lead tenant ensured the financial viability of the project and reinforced the drawing power of downtown Pittsburgh as a location for corporate headquarters. Subsequently (in May 1986), CNG announced that it and its subsidiary, Peoples Natural Gas, would lease 10 floors, or 219,000 square feet in the 32-story building and would become a limited partner in the development. As a result, the building was named CNG Tower.

Heinz Hall Plaza, from which developers acquired unused air rights to build CNG Tower, shown (under construction) in the background.

Public Funds. The project received public funds totaling $24.5 million. The city and county guaranteed $7.5 million in bonds split equally between them. The Auditorium Authority of Pittsburgh and Allegheny County issued $7.5 million in local bonds in June 1984 to allow for the purchase of all land necessary for the theater expansion; thus, it became the owner in perpetuity of the theater property. In March 1984, the federal government provided the city with a $17 million UDAG for loans to be used for theater renovation and expenses related to the tower complex.

The UDAG funds were provided in the form of two $8.5 million loans. Lincoln Property received $8.5 million for partial financing of a 650,000-square-foot office building and related subsurface work for a second 650,000-square-foot office building on the site. (By acquiring development air rights for $7.4 million from Heinz Hall, Heinz Hall Plaza, and the Benedum Center, LPC increased its development rights from 673,555 square feet to 1.3 million square feet, considerably enhancing the economic viability of the office site.) The Cultural Trust received the other $8.5 million loan to be used for the historic restoration/renovation of the theater.

The loan to Lincoln Property Company will be repaid to the Trust for Cultural Resources over an 82-year period. (The Trust will also receive 5 percent of the net cash flow over $19 million should the office development generate this amount after the eighth year.) Repayments of the loan are to be used by the Trust for community development in the cultural district, and for discounted tickets to targeted groups, certain free tickets for civic or public events, and so forth.

Economic Benefits

This project will result in the creation of approximately 950 new jobs in the office building and 235 new jobs at the Benedum Center, plus 1,175 temporary construction jobs. In addition, it could generate space for more than 5,000 permanent jobs and more than $3.5 million in new annual real estate, parking, amusement, and business privilege tax revenues to the city, county, and school district.

Additional economic benefits will result in:

- Investment in construction and secondary spending for local goods and services of more than $300 million.
- More than $5.8 million per year in increased downtown food, parking, and retail expenditures.
- Additional economic development opportunities within the surrounding cultural district, enabling Pittsburgh's tourist and entertainment markets to expand.
- Increased ticket sales of almost $7.5 million, providing an additional $750,000 in city amusement taxes.

Ownership/Management Structures

The title to the land for the CNG office building site is held by Penn-Liberty Holding Company (a non-profit corporation) for the Howard Heinz Endowment, the owner of the 1.5-acre tract. The Lincoln Property Company leased the tract for 52 years and may renew the lease for three successive 10-year terms.

Lincoln Property makes lease payments to Penn-Liberty Holding Company beginning at $600,000 per year, $250,000 of which goes to the Pittsburgh Trust for Cultural Resources. These payments will serve as an endowment to the Trust, providing seed money for cultural development of the surrounding area.

Although the Auditorium Authority owns the 42,000-square-foot Benedum Center property—purchased with the $7.5 million bond issue and proceeds from the sale of unused air rights to the tower developer—the site was transferred to the Pittsburgh Trust for Cultural Resources to manage.

Lynn Johnson

The Lincoln Property Company of Dallas and/or its subsidiaries will develop, own, and manage the office building towers. Designed as a 1.3 million-square-foot twin-tower, office/retail complex, the project will be built in two phases. CNG Tower, a 32-story office building containing approximately 615,360 leasable square feet (650,000 gross), is under construction by Lincoln Liberty, a subsidiary of Lincoln Property Company, Dallas, and is scheduled to be completed in August 1987.

Two-thirds of the building is pre-leased (for 10 years) to CNG, Peoples Natural Gas, and Allegheny International. Rents will range from $26.50 to $31.50 per square foot of net rentable area. Phase II, the second tower, will not begin until Phase I is 85 percent occupied

The Benedum Center for the Performing Arts will be home for the Pittsburgh Opera, Ballet, and Civic Light Opera; it will also host full-scale Broadway shows.

and the appropriate market conditions are met. A 10,000-square-foot plaza will be provided on the tower site to meet the open space requirement for the theater.

The Pittsburgh Trust for Cultural Resources was created in 1984 and is incorporated by the Allegheny Conference on Community Development. Using public and private contributions and revenues from the real estate development, the Trust will:

- develop and manage the Stanley Theatre/Benedum Center for the

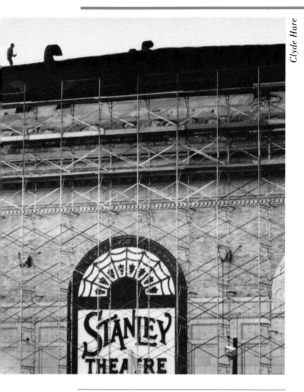

The existing Stanley Theatre will be carefully restored to form the new 2,800-seat Benedum Center for the Performing Arts. The theater's 1920s decor and ornate detail will be preserved while its backstage and support space will be expanded.

Performing Arts and help implement future theater projects in the district;

• initiate and coordinate a cultural district development process;
• provide district services and promotional activities; and
• facilitate additional development to enhance the area.

Development Process

The need for expanded cultural and entertainment facilities and the continued growth of Pittsburgh's corporate office and service economy made this project feasible. Moreover, the area surrounding Heinz Hall had deteriorated and was in need of revitalization. To upgrade the environment around Heinz Hall and in the surrounding Penn-Liberty district and to provide the initiative for cultural growth in downtown Pittsburgh,

the Howard Heinz Endowment initiated studies, mobilized other private and public interests, provided the venture capital necessary for the project, and launched the innovative private/public venture.

The development process involved several actions. First, a philanthropic Pittsburgh family acquired Heinz Hall and had it rehabilitated. Second, the Allegheny Conference on Community Development prepared a plan for the development of the area and the creation of a cultural district. And third, the project was moved along by the strong support from and active cooperation among private individuals, foundations, corporations, arts groups, and other volunteer groups with the city and many of its agencies, as well as with the county of Allegheny. For example, weekly meetings of a public/private task force established to coordinate the project were held in the mayor's office under the leadership of David Matter, the mayor's executive secretary. The group included the project consultants, developers, architects, representatives of the Heinz Endowment, the Allegheny Conference, and key members of the city administration, including the Urban Redevelopment Authority and the Department of City Planning. It was here that the proposed concepts were hammered out to achieve legal, economic, and design feasibility within political realities. The framework for the UDAG, air rights transfers, eminent domain procedures, and financing vehicles were orchestrated in these meetings while the project was being planned.

It is expected that this process will be repeated on additional sites in the surrounding cultural district. The combination of air rights transfers, charitable contributions, private investment, and public funds has helped translate a strong market for the arts into a development reality. The process also acts to preserve historically significant and/or low-rise facilities and to upgrade deteriorating neighborhoods.

Status

The first phase of the project is under construction, and by August 1987, the first tower and the restoration of the Stanley Theatre/Benedum Center for the Performing Arts should be completed and ready for occupancy.

All the necessary land has been acquired, cleared, and graded, and utilities have been relocated. Federal funds are available, the city/county bonds have been sold, and private financing through the sale of the first mortgage bond has been arranged. Leases for the first office tower have been signed with AI and CNG. Seventy percent of the office space has been preleased at an average rent of $28 per square foot for operating leases, and the owners anticipate the percentage to rise to 80 percent by the end of 1986.

Cushman & Wakefield, who is acting as the leasing agent, reports that lease inducements include the facts that the CNG Tower is the first "smart" building in Pittsburgh, fully geared to current office technology; and that it is located in the cultural district, a 12-block area surrounding the project and extending to the convention center.

Philanthropic contributions have been committed and pledged for more than the required $12 million needed for the Benedum Center. When completed, the renovated Stanley Theatre will have retained its 2,800-seat capacity. Its classical 1920s decor, including newly decorated and guilded interiors, domed ceiling, and ornate proscenium arch will have been restored. But as the new Benedum Center, it will have an enlarged and improved stage and a new six-story support building including two stage-sized rehearsal halls, one of which will act as an experimental theater. It will thus be possible to produce three different operas or other full-stage performances in any given week, thereby freeing Heinz Hall for use primarily as a concert facility. Financial projections show that the Center's renovation and new construction will cost about half that of new theater construction.

The Cultural Trust expects to manage and maintain the Benedum Center without outside financial support. This will depend, however, on the financial arrangements of air rights sales, loan repayments, and the completion and success of the tower complex, from which the Trust derives a share of the income to continue its management and development role.

The Fulton, a 1,500-seat theater, which is planned as a downtown home for local productions, is under option and will be renovated as the third, more intimate theater in the cultural district. A series of smaller theater facilities and surface parking are also planned.

Permanent staff has been hired to help meet the Trust's future development goals within the arts and entertainment district. It has been estimated that, aside from performance space, the cultural district has the potential to support 2 to 3 million square feet of new residential, hotel, office, parking, and open space development by the year 2000. Consultants envisage concomitant urban design amenities to include streetscape improvements such as landscaping, paving and lighting, new housing overlooking riverfront parks and walkways, and new eating places, clubs, and shops.

Overall, this innovative process will have a significant impact on the physical improvement of the corridor between Heinz Hall and the convention center, fueling the continued renaissance of Pittsburgh's Golden Triangle.

STEEL PLAZA/ ONE MELLON BANK CENTER

Corporate headquarters expansion spurred this nearly seven-acre project in downtown Pittsburgh, which includes the development of One Mellon Bank Center, a 54-story, 1.5 million-square-foot office and commercial tower; a 200-car garage; new streets; a major open space; and the Steel Plaza Station, which is the main station of the Light Rail Transit (LRT) system. Proposed are two additional office towers, a luxury hotel, and two small department stores.

The project was initiated when United States Steel Realty Development Division, a subsidiary of U.S. Steel, began plans to develop a megablock that it owned across from its corporate headquarters on Grant Street. At about the same time, the city was planning improvements in the area, and the Port Authority of Allegheny County Transit Division (PAT) was completing plans for its underground rail system in downtown Pittsburgh. Through cooperative interaction, PAT built its underground station—the Steel Plaza Station—and, at the same time, the supporting beams for U.S. Steel's proposed development above the station. It also built new, realigned city streets.

The Steel Plaza project site fronts on downtown Pittsburgh's Grant Street on the upper portion of the Golden Triangle between the

Grant Street—the location of some of Pittsburgh's most important civic and corporate buildings such as One Mellon Bank Center, the U.S. Steel Building, the Richardson Courthouse, and the City-County Building—is being reconstructed as a grand boulevard with median strips, brick paving, granite curbs, and light and sign posts, all of which are being adopted as standards for new downtown construction.

STEEL PLAZA/ONE MELLON BANK CENTER

Project Type: Joint development of underground Light Rail Transit (LRT) station and 54-story One Mellon Bank Center office tower.

Developers: Office tower: United States Steel Realty.

Transit: Port Authority of Allegheny County Transit Division (PAT).

Architecture/ Planning: Welton Becket Associates, Architects, New York; Pittsburgh Department of City Planning/Urban Redevelopment Authority.

Financing: Private $126 million for One Mellon Bank Center. Transit financed by a federal DOT grant (80 percent of the cost), with the remaining 20 percent financed by the state and county.

Status: Opening dates: office tower—1984; transit station— July 1985; proposed new complex (if approved) to begin construction 1988 and open 1990.

Granite curbs contributed to Grant Street's $13 million transformation.

courthouse and the U.S. Steel headquarters tower. Grant Street is home to various corporate headquarters and major buildings like Koppers Company, U.S. Steel, the Gulf Oil Building, the Frick Building designed by Daniel Burnham, the Union Trust Building (now called Two Mellon Bank), a major

hotel, the City-County Building, and the Allegheny County Courthouse designed by H.H. Richardson. The street itself is being reconstructed as a grand boulevard worthy of its abutting structures. New street lighting, paving, plantings, and sidewalks, together with the elimination of overhead wires formerly used by street trolleys, are transforming the street into a major aesthetic asset in downtown.

One Mellon Bank Center, a privately built and financed corporate headquarters structure, was dedicated in 1984 and is 85 to 90 percent occupied. The midtown LRT station was opened in July 1985. Plans for the remainder of the nearly seven-acre site include a $450 million to $500 million three-building complex to be built over the underground station. This proposed hotel/office/retail complex containing 3 million square feet of space is expected to begin within a year with the hotel and retail portions.

Financing

The Steel Plaza was originally conceived as a private development on privately held land. As executed, the project involved the participation of at least three public bodies and the construction of major public improvements, notably Pittsburgh's underground transit system and main station, and new public streets.

The allocation of land, responsibilities, and dollars between the private and public sectors was outlined in an agreement among United States Steel Realty (the developer of the One Mellon Bank Center office tower), the city, the Urban Redevelopment Authority (URA), and the Port Authority of Allegheny County (the developer of the Light Rail Transit).

One Mellon Bank Center, at an estimated cost of $126 million, was privately financed. United States Steel Realty developed the project for a major corporate tenant, on a portion of a seven-acre site that U.S. Steel acquired—through direct purchase or trade of surface and subsurface land—from various sources including Mellon foundations,[8] the city, the Urban Redevelopment Authority, and PAT.

The city used land as a financing tool to make civic improvements in the area. It bartered and leveraged land from on-site streets it would vacate to allow PAT to build new realigned streets in the project area, and to convince U.S. Steel to integrate its design plans with the Light Rail Transit construction to create desired civic spaces and to achieve other design criteria.

The Urban Redevelopment Authority sold a two-acre site—from the 95- to 102-acre Lower Hill re-

---

[8] Three foundations were involved: the Richard King Mellon Foundation, the Sarah Scaife Foundation, and the A.W. Mellon Educational and Charitable Trust.

One Mellon Bank Center, a 54-story office tower, rises between the Richardson Courthouse and the U.S. Steel Building. The Mellon tower was built as part of a joint development with the Steel Plaza Light Rail Transit Station.

Lynn Johnson

development area—to United States Steel Realty for $2.5 million. (The site was originally assembled in the 1950s as part of Pittsburgh's first federally assisted urban renewal project.) URA also became the instrumental agency responsible for various land swaps, street vacations, and agreements.

PAT spent for station development $29.4 million from a $480 million Urban Mass Transit Grant it received in 1979. The U.S. Department of Transportation covered 80 percent of the cost, with the remaining 20 percent shared by the state (16 ⅔ percent) and by the county (3 ⅓ percent).

Total public funds of $29.4 million were allocated as follows:
- $3.5 million—acquisition cost of a parking garage on the eastern edge of the site, originally owned by the Public Parking Authority (in 1980).
- $0.9 million—cost of additional property acquisition.
- $0.3 million—cost of demolition.
- $1.1 million—cost of relocation.
- $23.6 million—cost of tracks, signs, etc., for Steel Plaza Station.

PAT used the parking garage site (surface property) to trade for subsurface property as outlined in the master four-party agreement.

Ownership/Management Structures

Before the four-party agreement was made, landholdings on the Steel Plaza project site were as follows:
- The URA owned a two-acre parcel, part of the Lower Hill renewal project.
- The city owned streets to be vacated and realigned.
- PAT owned land acquired from the Public Parking Authority.
- U.S. Steel owned the Grant Street frontage of the parcel.

Land was acquired through land swaps and purchases as per the agreement. This agreement, prepared by URA in September 1981,

provided PAT with all subsurface rights necessary for the LRT and the Steel Plaza Station and all surface rights for ventilation shafts and access ways for the station; it provided the city with surface rights necessary for the realignment and construction of its streets; and it provided United States Steel Realty with the balance of subsurface and surface rights and all of air rights in the project area for use in its development. The last area consisted of three development parcels. On the parcel facing Grant Street, United States Steel Realty developed for the Dravo Corporation a 54-story tower and plaza, which it then sold to Mellon Bank, which now leases and manages the project under a sale/leaseback arrangement. United States Steel Realty owns, or has under option, the remaining development parcels that are being negotiated for sale.

Maintenance of the streets, the plaza, and the LRT is shared. PAT maintains the station and access to one surface station; United States Steel and Mellon Bank maintain and provide security for other areas and exits. PAT built realigned streets in accordance with city design standards and dedicated them to the city, which now maintains them.

PAT and United States Steel Realty agreed to install and maintain vertical and horizontal supports to protect both parties' structures. United States Steel Realty or another developer will construct over the underground transit facility a commercial structure supported by columns, walls, and footings that will also support the transit. Maintenance of these facilities will also be shared.

Development Process

The development of the Steel Plaza area, like many other projects in downtown Pittsburgh, reflects the city's corporate character and growth. The cooperative interaction of corporate and government leaders and the involvement of

various civic organizations and foundations brought about the rebuilding of a significant portion of downtown, to the mutual benefit of the private and public sectors.

The site includes a two-acre parcel of land that had been assembled by the Urban Redevelopment Authority as part of Pittsburgh's first federally assisted urban renewal project approved in 1955. A 1962 study by the Pittsburgh Regional Planning Association had recommended the area just east of Grant Street as the location for the main downtown station of a new public rail transit system, and planners at the time urged that the land in the general area be acquired to protect it for future public transit use. The Mellon foundations acquired the land to assure its orderly development, but plans for the transit system floundered and the properties were later sold to the United States Steel Realty Development Division in 1976. The United States Steel headquarters building occupied the site adjacent to these properties.

In 1976, PPG Industries, one of Gateway Center's first occupants (1953), and whose lease was expiring in 1983, began looking at downtown sites for a new headquarters facility that would meet its need to expand over the next 25 years. The Dravo Corporation, whose lease in another downtown tower also was to end in 1983, began a similar search two years later. The United States Steel site was attractive to both corporations. United States Steel was not interested in selling the site, preferring instead to joint-venture the development of a headquarters building designed to a major tenant's specifications. Initially, it hoped to retain an on-site building and to remain remote from any transit station connections.

Other corporate moves were being examined by Mellon Bank and Duquesne Light, which together foresaw a need of well over 1 million square feet of space. City officials, through the mayor's Development Council, were kept abreast of the corporate searches and development needs, and were eager to assist in the planning and execution of the expansion plans of these corporations to assure their continued presence and growth in downtown Pittsburgh.

PPG ultimately decided that it would develop its own building on a five-acre site closer to the Point—just east of Gateway Center off Market Square.

With PPG out of the picture, United States Steel forged an agreement with the Dravo Corporation, a major international construction and natural resources engineering firm, to be the anchor tenant in a new world headquarters tower. The company projected an ultimate need of 1.2 million square feet and had a peculiar requirement for large floor areas—36,000 to 40,000 square feet—for engineering task forces, in addition to normal administrative and staff office needs. The need for the engineering spaces controlled the architectural and site design, which required that the total site be cleared. Clearing the site supported four city specifications: for new streets—which meant cutting through the United States Steel–owned parcel; for connection to the transit system; for a civic open space; and for design compatible

The Steel Plaza Station was built to support the transit facilities as well as several Steel Plaza buildings.

Clyde Hare

with existing historic structures, which would become more visible when the site was cleared.

The Port Authority had received federal approval of its $480 million grant for the Light Rail Transit system in 1979, and moved to acquire and demolish a public parking garage on the development site in 1980, making a key parcel of land available for total site development. Ongoing meetings in the mayor's office with the URA, PAT, United States Steel Realty, and other participants, resulted in the agreement mentioned earlier outlining various land transfers and responsibilities. The URA would sell its two-acre parcel held over from the Lower Hill redevelopment parcel and oversee the various land swaps and purchases, street realignments, street furniture, and other site construction specifications. PAT would trade its parking garage land for subsurface rights under the United States Steel parcel. It would also build new streets and construct subsurface supporting beams and columns suitable for the proposed commercial development above ground. United States Steel increased its landholdings by about one-third through this deal. In February 1980, the chairman of United States Steel and the chairman of Dravo announced the proposed development of the 1.5 million-square-foot Dravo Tower on Grant Street across from the Union Trust Building, with new street alignments and pedestrian connections to the LRT Steel Plaza Station.

Construction on Dravo Tower began in April 1981. Mellon Bank had begun looking for expansion space and had purchased an existing downtown office building, One Oliver Plaza, in which Dravo was a major tenant, in anticipation of that space becoming available when Dravo moved into its new headquarters building. PAT began construction for the Light Rail Transit tunnel and station on Steel Plaza in 1981. In July 1982, Dravo and U.S. Steel signed a $450 million lease commitment for 25 years at a set rent. Dravo planned to move into

612,000 square feet and grow into 1.2 million square feet by the year 2000.

By the end of 1982, however, the economic recession was taking its toll on corporate capital programs; Dravo was undergoing economic retrenchment and had to reassess expenditures. The 1.2 million-square-foot office space expansion was no longer on the horizon. In a trade and solution resulting in still another swap in this project, Dravo and Mellon struck a deal whereby Dravo would stay in One Oliver Plaza, owned by Mellon. Mellon would retrofit the space and set the rent for 20 years for Dravo. Mellon Bank would move into the 54-story headquarters structure built on land once owned by Mellon foundations. The final scenario: Mellon Bank assumed Dravo's 25-year lease in the new tower and purchased the building from United States Steel. The tower's name was changed to One Mellon Bank Center.

By 1983, PAT was resurfacing the new city streets. In 1984, the dedication of One Mellon Bank Center took place, and on July 4, 1985, the Steel Plaza Station and the Light Rail Transit system were opened to the public. Development of the remainder of the site is being negotiated, and the prospects of a new hotel, and additional office, commercial, parking, and possibly residential uses are under consideration.

One Mellon Bank Center has since been purchased by a syndicator, and Mellon Bank is a major leaseholder in a sale/leaseback arrangement.

Public Participation

The Steel Plaza project is billed as a private development. In truth, although a tower could have been built on United States Steel's land without the involvement of public bodies, the cooperation and subsequent design changes brought about through the public/private partnership turned out to be a great asset aesthetically not only to the corporations, but also to the public agencies and to the city.

While the $125 million tower development was privately financed with United States Steel Realty as the developer and was designed to the specifications of the proposed major occupant, it had to adhere to criteria outlined by the City Planning Commission as part of the city's downtown development strategy. Also, Pittsburgh's zoning ordinance requires all new projects to have 20 percent in open space (60 percent in the case of Gateway), a need that was handsomely met in this project by the civic plaza that opened views to the historic Richardson Courthouse and the Union Trust Building across from the site. The integration of the two construction projects was physical in terms of support structures and aesthetic in terms of the amenities provided to the user/pedestrian. As executed through public intervention, the development implemented an urban design concept rather than an architectural monolith.

Status

One Mellon Bank Center is more than 85 percent occupied, with rents running at about $24 to $26 per square foot; 54,000 square feet of the retail space is 70 percent leased; and the open spaces are actively used. Representative of Pittsburgh's corporate growth, Mellon Bank has more than tripled its downtown space to almost 3 million square feet. The transit system is running and the Steel Plaza Station has underground access to the United States Steel building, One Mellon Bank Center, and the civic plaza. The new streets are finished and in use, improving the circulation pattern. Street lighting, furniture, and signage are in accordance with city design standards.

Negotiations are underway for additional development on the site (to be called Pittsburgh City Center) and construction is expected to begin in 1988 on a new hotel and retail space by the New York

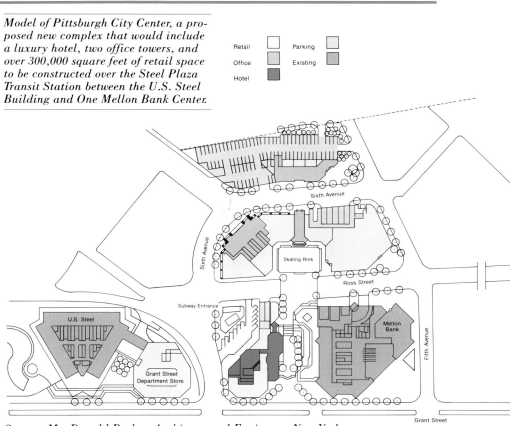

Model of Pittsburgh City Center, a proposed new complex that would include a luxury hotel, two office towers, and over 300,000 square feet of retail space to be constructed over the Steel Plaza Transit Station between the U.S. Steel Building and One Mellon Bank Center.

Source: MacDonald Becket, Architects and Engineers, New York.

City–based Mosbacher Group, which has the land under option.

The aesthetic benefits have been complemented by the economic benefits of this project. Because of it, the continued presence of at least two major corporations downtown has been assured. Pittsburgh has yet another headquarters tower scaling its skyline. Compared with the 500 jobs originally provided in the project area, the office tower alone now provides 8,000 jobs and has added 1.5 million square feet of office space downtown. Future development is expected to provide more than 10,000 additional jobs and the construction of a $400 to $500 million, three-building project by 1990.

The entire Light Rail Transit project is estimated to be a $600 million public investment that will ultimately generate $1.8 billion in private expenditures and employ 8,200 people.

This project presents another example of the positive effects that can result from well-orchestrated public and private cooperation in civic improvement. It illustrates the rapid corporate headquarters and services expansion in Pittsburgh and particularly the explosive growth of the banking industry. Between 1980 and 1984, the four major corporate moves mentioned in this case study were responsible for the construction of three office towers and the creation of more than 4 million square feet of space, together with retail and parking areas. PPG developed its own headquarters tower. Mellon Bank purchased a new tower and retrofitted two existing buildings, and a speculative office development (One Oxford Centre) brought almost 1 million more square feet of office space to the market in 1981 with Duquesne Light as an initial tenant.

Rendering of Liberty Center with the Vista International Hotel in the foreground. Liberty Center is part of Pittsburgh's expansion into the convention and tourism market.

LIBERTY CENTER/CONVENTION HOTEL AND OFFICE TOWER

Liberty Center is a $136 million downtown luxury hotel and office tower project standing on 2.4 acres of land adjacent to the convention center. When completed, it will include a 619-room, 25-story Vista International Hotel; 30,000 square feet of retail space; and a 500,000-square-foot, 27-story office building (Federated Investors Tower).

The city initiated this project as a key element in its efforts to boost tourist and convention business. Located at the upper end of the Golden Triangle and adjacent to the David L. Lawrence Convention Center, Liberty Center is the result of a concerted marketing effort to encourage development in an area that had been considered the back door of Pittsburgh's downtown core. The convention center, begun in 1977, was built on a piece of railroad property next to the tracks and Pennsylvania Station on the northeast corner of the Triangle, overlooking the Allegheny River. The Penn Avenue spine between the convention center and downtown was lined with empty lofts and its parallel thoroughfare, Liberty Avenue, was noted for its bars and pornographic shops. Adjacent to the center, the railroad terminal was used only as a waiting room and ticket counter for Amtrak's four daily trains. Although the area had potential because of its proximity to the office and cultural core of the city, the overall environment was one of blight and decay.

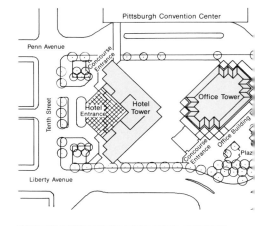

Site plan of Liberty Center.

Several activities strengthened the site's potential for development. The first was the construction of the convention center itself, which opened in 1981. Proposed transportation alterations would improve the traffic circulation and access to the area and would increase the flow of activity to and through the area. The Light Rail Transit terminal station was planned near the site; and the East Busway ends downtown at the Grant/Liberty intersection. The city was committed to making major street improvements at the intersection and on surrounding streets; Grant Street was being completely redone as a grand boulevard (at an estimated cost of $13 million). Moreover, although long vacant, the old Penn Central Railroad Station building and rotunda, designed by Daniel Burnham and designated a historic landmark, graced the area.

While earlier city administrators perhaps foresaw the potential of the area when the site was selected for the convention center in the 1970s, it was becoming disturbingly obvious to the subsequent Caliguiri administration and to civic leaders that private development was not occurring on the sites adjacent to the convention facility. In fact, Penn Central, which owned much of the land, had been unable to dispose of it.

In 1979, the city, working through the Urban Redevelopment Authority, interceded and purchased 2.4 acres of largely vacant land just south of the convention center, and had several blocks surrounding the center designated as an urban renewal area. It proceeded to generate interest in developing the same 104,000-square-foot parcel that Penn Central had been unable to market before the city acquired it. The URA put together a design program for a hotel development on the site, packaged it, and began an aggressive marketing program. It launched a design/developer competition, requesting proposals, and advertised its offering to help with a UDAG application. As well as putting in

escrow with URA a $25,000 good faith deposit, finalists had to present architectural schematics, a completely described financial package, and a description of the hotel and its management. The developer chosen, Grant Liberty Development Group Associates (GLDGA), proposed a well-designed, multiuse complex to reinforce the convention center and an office tower, as well as hotel, to enhance the financial feasibility of the project for the city. The Redevelopment Authority purchased the landmark Penn Central Station and office building across the street and made emergency repairs to assure its preservation and appropriate reuse.

LIBERTY CENTER/CONVENTION HOTEL AND OFFICE TOWER

Project Type: When completed, this project will include a 619-room, 25-story Vista International Hotel; a 500,000-square-foot, 27-story office building—the Federated Investors Tower; 30,000 square feet of retail space; a 600-car subsurface garage; 20,000 square feet of landscaped plazas; and a pedestrian bridge to the convention center.

Developer: Grant Liberty Development Group Associates (GLDGA)[1].

Owners: Liberty Center Venture, composed of GLDGA and Metropolitan Life.

Architecture: Urban Design Associates, Architects, Pittsburgh; Burt Hill Kosar Rittlemann Associates, Pittsburgh; The Architects Collaborative (TAC), Cambridge Massachusetts.

Construction: Primary: Mellon-Stuart, Inc., Pittsburgh; Forest City Dillon—modular building method used for hotel.

Financing: $136 million private and public, as follows:

Private loan	$99,000,000
Vista	3,000,000
Equity	12,896,000
UDAG	21,000,000
	$135,896,000

Status: Groundbreaking, December 1984; completion, December 1986.

---

[1] GLDGA is made up of the following five general partners who, in addition to being developers/owners, play other roles in the project:
- Urban Design Associates, Pittsburgh: developer, owner, and architect.
- Burt Hill Kosar Rittleman Associates, Pittsburgh: developer, owner, and architect.
- Beynon and Company, Inc., Pittsburgh: developer, owner, leasing agent, and part of management team.
- Joseph L. Muscarelle, Inc., Maywood, New Jersey: developer, owner, construction manager, and manager in joint venture with Beynon & Company; joint venture contractor with Mellon-Stuart, Inc., Pittsburgh.
- Forest City Enterprises, Inc., Cleveland: owner, developer, and subcontractor for hotel tower construction.

The 1.3 million-square-foot hotel/office building complex is nearing completion with Federated Investors as its anchor tenant. A private developer has under option the Penn Central Station building, which it plans to restore and convert to luxury apartments and commercial space. Transportation facilities are in place and the streets are being completed according to design criteria that include trees, landscaping, paving, light standards, and signage. The project anchors a cultural district, whose opposite end is balanced by CNG Tower/Benedum Center for the Performing Arts (discussed earlier).

Financing

Liberty Center is being privately developed through a joint venture involving Grant Liberty Development Group Associates (a private partnership) as developer and co-owner, and Metropolitan Life as co-owner and investor.

Total project costs are estimated at about $136 million. The city received a $21 million Urban Development Action Grant for loans to the project. Almost $115 million in private funds came from the following sources:

Metropolitan Life	$99,000,000	Permanent Financing
VISTA (who will manage the hotel)	$3,000,000	Hotel Development
Developer Equity	$12,896,000	Site Acquisition and Development
UDAG	$21,000,000[1]	Partial Construction and Permanent Financing
Total Cost	$135,896,000	

[1]Of which $150,000 is the URA administrative cost.

Liberty Center rendering showing the clock tower and the Federated Investors Tower in the foreground.

Initially, Grant Liberty Development Group Associates acquired the site from URA and designed and constructed the project, obtaining a construction loan of $99 million from Mellon Bank and Wells Fargo Bank, each of which assumed one-half the total amount. As shown above, GLDGA's own equity contribution was about $13 million.

After GLDGA has completed construction of the project, Metropolitan Life will make a $67 million permanent loan to the venture and will invest $32 million as equity funds. GLDGA will then own 40 percent of the project and Metropolitan Life 60 percent. Vista International, who will manage the hotel, also lent GLDGA $3 million as partial construction and/or permanent financing.

The URA actively participates as the original site owner, as a packager, and as a lender. The URA purchased the property in 1979 from the Penn Central Railroad for $4.135 million using a five-year loan at 7 ½ percent interest, secured by $2 million in government securities and a land mortgage. The property was sold to Grant Liberty for $5.076 million plus closing costs.

GLDGA acquired two loans from URA: $2.914 million in a purchase money mortgage for the real estate, $2 million of which is to be repaid by November 1986; and $20.850 million in federal UDAG funds of which up to $18.850 million can be in construction costs and up to $2 million in necessary postopening rent-up costs on the VISTA International Hotel.

The URA loan to the developer of $20.850 million from UDAG funds has an 8 percent interest (to come out of the project's net cash flow) with a balloon payment of the principal at the end of the 15th year. URA may share in 20 percent of excess "profits" in years 6 to 15.

UDAG repayments are committed to a capital reserve fund for the convention center and to activities eligible under Title I of the Housing and Community Development

Act of 1974. Street improvements to be provided by the city have been included in recent city capital budgets and will be financed by a combination of federal and local money.

Were it not for URA's aggressive action in purchasing the site, marketing it, and offering technical and financial assistance to the developers, the project could not have been realized as planned.

Status

Federated Investors Office Tower has been topped off, and the Vista International Hotel is under construction—using the precast concrete modular building method patented by Forest City Dillon, Inc.—and should be completed by December 1986. The tower's anchor tenant, Federated Investors, Inc. (a subsidiary of Aetna Life Insurance Company), is to lease about one-third of the building on the top nine floors. The hotel manager is working on marketing the hotel; leasing agents are promoting the retail and other space. Rentals for office space will average $23 to $28 a square foot. Rentals for retail space for about 20 to 25 specialty shops should average about $40 a square foot.

The owners anticipate an increasing demand for downtown office space from financial institutions, insurance companies, law firms, and high-tech firms that are expanding. They are confident that the complex will be fully occupied within three years, citing as highlights the office tower's walkway to the hotel through a four-story podium area that will have meeting rooms, retail shops, upscale restaurants, lounges, and a fitness center. Hotel room service will be available to office tenants. The hotel has also been designed to serve the convention center by providing it with additional ballroom and kitchen facilities when needed. A pedestrian bridge connects the hotel to the convention center.

Two landscaped plazas containing 20,000 square feet will replace

the formerly desolate area, and will establish an appropriate setting for the David L. Lawrence Convention Center, as well as augment the facilities offered to tenants and users.

Streets are being improved based on downtown design standards established by the city planning commission. A troublesome intersection at Grant and Liberty streets will be realigned; overhead wires will be eliminated; and the streets will be lined with trees, planters, attractive curbs, paving, new light standards, and signs.

With the downtown expressway loop nearly complete, motorists entering the city from the north can easily see the project. East Busway and subway terminals will also improve access to the area.

Liberty Center itself has generated about 500 construction jobs and is expected to produce over 1,500 new permanent jobs. Tax increases to the city are projected at $2 million annually. Private investment for development will be $115 million, or $5.50 for each public dollar.

Development of this hotel complex has sparked interest in additional improvements in the surrounding area. Developers propose to transform the Penn Central Railroad Station building into 240 luxury apartments and 24,000 to 50,000 square feet of retail and commercial space, with 150 parking spaces. Rents will range from $750 to $900 a month. The Penn Station Historic Joint Venture Corporation plans to spend $25 million to renovate the site, and market it as the "Pennsylvanian."

Other surrounding buildings are being privately renovated for office and other reuse. The establishment of the Cultural Trust and the Cultural District and the resulting activity will support rehabilitation and improvement of the Penn-Liberty corridor, which is anchored by the convention center and the hotel complex at one end, and by Heinz Hall and the Gateway at the other end. Most recently, serious proposals have been made to create an ententainment district and/or festival marketplace in the area immediately above the convention center development. Preliminary estimates project a private investment of $336 million, a public investment of $35 million, increased local tax revenues of more than $3 million ($600,000 net annually), and over 7,000 permanent jobs.

The city's and the URA's marketing effort is proving successful and will undoubtedly act as a catalyst to hasten the private development of an area that would have remained moribund were it not for public intervention. Clearly, this project will tap the tourism and convention market that Pittsburgh has begun to pursue.

FUTURE CHALLENGES

While downtown Pittsburgh is experiencing a building boom, and the economy is diversifying, growing, and producing new jobs in the service sector, problems are emerging that could either slow the momentum of Renaissance II or could mark the beginning of yet another renaissance.

Although the number of jobs is increasing in Pittsburgh, the area's 7.8 percent unemployment rate is still above the national average of 7.1 as reported in June 1986. Unemployment has been most severe in the region's traditional industries, especially the steel plants in the Monongahela and Ohio valleys. Employment in the steel industry declined by nearly 50 percent in four years, and changes in the world market suggest that this trend will not be reversed. Mill and factory workers have lost jobs and communities have lost their sustaining industries, many of which have been anchors for the local economy for 100 years. And while job gains outnumber losses, the gains are in the nonmanufacturing and service sectors. New employment opportunities and new business activity have to be developed for those areas that have undergone permanent change and suffer from a reduction in jobs. Continued economic diversification is essential. Efforts to develop more effective systems for training and retraining the workforce will contribute to economic development.

More detailed economic analyses and recommendations are outlined in the Allegheny Conference's 1984 report, *A Strategy for Growth: An Economic Development Program for the Pittsburgh Region*. Mobilized by the Conference, task forces were formed to study how to bring about a change in the structure of the economy that would affect workers and corporations alike. New headquarters, new technologies, and new markets are being sought by the business and university community in cooperation with the public sector, as a result of the 1984 study and its proposals. The study programs are geared toward long-term growth and a positive change in the trend. They build on earlier Conference efforts toward diversification of the Pittsburgh economy—the formation of the Regional Industrial Development Corporation (RIDC) in 1955, and Penn's Southwest Association in 1972—to attract new jobs and new investment by encouraging industry and businesses to locate and expand in the area.

Although significant transportation improvements have been made, the region's infrastructure—roads, bridges, airports, as well as water, sewage, and other basic systems—are all in need of repairs and improvements that are estimated to cost $9 billion between now and 1990. A recent study projects a funding shortfall of $5.5 billion. Yet economic growth and development cannot continue without upgraded access and support systems.

Specific projects that will mold the future of the city will be the new Technology Center on the former J&L Steel Plant site, a proposed science center, an entertainment district, the development of Herr's Island, and a festival market. These projects call for an investment of almost $630 million of which $200 would be public dollars. Public and private entities, together with the city, will determine priorities and alternatives and where to commit scarce funds. Other challenges facing the city are the needs of the homeless and of those who are unable to afford housing without subsidies. These challenges, as well as the ongoing reclamation of the city's waterfronts, the $400 million proposed expansion of the airport, and continued economic growth will shape the strategy for Pittsburgh's future development.

Pittsburgh and Pittsburghers have established a track record as problem-solvers. Generally recognized as a bootstrap community, the city benefited greatly from the availability of significant federal financial assistance stemming from the Housing Act of 1949 and other federal and state programs that are now ebbing under the current public attitude of fiscal restraint and conservatism. Perhaps the greatest future challenge will be in finding solutions without the federal assistance that made so much possible in the past.

Downtown as viewed from Spring Hill—one of Pittsburgh's residential neighborhoods within easy reach of the central business district.

LESSONS LEARNED

Four key factors contributed to the success of the Pittsburgh revitalization: public/private cooperation; professionalism and organization; creative financing tools; and initiative, the ability to take risks, and the integrity of the many entities involved. Pittsburgh has learned that revitalization should focus on:
- neighborhoods;
- renovation and rehabilitation, including historic preservation;
- good design and amenities, including cultural facilities, institutions, and open spaces;
- facilitation and provision of guidelines for corporate development;
- improved public access to waterfronts;
- improved transportation facilities;
- the leveraging of private funds with public resources;
- use of aggressive marketing techniques;
- promotion of mixed-use development; and
- diversification of the city's economy.

PUBLIC/PRIVATE COOPERATION

The key to Pittsburgh's rebirth has been public/private cooperation. Business leaders have been actively involved with the redevelopment of the city since the early days of urban renewal. They proposed the formation of the Urban Redevelopment Authority, and, as part of its board of directors, helped set policy along with the mayor. This spirit of cooperation between government and business leaders, regardless of political affiliation, has been the cornerstone of

William Metzger/Courtesy Neighborhoods for Living Center, Pittsburgh

Pittsburgh's success. Corporations, individuals, charitable foundations, public agencies, and citizen groups have all functioned as initiators and/or participants in large-scale urban development.

PROFESSIONALISM AND ORGANIZATION

The Pittsburgh experience also provides evidence of the need for skilled professionals and organizations to implement a long-term redevelopment plan. Pittsburgh was particularly blessed in having enthusiastic and creative professionals in the public and private sectors.

CREATIVE FINANCING TOOLS

Like many U.S. cities, Pittsburgh has received vast sums of federal funds. But it began redevelopment with private funds and therefore provides a useful role model for the present day with its scarcity of federal funds. Many of the innovative financing tools were described earlier. Of particular significance are the arrangements made by the Pittsburgh Trust for Cultural Resources to channel public, private, and philanthropic funds to revitalize the downtown and to promote cultural facilities and the arts. Acting as a receptacle for charitable donations, air-rights purchase funds, UDAG loan repayments, and transfer of tax advantages, the Cultural Trust is a vehicle worth replicating.

Pittsburgh also has used strategically its zoning and development controls, design criteria, open space requirements, and other controls to shape desired reuse and design criteria, thereby aiding direct public investment. In addition, public expenditures on amenities have helped promote private investment.

INITIATIVE, RISK TAKING, AND INTEGRITY

Exercising initiative and taking risks are the intangible aspects that make for great leadership and partnerships. The risks taken by a handful of Pittsburgh businessmen who initiated redevelopment were matched by the risks taken by those supporting them. The latter included the public officials who defended the constitutionality of the enabling legislation and the corporations that invested in the city when the advantages of doing so were not clear.

SUMMARY

In spite of Pittsburgh's resourcefulness, neither the public nor the private sector can manage development alone. With all the sophisticated mechanisms, leveraging, and creative planning employed through the years, the need has continued to exist for cooperation between federal, state, county, and local governments, on the one hand, and corporations, civic and philanthropic organizations, and local residents, on the other hand. Knowing this may be Pittsburgh's greatest lesson learned.

ST. LOUIS

ST. LOUIS
A COMMENTARY

T hose who witnessed the transformation of the city of St. Louis during the past few decades have had their faith in urban vitality restored. Eulogies of St. Louis written and delivered by some were indeed premature. A city that was seen as moribund by hardened realists was viewed as a development opportunity by imaginative entrepreneurs. Those who thought that restoring cities would be unremunerative were proved wrong.

As the authors of this chapter point out, St. Louis used all three levels of government to encourage private developers. The resulting strategy relied on many components, all of which deserve credit: the Community Development Block Grant program for allowing needed federal funds to be allocated by local officials in ways most

Major strides have been made in the revitalization of downtown St. Louis.

beneficial to their jurisdiction's circumstances; the federal income tax code for being sensitive to historic preservation; the Urban Development Action Grant program for providing key capital; the state of Missouri for enacting statutes that allowed private firms to use public authority for public purposes; elected and appointed officials of the city of St. Louis for being the creative brokers between the public and private sectors; major corporations like Mercantile Bank and Ralston Purina for having the enlightened self-interest to take the long view; and—most of all—urban entrepreneurs like Leon Strauss of Pantheon Corporation, who ultimately made it all happen.

As a result of these successes, especially those of the past decade, the question concerning St. Louis is no longer whether it will survive, but whether it will be able to sustain the momentum of its residential and employment comeback. The likelihood is that it will not continue this pace of redevelopment but will instead simply consolidate and maintain its recent successes, experiencing little additional growth.

The city of St. Louis, at the heart of the metropolitan area but containing only a small part of the land mass and less than 20 percent of the population, has once again become a factor in the overall housing market. This can be attributed to the increased desirability of inner-city living among some segments of the population and, as the following chapter emphasizes, to the public financing that has reduced developers' costs, resulting in rents and sale prices that are competitive.

But availability of federal support, either through the Community Development Block Grant's front door or the income tax code's rear entrance, is dwindling. CDBG's funding is declining, and the Tax Reform Act of 1986 has lowered the worth of historic rehabilitation and dramatically reduced the tax benefits of real estate investment.

As there are fewer subsidies for city housing, the price of urban housing in relation to the price of housing in the rest of the metropolitan area should increase, thus lowering the demand for residences in the city. Moreover, many of those preferring city living—the so-called urban pioneers—have already made the trek inward and the age cohort (18 to 39) from which most of them came is declining in number. In short, the relative price of city housing is likely to rise, while the city's original supply of units is decreasing. Together, these two factors do not bode well for additional growth in the city.

A June 1986 Abt Associates survey of both urban and suburban residents, conducted for the Mayor's Task Force for Improved City Services, supports this concern. Although 88 percent of the suburbanites agreed that conditions were improving in the city and although a large percentage gave the city high ratings as a location for sports events (82 percent), cultural activities (82 percent), and shopping (78 percent), a strong percentage rated it much lower as a place in which to live (49 percent) or to raise a family (46 percent).

More directly, only 6 percent of suburbanites responded that they would prefer to live in the city, whereas 31 percent of the city residents opted for the suburbs. Those wanting to move out of the city were usually married couples under 40, almost half of whom said they would rather be in the suburbs. Virtually none of the suburbanites who wanted to move to the city have children.

From the standpoint of competitiveness, St. Louis's housing will not do well among the prototypical household of the 1990s: couples and single parents between 30 and 50 with one or two children. The reasons are no doubt varied, but two dominate: the perceived lack of quality in the city's public schools, and concern about the safety of children living in the inner city. The first can sometimes be dealt with by using parochial or private schools, but even that tactic carries a price that must ultimately be reflected in the housing market.

Paradoxically, the very instrument—Missouri's Chapter 353 law—that has stimulated physical revitalization has weakened the financial base for human development. A May 1985 report by Washington University economists Arthur T. Denzau and Charles L. Leven to the St. Louis Board of Education's Community Advisory Committee estimated that Chapter 353 tax abatement is costing the city's public schools almost $6 million a year and that the 1986 present value of all 353 abatement exceeds $40 million.

For each $1 the city abates in property taxes, $.057 is denied the St. Louis public schools. Moreover, given the nature of the city's taxation system, the public schools do not share in either the tax gains from sales or from earnings that redevelopment produces. Although the revenues lost to the schools are only about 3 percent of the School District's total budget, they would nevertheless represent a significant contribution to improved public education, which is key to increasing the demand for city housing.

Much is being done to improve the city's public schools through innovative voluntary desegregation partnerships with most of St. Louis County's districts, through implementation of new curricula, through magnet schools, and through the mayor's use of his substantial political skills on education's behalf. Even so, perceptions of the quality of public schools will undoubtedly lag behind any actual improvements to schools—if and when they are made. For the foreseeable future, parents who have the wherewithal to make a choice will, more often than not, choose suburbia over the city.

The opening of St. Louis Union Station as a mixed-use project is symbolic of the renewal of St. Louis.

Because of the public's image of the city's schools and because of diminishing federal support, St. Louis will have to work even harder to attract residents without children: young singles and empty nesters. The most likely scenario for the next decade would be for the city to strengthen its role as a significant residential alternative for those without children. The chief inducements would be that the city is both convenient—and exciting.

E. Terrence Jones is a professor of political science at the University of Missouri–St. Louis, St. Louis, Missouri.

INTRODUCTION

The Gateway Arch is the hallmark of St. Louis.

Editor's note: *Unless noted otherwise, all photos in this chapter are by Claudia Burris/East-West Gateway Coordinating Council or by Sylvia Richter Drain/Team Four.*

St. Louis continues to ride the crest of a wave of dramatic revitalization. The city's neighborhoods, as well as its downtown, echo with the sounds of new construction and rehabilitation. Lambasted in the national press following the release of the 1980 census, the city now receives kudos on its redevelopment. Above all, St. Louis has developed a decisive optimism about itself, its role in the nation's economy, and its future. The resurgence that began in the early 1970s, after nearly three decades of physical, social, and economic stagnation, is now readily apparent to residents and visitors alike.

Two major developments of the 1960s—the Gateway Arch and Busch Stadium—symbolize and continue to fuel the city's redevelopment. The soaring arch, designed by Eero Saarinen, has gained nationwide recognition as the "gateway to the West." Residents of St. Louis, however, also see it as an expression of the pride and hard work vested in their city, set midway in the nation on its most famous river.

Busch Stadium, built in 1967 as the home of the Cardinals, was one of the first major private developments in St. Louis since pre–World War II. It demonstrated to the private investment community that the city of St. Louis could be profitably adapted to serve the needs of postindustrial society. The stadium—and several related commercial/office projects including Mercantile Center, Boatmen's Bank Tower, Marriott's Pavilion Hotel, and General American Life Insurance Company's headquarters—greatly bolstered investor confidence in the downtown, eventually spurring the recent development of two of the nation's largest mixed-use projects: St. Louis Union Station and St. Louis Centre. The historic and long-mothballed Union Station was brought back to life by Oppenheimer Properties and the Rouse Company. St. Louis Centre, developed by Melvin Simon & Associates and the May Company, is the nation's largest downtown indoor shopping mall with four levels connecting two major department stores.

This chapter chronicles the reversal in urban disinvestment that characterized St. Louis for so long. Most important, it focuses on the private sector's role in redeveloping an old city, creatively, diversely, and profitably, and on the public sector's role in fostering an economic and social environment within which the private sector was and is willing to take the risks necessary to rebuild St. Louis.

STATISTICAL BACKGROUND

Some statistics on the city of St. Louis, taken at decade intervals in 1960, 1970, and 1980, reveal its bleak story.

- Overall city population plummeted from 749,700 in 1960 to 453,100 in 1980, a 40 percent decline.
- Of 18 planning areas established by the city's Community Development Agency, only one showed net growth and only one remained stable. All others had population losses from 1960 to 1980 ranging from 14 to 73 percent.
- Meanwhile, in suburban St. Louis County, which is independent of the city, the population increased 38 percent, from 704,100 in 1960 to 973,900 in 1980.
- From 1960 to 1980, the metropolitan area population remained fairly stable at 2.4 million.
- The number of housing units in the city declined from 263,000 in 1960 to 202,000 in 1980, a 23 percent drop.
- Housing over 20 years old in 1960 totaled 89 percent of all units. By 1980, 85 percent of all units were

more than 20 years old (although only 61 percent were older than 40 years, which was a decrease of 48 percent in the number of units built before 1940).

- Employment in the city dropped 12 percent, from 355,900 in 1970 to 323,300 in 1980, while metropolitan area employment increased by more than 20 percent.
- Per capita income in 1980 in the city (in constant 1982 dollars) was $7,480, only 8 percent higher than in 1970. Suburban St. Louis County's per capita income, on the other hand, was $11,720 in 1980, having increased 16 percent since 1970.

TURNING POINTS

In 1973, the Rand Corporation published a research report on urban decline, which used St. Louis as a case study. Examining the causes, symptoms, and effects of urban decline, the report, though critical, had a "rally-'round-the flag" effect throughout the St. Louis region. While many of the forces that would eventually make St. Louis a redevelopment showcase were already at work, the Rand report became the catalyst for concerted action.

The Rand analysis was based on the 1970 census data, which documented dramatic losses in St. Louis's population and housing through the 1960s. Rand conducted extensive research on the effects on the city of highway construction, real estate tax policies, availability of developable land, and a conservative banking community. It also surveyed industrial developers and contrasted the already relatively slow economic growth of the metropolitan area as a whole with the city's decline.

Rand's suggestions were best summed up in a single paragraph of the report:

> The fact that St. Louis has already undergone major economic and population decline raises the possibility that the attendant accumulating inventory [of land and buildings] may initiate a new set of conditions in the city that will gradually mitigate or

FIGURE 5-1
TOTAL POPULATION: CITY OF ST. LOUIS AND METROPOLITAN AREA, 1960–1990

	City of St. Louis	Average Annual Change	St. Louis Metropolitan Area[1]	Average Annual Change
1960 Census	749,700	–	2,161,000	–
1970 Census	622,200	–1.7%	2,429,000	1.2%
1980 Census	453,100	–2.7%	2,377,000	–0.2%
1986 Estimate	421,000	–1.2%	2,401,800	0.2%
1990 Projection	401,100	–1.2%	2,417,400	0.2%

[1] Includes the Missouri counties of St. Louis City, St. Louis, St. Charles, Jefferson, and Franklin; and the Illinois counties of St. Clair, Madison, Clinton, Monroe, and Jersey.
Sources: U.S. Bureau of the Census; and St. Louis Chapter, American Statistical Association.

FIGURE 5-2
COMPONENTS OF POPULATION CHANGE: CITY OF ST. LOUIS COMPARED WITH METROPOLITAN AREA, 1980–1986

	City of St. Louis	St. Louis Metropolitan Area
1980 Census	453,100	2,377,000
Net Natural Increase 1980–1986	9,750	93,000
Net Migration 1980–1986	–41,850	–68,200
1986 Estimate	421,000	2,401,800

Source: St. Louis Chapter, American Statistical Association.

FIGURE 5-3
AVERAGE ANNUAL CHANGES IN POPULATION, HOUSING, INCOME, AND EMPLOYMENT: CITY OF ST. LOUIS, 1970–1980 AND POST-1980

	1970–1980	Post-1980[1]
Population	Down 2.7% per Year	Down 1.2% per Year
Housing Units	Down 1.5% per Year	Down 0.1% per Year
Per Capita Income[2]	Up 0.8% per Year	Up 0.5% per Year
Employment	Down 0.9% per Year	Down 1.8% per Year

[1] Population as of January 1, 1986. Housing units as of December 31, 1985 (excludes rehab of 7,275 existing units). Personal income through 1983. Employment through third quarter, 1985.
[2] Constant 1982 dollars.
Sources: St. Louis Chapter, American Statistical Association; St. Louis Community Development Agency; U.S. Bureau of the Census; and Missouri Division of Employment Security.

even reverse the downward trends of the past. Theoretically, any urban jurisdiction can "bottom out," as large blocks of inexpensive empty land stimulate new forms of investment.[1]

As it turned out, St. Louis's decline had indeed "bottomed out" in the early 1970s; in fact, the growing availability of land and buildings in a city of brick structures began to stimulate new forms of investment. These forms were diverse and adapted to the particular resources, risks, and politics of the many and varied neighborhoods—including downtown.

The new forms of private investment would not have emerged, however, had it not been for the parallel emergence of a new attitude at city hall and the availability of significant outside resources. City government began to shift its stance from direct involvement in redevelopment, principally through urban renewal, to indirect involvement through creating a private business climate aimed at lowering the risks of inner-city investment to a level competitive with the suburbs. The private investment/development sector could then implement creative solutions to disinvestment.

Initial outside resources came primarily in the form of Community Development Block Grants (CDBGs). Since 1975, St. Louis has received over $311 million in CDBG funds as a result of the federal allocation formula's heavy emphasis on poverty and age of housing. St. Louis's stock of old, brick residential and nonresidential buildings has suffered the ravages of classic urban abandonment, but without widespread loss of the physical structures themselves. Thus, the city has an unusually large inventory of buildings and, consequently, a healthy allotment of CDBG monies. Other federal aid has consisted of Urban Development Action Grants, Small Business Administration loans, and the

Neighborhood Business Revitalization loan program.

The state of Missouri helped the city by enabling it to establish privately controlled redevelopment areas and by legislating numerous tax and property acquisition incentives, including the highly successful Urban Redevelopment Corporations law (Chapter 353), the Land Clearance for Redevelopment law (Chapter 99), and the Planned Industrial Expansion law (Chapter 100). The state has authorized extensive use of industrial revenue bonds; St. Louis has created a state-enabled enterprise zone; and the state allows tax credits for corporations that donate to neighborhood revitalization efforts. The state has created special business districts with additional taxing power; tax increment financing is now possible; and the Missouri Housing Development Commission has loaned millions of dollars to city developers.

The city set up two innovative housing programs, both using Community Development Block Grants. The Housing Implementation Program (HIP) provides low-interest "gap" financing loans to rental housing developers and the

For Sale Incentive Program (FSIP) provides financial incentives to buyers who will occupy homes they purchase. Together, these programs have helped build and rehabilitate more than 10,700 housing units since 1978. Furthermore, an unusual set of city programs intended both to boost civic pride and to assist in fostering solid residential communities has been underway for the past five years. Operations Impact, Brightside, and Safestreet are geared, respectively, toward enforcing the building code; cleaning up and beautifying yards, streets, and alleys; and reducing crime.

This activity has had the following results:
- The number of redevelopment projects using some form of city financial assistance totaled 830 from 1960 through 1985, with 86 percent of these assisted projects approved since 1980. (See Figure 5-8.) The development cost of the projects since 1980 alone is $2.1 billion (in constant 1985 dollars), 66 percent of the total since 1960. (See Figure 5-4.)
- In the early 1970s, nonresidential investment in projects exceeding $100,000 in St. Louis proper rep-

[1] Rand Corporation, *St. Louis: Final Report*, August 1973.

FIGURE 5-4
SUMMARY OF ST. LOUIS DEVELOPMENT TRENDS: 1958–1986

	1960–1979	1980–1986
Redevelopment Projects Using Any Form of Public Financial Assistance in Constant 1985 Dollars	$1.1 billion ($55.5 million per year)	$2.1 billion ($301.5 million per year)
	Early 1970s	**Early 1980s**
Commercial Development in Projects Costing $100,000 or More (City as Percent of Metro Area)	3%	35%
	1958–1979	**1980–1986**
Downtown Development Activity in Constant 1985 Dollars	$1.57 billion ($71.4 million per year)	$1.63 billion ($232.8 million per year)

Sources: St. Louis Regional Commerce and Growth Association; Downtown St. Louis, Inc.; and St. Louis Community Development Agency.

FIGURE 5-5
DEVELOPMENT ACTIVITY IN DOWNTOWN ST. LOUIS[1]
COMPLETED OR UNDERWAY: 1958–1986

Type of Development	Current Dollars	Constant 1985 Dollars	Key Elements
Arch Memorial	$ 43,055,000	$ 120,739,000	
Churches	4,405,000	8,985,000	
Cultural/Recreational/Boats	127,980,000	215,824,000	
Highways and Streets	76,709,000	164,609,000	
Hotels and Motels	305,016,000	395,504,000	16,199 rooms
Industrial	7,500,000	8,870,000	
Office Buildings	1,049,976,000	1,432,527,000	18,971,480 square feet
Other Public Improvements	2,950,000	5,721,000	
Parking Structures	74,081,000	139,154,000	21,747 cars
Residential	202,700,000	372,005,000	4,101 units
Retail	334,195,000	351,509,000	4,543,800 square feet
Transportation Terminals	3,225,000	8,783,000	
Total	$2,231,792,000	$3,224,230,000	

[1] Area bounded by riverfront, 21st Street, and Chouteau and Cass Avenues.
Source: Downtown St. Louis, Inc., March 1986.

FIGURE 5-6
INVESTMENT IN DOWNTOWN ST. LOUIS:
1958–1986

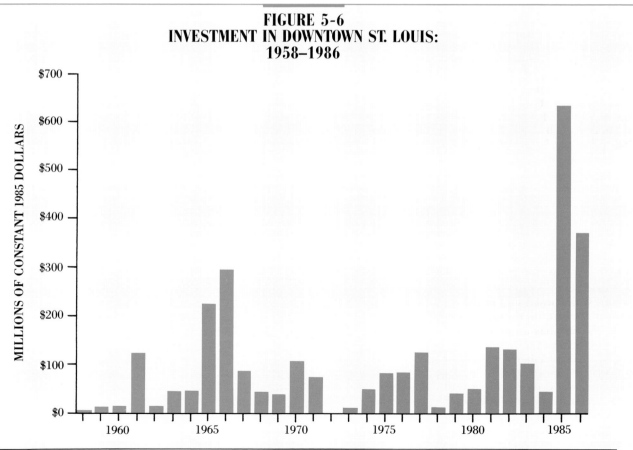

Sources: Downtown St. Louis, Inc.; Team Four Research.

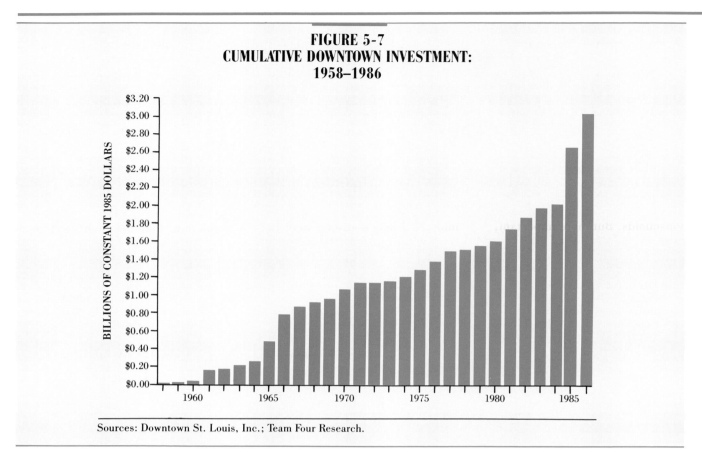

FIGURE 5-7
CUMULATIVE DOWNTOWN INVESTMENT:
1958–1986

BILLIONS OF CONSTANT 1985 DOLLARS

Sources: Downtown St. Louis, Inc.; Team Four Research.

resented only 3 percent of all St. Louis metropolitan development of that scale. The same data source for 1980 through 1985 shows that St. Louis proper attracted over one-third of these investments.

- Downtown St. Louis has benefited from $3.2 billion of investment (in constant 1985 dollars) since 1958, 51 percent of it since 1980. (See Figure 5-7.)
- As of early 1986, 23 downtown construction projects were already underway or planned, involving investment totaling $270 million (in current dollars), compared to a total of 36 projects developed in 1985 costing $639 million (in current dollars).

Investment has also spread well outside downtown. As noted before, since 1980, more than 10,700 housing units have been rehabilitated or constructed. St. Louis has become a national model for its neighborhood revitalization proj-

ects, including the well-publicized success stories of the Washington University Medical Center Redevelopment Area; the new and rehabilitated housing created by the Pantheon Corporation in Skinker-DeBaliviere, which 10 years before had been one of St. Louis's most deteriorated neighborhoods; new and rehabilitated housing in and adjacent to downtown; and commercial renovation and construction throughout the city as developers and investors recognized the buying power of city residents and their renewed pride in city living.

THE CAUSES AND SYMPTOMS OF DECLINE

The reasons for St. Louis's decline—which are the same for many cities—are simple to understand. In the early 1950s, the city's population peaked at more than 850,000 (compared to about 421,000 today) within geographic boundaries unchanged since 1876

and fixed at 61 square miles. By almost any standard, St. Louis was overcrowded. The Depression and World War II effectively stopped housing construction in both the city and the suburbs, and the housing stock was growing old. The general postwar migration to the suburbs for jobs and houses left behind a shocked city with no realistic opportunities for annexing suburban areas.

As elsewhere, this migration was assisted and exacerbated by the availability of federal mortgage insurance and interest deductions on income taxes for the purchase of single-family homes. Less than a third of the city's housing stock was (and is) for single families, and even less was (and is) owner-occupied. Furthermore, the city's housing stock was old and generally poorly maintained, not an easily mortgageable product. Existing residents were also relatively old, and because of the Depression and war years when grown children could not easily find homes to buy or rent, households remained large. Such pent-up demand exploded in the ensuing 20 years as younger families left home and the city to buy new homes where they were being made available—the suburbs. Meanwhile, their parents remained behind—reduced households in large houses.

Federal highway construction also affected housing in St. Louis, as it did in other cities. Right-of-way purchases displaced urban households. But more important, commuting from suburban residences to city jobs became easy. As time went on, of course, this easy access also helped the suburbs lure city firms to new suburban business and industrial parks. Thus, the central city lost its long standing as the primary place of employment.

Furthermore, the suburbs had no overpowering desire or reason to assist the city. They continued to experience robust growth while the city lost jobs, housing, and people. St. Louis has a long history of discord with St. Louis County, the principal suburban county. This lack of political solidarity carries over into the 90 incorporated suburban municipalities in St. Louis County, ranging in size from a few hundred people to nearly 50,000. The region is further fragmented into 113 school districts, 10 counties, 200 municipalities, 281 special districts, and two states connected by a series of bridges, about half of them badly worn. The Mississippi and Missouri Rivers are also no small barriers to regional unity.

Several attempts to reunite the city and the county have failed miserably in the past century.

St. Louis has a "weak-mayor" form of government that consists of a board of 28 aldermen and its president, who is elected at large. The board president has equal authority with the mayor and the elected comptroller in determining the city's budget, a situation that further dilutes the power of the executive branch. The county is headed by a county executive, whose leadership is limited by the presence of many municipal mayors who have greater powers within their own jurisdictions than the county executive has over the county.

Such conditions prompted a detailed 1982 research report on the economic development problems caused by political fragmentation in St. Louis. The report found that governmental structures and civic leadership in the St. Louis area are severely fragmented and that

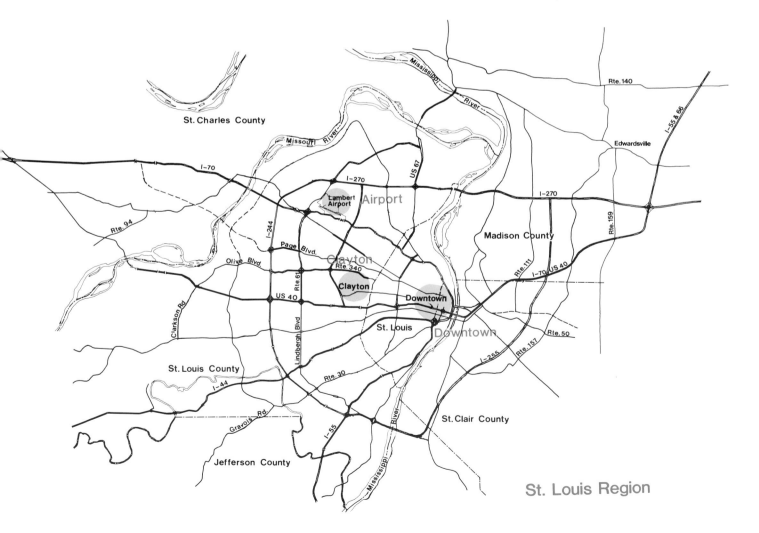

St. Louis Region

"fragmentation results in an inability to act decisively on major problems facing the region."[2]

With its percentage of the region's population slipping, St. Louis had also to cope with postwar urban decay. Complicating this struggle was the city's inability to annex land for future growth and its lack of financial and human resources to solve major problems—including an increasing ratio of low-income households.

Nevertheless, some attempts to unify the region were successful and have fostered a more cooperative spirit among leaders. The city, in particular, has benefited from these joint efforts, which give residents more opportunities to share the resources of other communities in the region. The first major cooperative program was the Metropolitan Sewer District (MSD), which was set up in 1954 and which currently oversees the storm and sanitary drainage system throughout the city and most of St. Louis County (eight other counties are part of the metropolitan area). MSD removed responsibilities for sewer control from general and political forces, and, more important, it assumed the responsibility of coordinating sewer projects for nearly 1.5 million people, 60 percent of the region's population.

Other positive forms of regionalism include the Bi-State Development Agency (a metropolitan mass transit system), the Zoo-Museum District, the Junior College District, the St. Louis Convention and Visitors Commission, and, most recently, the St. Louis Regional Medical Center (merging the St. Louis City and St. Louis County public hospitals). Regionalism also extends to school desegregation through a voluntary busing program involving the St. Louis City public schools and every public school district in St. Louis County.

These and other nonpolitical examples of cooperative efforts have enabled St. Louis to benefit to some degree from general economic growth throughout the region, while remaining politically separate. Thus, the city has maintained a firm hold on the region's economy, culture, and leadership. Located in the city, for example, are MSD's headquarters, the St. Louis Zoo and all museums in the Zoo-Museum District, one of three St. Louis Community College campuses as well as its administrative offices, the offices of the St. Louis Convention and Visitors Commission, the regional public hospital, and the headquarters for the Bi-State Development Agency.

In the last 20 years, St. Louis has gone far toward correcting its postwar decline by implementing a large number of innovative development programs aimed at greatly improving its quality of life, and thus reducing the risks of investing in an old city.

[2] "Fostering Development in Metropolitan St. Louis: The Need and Options for Governmental Reorganization in St. Louis and St. Louis County" by Dana L. Spitzer, director of Regional Government Affairs, Monsanto Company. Submitted to John W. Hanley, chairman, The City-County Task Force of Civic Progress, and former chairman of the Monsanto Company, December 1982.

REDEVELOPMENT STRATEGY

Exterior view of St. Louis Union Station's headhouse.

St. Louis has had no grand strategy for revitalization, in terms of a formally adopted physical blueprint for public and private action. But an evolving public policy framework—as reflected in urban renewal, redevelopment corporations, and CDBG programs—has guided development patterns and reinvestment according to both public goals and private market realities.

This policy framework is based upon two fundamental principles:

• **Reinvestment within the city should build on existing sources of strength.** Initial development actions were concentrated within or immediately adjacent to the central corridor that begins downtown at the Gateway Arch and extends to the western fringe of suburban development. This corridor contains the lion's share of the region's major medical, cultural, and higher education facilities, as well as its office employment centers. The private sector chose the strongest opportunities for joint public/private investment within this corridor.

• **With a growing base of stability and strength, the process of shoring up the weaker areas of the city must proceed.** As reinvestment along the central corridor proved successful, the city has used development incentives to encourage investors to expand their horizons to revitalize many diverse older neighborhoods and commercial areas on the city's north and south sides. The focus of public investment has thus shifted to other areas of the city that were earlier perceived as too risky. More recently, this policy has led to less reliance on the private market and greater emphasis on public guidance of investment policy in other areas of the city.

When a city is economically, socially, or politically unstable, investment in its future decreases proportionately. After World War II, St. Louis found itself in just such a position, as did many other cities in the United States. Overcrowded urban areas were abandoned for suburban open spaces; old houses and buildings were considered unadaptable to new lifestyles; old industries were discarded for new technologies and business practices; and racial and economic prejudices fostered large-scale urban segregation. Thus, St. Louis had to devise plans to overcome disinvestment and to compete with its suburbs to survive as a vital component of the metropolitan area.

Like many cities, St. Louis turned to urban renewal, which, enabled by state law and federal programs, allowed the city to clear slums. Relatively large developable parcels of land were then assembled and made available to private investors and developers.

This limited strategy helped to improve investment conditions. But there was a long way to go. The city had (and still has) many disinvestment problems that went well beyond the availability of land. Planning did not include the private sector, which would have known more about the economic realities of certain public actions. And the private market responded poorly when urban renewal was undertaken without market rationale.

Missouri, however, had an unusual tool with which to encourage redevelopment in its cities. At about the same time that the federal government passed legislation supporting state and locally sponsored urban renewal in the late 1940s, the state of Missouri passed the Urban Redevelopment Corporations law (Chapter 353, RSMo). This law enabled cities in the state to confer on private, limited-dividend corporations some key public powers and incentives to encourage redevelopment.

Chapter 353 allows the city of St. Louis to pass on its power of eminent domain and confer real estate tax abatement to a project developed by a private, for-profit redevelopment corporation formed to implement a private redevelopment plan for an area legislatively designated as blighted.

Chapter 353 has encouraged private interests to undertake small- and large-scale projects using numerous types of directorships and management structures, sources of revenue, goals, and measures of success. Although standard in high-growth and suburban areas, private business plans for development in the inner city were frequently difficult to achieve because of the perceived market risks and local government bureaucracy. Chapter 353 encourages the private sector to take the initiative in selecting targets for development and, in doing so, to take much stronger control of the risks to be borne. As a result, a redevelopment industry emerged to take advantage of the myriad urban development opportunities in the city rather than relying on public initiatives, planning, and implementation.

The first real test of Chapter 353's flexibility and power came with the redevelopment of the area that now includes Busch Memorial Stadium (built in 1967) in downtown St. Louis. The stadium and several parking facilities related to it were developed by the Civic Center Redevelopment Corporation, a private 353 corporation established by a coalition of major downtown business and financial interests. (It was recently acquired by and is today a wholly owned subsidiary of the Anheuser-Busch Companies, Inc.) Thus, prominent civic leaders who realized the importance of revitalizing the dying CBD saw an opportunity to do so by means of a privately controlled 353 corporation. They proceeded to show the entire state that such a corporation could accomplish a great deal in six years (a relatively short time for that era) and could

ultimately yield a return on the original risk capital.

Based on this success, more than 70 other 353 corporations have been created in St. Louis over the past two decades. Kansas City has also benefited substantially from the 353 law, as have many smaller cities since the late 1970s, when the state legislature changed the law to allow most communities in the state to use Chapter 353.

Most significant, the success of the Busch Memorial Stadium using Chapter 353 brought with it the realization that the city government's role in redevelopment should be to establish and maintain an economic climate in which the private developer is willing to take risks. This, in turn, encourages the growth of an urban development industry that makes the city more competitive with the suburbs.

Lessening the risks meant not only increasing private control, but also lowering development costs so that potential economic losses are minimized. To achieve this, the city has relied heavily on CDBG monies, UDAGs, and other federal resources to provide low-interest and "gap" financing and public capital improvements to reduce the costs of doing business in the city. Further steps involved cleaning up neighborhoods, reducing crime, enforcing building codes, managing traffic flows more adroitly, and increasing the participation of city residents, businesses, and the private development sector in deciding public planning issues.

Evolving over four successive mayoral administrations since the mid-1960s when the Gateway Arch and Busch Stadium were built, St. Louis's redevelopment strategy has remained relatively consistent, changing naturally, not in fits and starts as new mayors entered city hall. Paralleling this has been a consistency of leadership. Aldermen, city officials, developers, and residents supporting the private market initiatives under Mayor Cervantes in the early 1970s remain in the forefront of the revitalization effort, although most

now hold different positions. A critical element, therefore, in pursuing a long-term, consistent redevelopment effort has been to do so without alienating or losing the people who know best how the redevelopment strategy works and how it is intended to evolve. This consistency of goals and of dedicated leaders has been the cornerstone of St. Louis's revitalization.

Lafayette Square townhouses.

KEY REDEVELOPMENT TOOLS, MECHANISMS, AND INCENTIVES

OVERVIEW

The St. Louis redevelopment story has been made possible, in part, by a wide range of available development tools and incentives. This menu of laws, programs, and funding sources enables city officials, businesses, developers, redevelopment organizations, and neighborhoods to select the most appropriate means for accomplishing their common goals. In general, these goals attempt to adjust market forces so that city locations become reasonably competitive in the real estate marketplace.

These tools have been developed in response to and in anticipation of problems that inhibited development in St. Louis. In many cases, multiple programs are combined to tailor a set of tools and incentives that best suits the needs of a particular project or area. The result has been a "custom-built" public/private partnership designed to take advantage of the distinctive characteristics of a particular project or area.

The city's three major programs and financing mechanisms for redevelopment are:
- The Urban Redevelopment Corporations law (Chapter 353, RSMo).
- The city's Housing Implementation Program (HIP).
- The city's historic district program and use of investment tax credit incentives.

Although these are not the only programs available in St. Louis, they constitute the principal, city-based tools used today from which other programs have evolved. The Housing Implementation and For Sale Incentive Programs make extensive use of federal Community Development Block Grants; thus, tools are combined with incentives. The city's historic district program builds upon the investment tax credit created by the federal income tax system. The Chapter 353 program is based on state-enabling legislation allowing municipalities to tailor their own private development programs to meet local objectives.

The city of St. Louis and its developers have used extensively all of the following programs. (Tax increment financing is still being tested in the Missouri courts.)
- Land Clearance for Redevelopment Authority, Missouri Statutes, Chapter 99 (urban renewal).
- Planned Industrial Expansion Authority, Missouri Statutes, Chapter 100.
- Missouri enterprise zones.
- Special Business District, Missouri Statutes, Chapters 32 and 71.
- Community Development Block Grants.
- Urban Development Action Grants.
- Small Business Administration loans.
- Neighborhood revitalization loans.
- The city's For Sale Incentive Program (FSIP) to encourage homeownership.
- Other city programs: Operation Impact, Operation Brightside, and Operation Safestreet.

St. Louis has also been notably successful in applying for and receiving UDAG awards. As shown in

FIGURE 5-8
CDA-ASSISTED SITES BY FORM OF ASSISTANCE: 1960–1985

Form of Assistance[1]	Assisted Projects			Total Development Cost[2]		Average Cost (In Millions)
	Number	Percent	In Millions	In Millions	Percent	
UDAG	28	3.4%	$ 78.7	$ 461.6	17.2%	$16.5
IRB	156	18.8	357.5	503.7	18.7	3.2
SBA 503	96	11.6	15.5	71.5	2.7	0.7
HUD 108	15	1.8	2.3	14.5	0.5	1.0
HIP	139	16.7	70.1	400.6	14.9	2.9
FSIP	104	12.5	5.1	41.5	1.5	0.4
Pub. Imps.	11	1.3	3.0	148.3	5.5	13.5
Other	44	5.3	9.8	27.1	1.0	0.6
353	355	42.8	–	1,758.9	65.4	4.4
99	141	17.0	–	1,101.0	40.9	7.8
100	67	8.1	–	154.0	5.7	2.3
Total[3]	830	100.0%	$542.0	$2,690.6	100.0%	$ 3.2

[1] UDAG   Urban Development Action Grant
   IRB   Industrial Revenue Bonds
   SBA 503   Small Business Administration Loans
   HUD 108   HUD Section 108 Neighborhood Business Loans
   HIP   Housing Improvement Program
   FSIP   For Sale Incentive Program
   Pub. Imps.   City-Funded Public Improvements
   353   Chapter 353 Redevelopment Corporations Project
   99   Chapter 99 Urban Renewal Project
   100   Chapter 100 Industrial Development Project

[2] Total cost of projects supported by each form of assistance.

[3] Totals are less than sum of the above numbers. The differences are caused by the use of multiple assistance programs by some projects.

Source: St. Louis Community Development Agency, Assisted Sites Inventory, December 1985.

ABOUT URBAN REDEVELOPMENT CORPORATIONS

- A redevelopment corporation formed under the Chapter 353 Urban Redevelopment Corporations law must be a private, for-profit operation with limited dividends.

- It must operate within a city-approved redevelopment plan for an area designated as being economically and/or physically blighted.

- It may acquire property by negotiation or by "borrowing" a city's powers of condemnation; it may hold and redevelop property, or sell or lease property to others.

- The corporation may receive and/or pass through property tax abatement on new assessment, up to full abatement for years 1 through 10 and 50 percent abatement for years 11 through 25. It must make payments in lieu of taxes to avoid a drop in tax revenues. It cannot benefit, however, from Industrial Development Authority bond financing where tax abatement is also allowed.

- The corporation may benefit from the Land Clearance for Redevelopment Authority (Chapter 99, urban renewal) bond financing if the project is in a URA area.

Figure 5-8, the city had received 28 UDAGs by the end of 1985, totaling nearly $80 million. The grants have supported projects ranging from such major commercial redevelopments as St. Louis Centre and Union Station to neighborhood economic development in the Union-Sarah area in the city's West End. Overall, UDAG-supported projects have incurred development costs of $461.6 million, which amounts to an average leverage ratio of $1 of UDAG money for every $4.90 of development costs from other sources.

The number of individual development projects assisted from 1960 through 1985 by these and related programs totals 830 and represents an overall investment of nearly $2.7 billion (in current, non-inflation-adjusted dollars). In addition, the downtown area alone has attracted approximately $1.1 billion in investment above and beyond the downtown projects, which were assisted by the various programs noted.

CHAPTER 353 URBAN REDEVELOPMENT CORPORATIONS LAW

The Chapter 353 Urban Redevelopment Corporations law is clearly the "top gun" in the St. Louis redevelopment arsenal. It was enacted in 1949 to enable local governments to provide eminent domain and partial tax relief as the essential incentives to induce private redevelopment corporations to undertake development within blighted areas. Since 1960, there have been 72 separate "353" development areas formed, accounting for a total investment of $2.046 billion (not adjusted for inflation).

A developer who wishes to take advantage of the incentives provided by Chapter 353 must be incorporated in the state of Missouri as a Chapter 353 Redevelopment Corporation. The corporation first approaches the city with a formal 353 plan for the area to be redeveloped. The plan must take into account not only physical redevelopment, but also the housing and social needs and wishes of both the present residents of the area as well as new residents who might be attracted by the improvements. Displacement and relocation of residents are principal concerns and must be addressed in the corporation's plan.

When the plan is approved, the corporation is appointed the 353 developer of the area and is granted tax abatement and eminent domain powers as needed to implement the intended revitalization efforts. The city retains overall control through its powers to designate blighted areas and to approve plans.

A key feature of the Chapter 353 law is that redevelopment in the city can be implemented more efficiently because private developers are responding to perceived market opportunities and are often able to move faster than a public authority

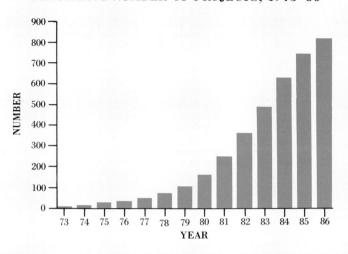

FIGURE 5-9
CDA-ASSISTED SITES BY YEAR:
CUMULATIVE NUMBER OF PROJECTS, 1973–86

Sources: St. Louis Community Development Agency; Team Four Research.

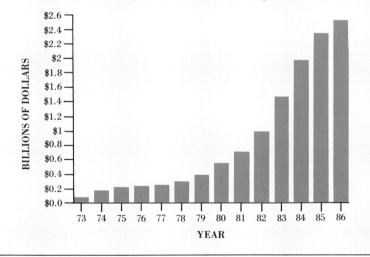

FIGURE 5-10
CDA-ASSISTED SITES BY YEAR:
CUMULATIVE DEVELOPMENT COST, 1973–86

Sources: St. Louis Community Development Agency; Team Four Research.

to get the job done. They usually have a pool of skilled professionals to call upon and they are in touch with the market—that is, they know about the potential residents or commercial tenants in the area. Unlike the days of urban renewal when the city was the principal re-

development leader, the 353 law allows the city to play a far less dominant role. At the same time, the city is in a position to help private developers achieve their goals (many of which are the city's goals) more inventively, efficiently, and profitably.

FIGURE 5-11
MAJOR CHAPTER 353 UMBRELLA REDEVELOPMENT CORPORATIONS IN THE CITY OF ST. LOUIS: 1985

Name of Redevelopment Area or Corporation	Total Development Costs[1] (In Millions)	Number of Individual Projects
City Center	$ 39.5	23
Civic Center	261.1	14
Laclede's Landing	56.2	27
Lafayette Square	21.6	14
LaSalle Park	42.4	18
Manchester Chouteau	18.6	18
Maryland Plaza	31.9	27
Mayco	275.4	9
Midtown Medical Center	21.2	17
Pershing/DeBaliviere	68.9	21
Samuel McCree	1.7	10
Washington University Medical Center	115.1	67
Washington Avenue	50.0	6
Total	$1,003.6 (57%)	271 (76%)
Total, All 353 Projects	$1,758.9 (100%)	355 (100%)

[1] Stated in current dollars (not adjusted for inflation).
Sources: St. Louis Community Development Agency, Assisted Sites Inventory, 1985; and Downtown St. Louis, Inc.

Many of the 72 redevelopment areas using Chapter 353 involve only one individual building; others involve many structures that share a common plan. The 67 separate projects in the area controlled by the Washington University Medical Center Redevelopment Corporation represent the largest number of projects under one 353 corporation. Most of the new downtown office buildings represent single projects, each of which required assembling several separately owned lots. Single-project areas are scattered throughout the city for residential and commercial purposes.

The results of the 353 process may be summarized as follows:
• The 353 program has created numerous permanent and construction jobs. For example, the recently completed St. Louis Centre downtown shopping mall created 2,500 full- and part-time jobs and 913 man-years of construction work. The city will receive over $2 million in additional sales tax revenue from the mall.

FIGURE 5-12
MAJOR SINGLE-PROJECT CHAPTER 353 REDEVELOPMENT CORPORATIONS IN THE CITY OF ST. LOUIS: 1965–1985

Name of Redevelopment Area or Corporation	Total Development Costs[1] (In Millions)	Number of Individual Projects	Key Elements
500 Broadway Building (Office)	$ 12.0	1	256,000 square feet (new)
Adam's Mark Hotel	105.0	1	907 rooms (new)
Boatmen's Tower (Office)	28.0	1	500,000 square feet (new)
Chase Hotel	21.6	1	385 rooms (renovated)
St. Louis Place (Office)	35.0	1	315,000 square feet (new)
Mansion House Center (Apartments, Hotel)	52.0	1	800 apartments (new) 450 rooms (new)
Del Coronado Apartments	13.0	1	198 apartments (new)
S.W. Bell Telephone Headquarters (Office)	120.0	1	1,500,000 square feet (new)
Gateway Mall (Office)	70.0	1	426,000 square feet (new)
St. Louis Union Station (Retail, Hotel)	140.0	1	160,000 square feet (new) 550 rooms (new)
Total	$596.6 (34%)	10 (3%)	
Total, All 353 Projects	$1,758.9 (100%)	355 (100%)	

[1] Stated in current dollars (not adjusted for inflation).
Sources: St. Louis Community Development Agency, Assisted Sites Inventory, 1985; and Downtown St. Louis, Inc.

- More than 7,500 housing units (both new and rehabilitated) have been developed in designated 353 areas.
- Approximately 22 million square feet of commercial and industrial space, 5,500 hotel rooms, and 14,000 parking spaces have been developed under the program.
- Of the 72 approved plans, 31 (46 percent) are related to neighborhood development, which will provide housing and support facilities.
- More than $1.7 billion has been invested in new construction and rehabilitation projects in downtown St. Louis under the 353 program.

HOUSING IMPLEMENTATION PROGRAM

The Housing Implementation Program (HIP) represents the centerpiece of St. Louis's public/private partnership for housing development. Begun in 1978, it is one of the most effective of the programs devised by the city to leverage private investment with critical public funding, to bolster neighborhood stability, and to assist in the production of needed housing that would otherwise be economically infeasible. HIP is nationally recognized for its innovative and successful approach to housing. From 1978 through 1984, HIP funds, allocated from the city's Community Development Block Grant program, have assisted in the production of more than 6,500 rental units, one-third of which benefit low- and moderate-income families.

The St. Louis Community Development Agency publicly advertises, on a regular basis, for housing development proposals that require some form of cost subsidy to be financially feasible. The winning proposals—selected on the basis of need for the proposed housing, project feasibility, favorable leverage ratios, and developer capability—are awarded HIP financial assistance or are directed toward other programs. Projects may involve new construction or rehabilitation.

HIP functions much like the UDAG program. Development risks are often greater in inner-city areas than elsewhere, making it difficult or impossible for developers to obtain conventional financing either in adequate amounts or at interest rates competitive with other investments. To obtain a reasonable return on investment, the developer would have to charge housing rents well in excess of what the market would be willing to bear. To bring rents down to a level that the market will readily absorb requires cutting the developer's costs, including the cost to borrow money. When these figures are calculated, a gap usually exists between what the project will cost to build and what the market will pay in rent. Like UDAGs, HIP fills this gap.

HIP money is typically treated in the form of low-interest or no-interest, subordinated loans. The program does not subsidize rents; it provides a one-time subsidy of the developer's costs. The money is returned to the city over time as the loans are repaid. Occasionally, the city takes a modified equity position in the project in return for HIP funding. The money is thus returned as "profits" that the city can then channel back into development support.

HIP's most recent major tactical change has been to direct its limited, but highly leveraged, resources to specific target areas to provide the greatest benefit in catalyzing overall city revitalization. In addition, HIP is providing funds to complete major redevelopment projects begun in the last decade. Analysis shows that nearly all of the HIP-supported housing is located in the types of neighborhoods for which the program is intended.

The target areas are defined as key transition neighborhoods between stable and more severely deteriorated areas. Priority is given to rehabilitation projects, in order to return substandard or vacant dwellings to usable condition. But new infill construction is also encouraged when done jointly with

neighborhood-based, not-for-profit corporations. HIP reviews and changes target areas each year, depending on overall neighborhood improvements.

In addition to other funding sources, HIP has been used in conjunction with Urban Development Action Grants, with the Section 8 rental assistance program, with FNMA and GNMA programs, with Section 221d (4) construction, with bonds from the Missouri Housing Development Commission, and with the Missouri Chapter 353 Urban Redevelopment Corporations law.

HIP began officially in 1978 when the first round of eligible projects was announced. Since then, 80 separate developers have participated in HIP. Private developers often form joint venture relationships with neighborhood-based housing organizations, though the more experienced neighborhoods frequently act as their own developers. Most developers have used HIP for only one project, while a few—such as the Pantheon Corporation and McCormack, Baron & Associates—have used the program a number of times.

A total of 80 developers received HIP assistance for 140 separate projects constructed through the end of 1984. The 140 projects range in size from one housing unit to 309, and total 6,523 units. This makes an average of 47 units per project, but more revealing is the median, which is 28 units per project. The great majority of HIP-supported projects are relatively small (under 30 units).

The HIP program spent approximately $38.4 million between 1978 and 1984 and was used to leverage about $263.3 million in total development costs. While the total costs may include other nonprivate sources of money, the leverage ratio for total costs (less HIP contributions) is an impressive overall 1:6. In other words, HIP has been able to generate $6 of "other" housing investment for every $1 from the HIP program.

FIGURE 5-13
HOUSING IMPLEMENTATION PROGRAM: DEVELOPMENT INVESTMENT BY YEAR, 1978–1984

Year	HIP Allocation (In Millions)	Other Investment (In Millions)	Total Investment (In Millions)	Leverage Ratio[1]	Total Units Supported
1978	$ 2.1	$ 6.2	$ 8.3	1:3	646
1979	3.6	19.9	23.5	1:6	721
1980	4.9	37.9	42.8	1:8	1,103
1981	5.7	51.5	57.2	1:9	1,355
1982	7.4	30.9	38.3	1:4	861
1983	8.0	48.6	56.7	1:6	1,028
1984	6.7	29.8	36.5	1:4	809
Total	$38.4	$224.8	$263.3	1:6	6,528

[1] $1 of public HIP funds per $X of other development costs.
Source: St. Louis Community Development Agency.

FIGURE 5-14
HOUSING IMPLEMENTATION PROGRAM
TOTAL INVESTMENT IN HIP PROJECTS

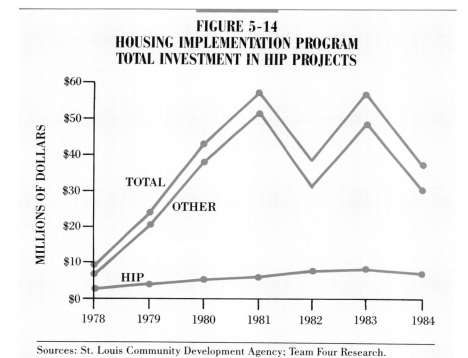

Sources: St. Louis Community Development Agency; Team Four Research.

HISTORIC DISTRICT PROGRAM AND THE INVESTMENT TAX CREDIT

When the Economic Recovery Tax Act of 1976 was passed authorizing an investment tax credit (ITC) of 10 percent for rehabilitation expenditures on certified historic structures, and in 1981, when the ITC was increased to 25 per-

cent, St. Louis was ready. Long before the enactment of these laws, the city had actively fostered the concept of historic preservation and by 1976 had already designated many local historic districts and buildings in accordance with the standards set by the National Park Service. Thus, St. Louis was in a position to take maximum advantage of the investment incentive program.

Designated in 1972 as St. Louis's first historic district, the Lafayette Square neighborhood led the city's program of revitalizing residential areas. Designation as a historic district protected the historic and architectural character of the area by preventing demolition of significant structures and haphazard renovations, and by encouraging historically sensitive rehabilitations and, eventually, infill construction. It also protected and upgraded property values in the neighborhood.

This technique was quickly applied in other parts of the city where demand was growing for improved housing and commercial opportunities and where architecturally or historically significant structures and districts warranted preservation and rehabilitation. As shown in Figure 5-15, 17 major areas had been designated historic as of late 1985.

A 1985 report by the St. Louis Urban Investment Task Force compiled the statistics shown in Figure 5-15, which illustrate the impact of the ITC and previous measures.[3] Some $503.2 million of historic rehabilitation occurred or was underway between 1977 and 1985, the period covered by both the 1976 and 1981 tax reform measures. Of this amount, $435.6 million occurred under the ITC program. Therefore, 87 percent of the total amount invested during this period was for projects initiated since 1982.

The data also indicate that the ITC program helped provide 4,204 housing units and the renovation of 679 individual buildings. From 1977 through 1981, the related accelerated depreciation program helped provide 759 housing units and 135 individual buildings. Thus, encouraging the renovation of historic structures in St. Louis through the federal tax system re-

[3] St. Louis Urban Investment Task Force, "The Impact of the Investment Tax Credit on Neighborhood, Commercial and Downtown Development and Historic Preservation in St. Louis," September 1985.

FIGURE 5-15
HISTORIC REHABILITATION ACTIVITY IN CITY OF ST. LOUIS:
1977–1985 PROJECTS COMPLETED AND IN PROCESS[1]

Historic Area	Pre-ITC 1977–1981 Amount (In Millions)	Housing Units	Bldgs.	With ITC 1982–1985 Amount (In Millions)	Housing Units	Bldgs.	Total 1977–1985 Amount (In Millions)	Housing Units	Bldgs.
Benton Park	–	–	–	$1.100	15	5	$1.100	15	5
Downtown	–	–	–	223.432	190	17	223.432	190	17
Central West End	21.165	619	57	62.822	1,100	110	83.987	1,719	167
Clemens House	–	–	–	5.263	114	13	5.263	114	13
Compton Hill	.775	7	3	7.343	205	37	8.118	212	40
Crittenden	–	–	–	.513	17	2	.513	17	2
Hyde Park	.295	NA[3]	5	16.408	455	105	16.703	455	110
Laclede's Landing	21.537	–	15	10.480	–	10	32.017	–	25
Lafayette Square	1.636	4	16	5.903	109	37	7.539	113	53
LaSalle Park	.791	12	4	8.114	69	29	8.905	81	33
McKinley Fox	–	–	–	.480	12	2	.480	12	2
Midtown	.060	NA[3]	1	17.924	161	8	17.984	161	9
Murphy Blair	–	–	–	1.720	41	2	1.720	41	2
DeBaliviere	–	–	–	14.805	384	47	14.805	384	47
Shaw	–	–	–	7.048	202	21	7.048	202	21
Soulard	5.661	117	30	22.876	491	158	28.537	608	188
Tiffany	–	–	–	9.849	224	61	9.849	224	61
Visitation	–	–	–	3.211	170	6	3.211	170	6
Scattered Sites	15.644	NA[3]	4	16.342	245	9	31.986	245	13
Totals	$67.564[2]	759	135	$435.633	4,204	679	$503.197	4,963	814
Percent of Total	13%	15%	17%	87%	85%	83%	100%	100%	100%

[1] Expenditures include only ITC-eligible expenses. Therefore, total development costs may be an additional 20 to 25 percent.

[2] Investment amounts from 1977 through 1981 represent qualified historic rehabilitation expenditures only and do not include other development that occurred in the neighborhoods/areas.

[3] Data on housing units produced are either incomplete or unavailable for these projects from 1977 through 1981.

Sources: St. Louis Urban Investment Task Force, "The Impact of the Investment Tax Credit on Neighborhood, Commercial and Downtown Development and Historic Preservation in St. Louis," September 1985. Also based on data provided by the U.S. Department of the Interior and discussions with developers.

sulted in the rehabilitation of 814 buildings and 4,963 housing units (although not all buildings contain housing).

When one compares these results with the overall assisted redevelopment in St. Louis summarized in Figure 5-8, it is clear that the historic district program contributes strongly to redevelopment in St. Louis. This figure also indicates those projects that have received some form of public assistance since 1960. The total investment (in current dollars) of these 830 projects is approximately $2.691 billion. Historic renovation programs have played a part in at least $503.2 million—or about 19 percent—of this total.[4]

As noted earlier, the historic neighborhoods that were established before the institution of the

[4] As indicated in Figure 5-15, the expenditures shown reflect only the ITC-eligible costs, not necessarily all the costs of a particular development. The St. Louis Urban Investment Task Force suggests that historic-related development may actually be 20 percent to 25 percent higher.

ITC have experienced a significant increase in rehabilitation development as a result of the ITC. Areas like the Central West End, Compton Hill, Hyde Park, Lafayette Square, LaSalle Park, and Soulard all experienced rehab investment during the period from 1977 through 1981. But the level of investment increased dramatically between 1982 and 1985.

It is also important to note that, although the ITC has achieved significant results, the job of revitalizing these and other neighborhoods is far from complete. In the Soul-

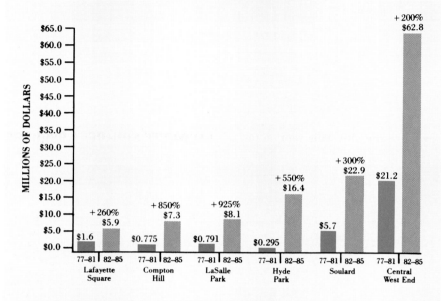

FIGURE 5-16
INVESTMENT IN HISTORIC REHABILITATION ACTIVITY IN SELECTED ST. LOUIS NEIGHBORHOODS: 1977–1981 AND 1982–1985

Source: St. Louis Urban Investment Task Force, "The Impact of the Investment Tax Credit on Neighborhood, Commercial and Downtown Development and Historic Preservation in St. Louis," September 1985.

the use of the ITC program, according to the National Trust for Historic Preservation. Between FY 1982 and FY 1985, St. Louis used the tax credit for 458 projects (many of which include more than one building). New Orleans, which ranked second at the time, used the ITC for 171 projects.

CONCLUSION

In summary, while St. Louis's old neighborhoods have contributed in the past to an image of deterioration and obsolescence, they contain an abundance of significant buildings in terms of their place in history and their architectural qualities. With the quickening interest nationwide in historic preservation, St. Louis has been able to take advantage of programs that encourage the preservation of older, attractive structures. At the same time, construction technology has grown more sophisticated, making possible efficient adaptations of old buildings to reflect present needs. The city's home-grown policy of setting aside significant historic and architectural areas to preserve them has given it a head start in exploiting the tax advantages of rehabilitation, which is also improving the quality of urban life.

ard neighborhood, for example, investment in historic rehabilitation since 1977 has assisted in the renovation of some 300 structures—but this is out of an approximate total of 1,100 structures in the neighborhood. It is also not clear how the change in the tax law will affect the continued renovation of historic structures.

Through the federal fiscal year of 1985, St. Louis led the nation in

ALTERNATIVE APPROACHES TO REDEVELOPMENT

The St. Louis experience is notable for the many varied approaches to redevelopment that have emerged. Neighborhoods, churches, major institutions, large corporations, and private developers have led efforts to revitalize the city. This section focuses on some of the most prominent examples of redevelopment resulting from their efforts.

Though representing the types of redevelopment efforts occurring in St. Louis, these examples do not necessarily represent the best projects, nor do they come close to representing all projects. For example, there are at present 72 approved Chapter 353 redevelopment areas. Only three are individually addressed in this section, while another four are referred to in discussions of downtown St. Louis. Two of the areas discussed here, in fact, have been unassisted by Chapter 353.

LAFAYETTE SQUARE: A PRODUCT OF NEIGHBORHOOD LEADERSHIP[5]

Description

Lafayette Square began in the 1860s as a fashionable residential

[5] Prepared with information provided by Laurel Meinig, executive director of the Neighborhood Marketing Services, Inc., and Bob Stewart of the Lafayette Square Restoration Committee.

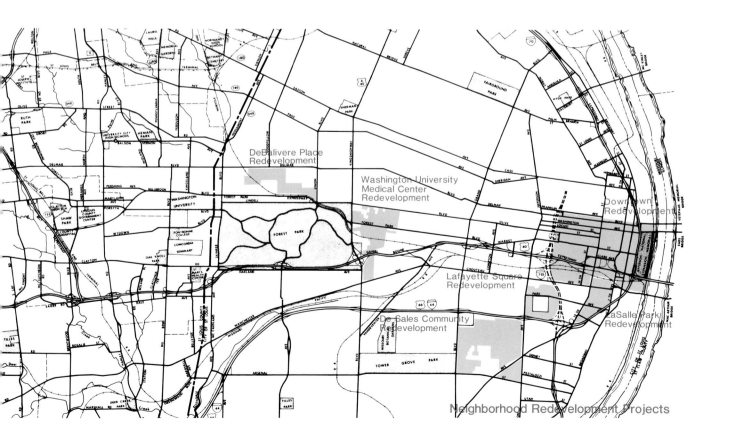

Neighborhood Redevelopment Projects

neighborhood on the near South Side of St. Louis, and reached its height between 1875 and 1890. Many large, well-constructed houses were built around Lafayette Park, the city's first major park, named after the famous French patriot to commemorate his visit to the city in the early 1800s. When redevelopment of the neighborhood began in the late 1960s, approximately 400 of these original structures remained. They provided a variety of Victorian architectural styles from small Federal row houses and elegant two- and three-

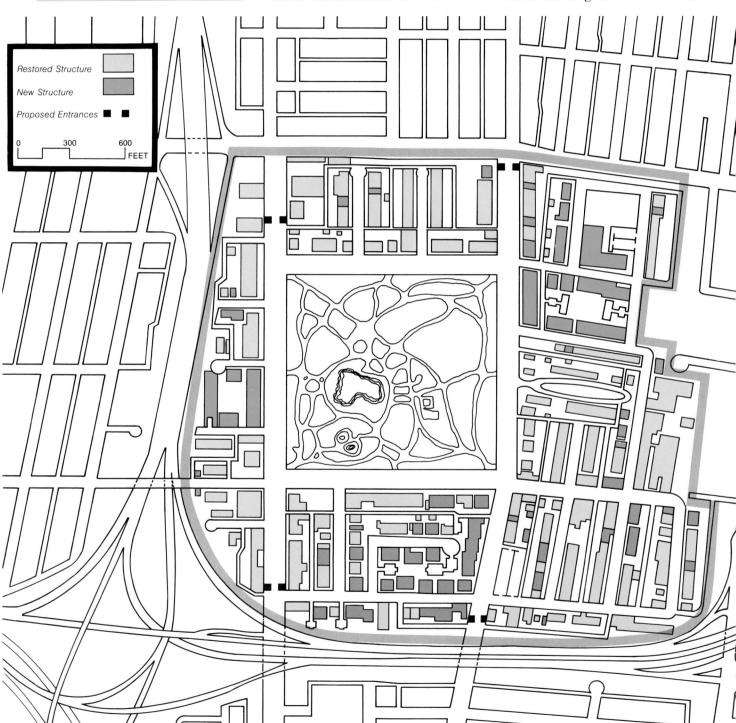

Lafayette Square Restoration Plan.

Restored Structure

New Structure

Proposed Entrances

0   300   600
FEET

Source: St. Louis City Planning Commission, fall 1971.

story townhouses to great eclectic mansions.

Lafayette Square is located just south of downtown between 18th Street on the east, Jefferson Avenue on the west, Chouteau Avenue on the north, and Interstate 44 on the south. When the Lafayette Square Restoration Plan was prepared in 1971,[6] most of the larger houses had been subdivided into rental apartments or into rooming houses. Although most of the houses lent themselves to restoration, some had deteriorated so badly that they were no longer restorable. Many houses had already been demolished. Those investing in the neighborhood have been inspired by the opportunities and challenges of restoration. Strong interest in preserving architectural detail of individual houses must, however, be correlated with the more basic objective of the 1971 plan, which is the overall revitalization of the neighborhood.

Aside from its impressive old homes, Lafayette Square attracts residents because it is a prime center-city location. While commercial redevelopment was underway downtown, urban renewal was shifting from a program of land clearance to one of preservation and restoration. Lafayette Square became the first resident-based renovation effort in the city, launching the recent revolution in urban living in St. Louis. The redevelopment effort in LaSalle Park (discussed later), east of Lafayette Square, began at about the same time. But whereas LaSalle Park's plan was originally based on widespread clearance and had the benefit of a major corporate sponsor and investor—the Ralston Purina Company—Lafayette Square residents pushed for a city redevelopment policy based on the preservation of architecturally and historically significant buildings.

[6] The plan was prepared by the St. Louis City Planning Commission in cooperation with the Lafayette Square Restoration Committee and the Lafayette Park Neighborhood Association.

Typical renovated townhouses in the Lafayette Square neighborhood.

Financing

Until the middle 1980s, when relatively large-scale infill construction began, the renovation of Lafayette Square had been almost entirely the effort of private individuals, although the neighborhood's resident organizations coordinated this effort. Therefore, statistics on financing the renovation of many houses are not readily available.

The issue of financing was, nevertheless, of critical importance in Lafayette Square—particularly when buyers were unable to obtain financing from private lending institutions in the early years. The neighborhood did not readily demonstrate a long-term future nor did "comparables" for post-rehabilitation appraisals exist. These factors made the properties highly affordable: they could be bought for the amount of a downpayment on a home in a better neighborhood or in the suburbs. Financing was needed, however, for the major repairs and improvements required on each property. These improvements typically cost much more than the purchase price of the property, and obtaining loans under such conditions was extremely difficult.

Owner/occupants therefore personally financed most of the early renovation work. The phrase "sweat equity" took on real meaning as residents undertook rehabilitation work themselves rather than contracting for it. Even finding contractors and craftsmen skilled in the kinds of construction work necessary was difficult in those days. The rehab industry had no niche in the construction industry.

Leading in efforts to resolve these problems, however, was the Mercantile Bank, an institution that continues to thrive on St. Louis's rehab industry. One of the region's largest banks and located downtown, Mercantile became in the early 1970s a major force in the rebuilding of the central city. Among many of its then progressive financing decisions was a commitment to give construction loans to individual homeowners who rehabilitated their homes themselves.

Newly constructed infill townhouses, which echo the Victorian architecture of the neighborhood, have been popular with homebuyers.

These loan accommodations were key to revitalizing many neighborhoods, first among them, Lafayette Square.

Development Process

By the early 1980s, Lafayette Square had succeeded in attracting and keeping residents who, in turn, had helped to revitalize and preserve an elegant St. Louis neighborhood. This success soon attracted developers interested in constructing infill housing to complement the existing Victorian architecture. Infill projects have been financed principally by Mercantile Bank and the Missouri Housing Development Commission (MHDC), the state's housing finance agency.

Direct financial assistance to stimulate neighborhood development had become, by the mid-1980s, a well-established policy of the city. The principal mechanism in the case of owner/occupant developers is the For Sale Incentive Program (FSIP) administered by the city's Community Development Agency using Community Development Block Grant funds. This program subsidizes the purchaser's costs so that the developer is better able to market the newly built housing. In Lafayette Square, as in LaSalle Park and several other neighborhoods, the FSIP program has been instrumental in selling ownership housing competitively and thereby encouraging sharp increases in the percentage of owner-occupied homes in the city's neighborhoods.

Status

The Lafayette Square of the 1980s barely resembles the run-down neighborhood of the 1960s, in which shabby Victorian houses overlooked a block-sized park full of overgrown vegetation and rusting, rotting furniture and fences. Today, virtually every house has been restored to its former stately appearance while a few continue to be wrapped in scaffolding. Vacant lots are scarce. The matching new townhouses fill a critical void in this urban neighborhood and give it a finished and lived-in appearance. Lafayette Square is the city's first historic district and is listed on the National Register of Historic Places.

Lafayette Square would not be what it is today had it not been for resident leadership and a true pioneering spirit among those who took the great personal and financial risks required to renovate the neighborhood. Renovated houses in

Luxury townhouses have been built across from historic Lafayette Park.

the square now sell for $50,000 to $180,000. The few remaining shells in need of major rehabilitation are priced upwards of $15,000, whereas in the early 1970s, most shells were selling for under $1,000.

DESALES COMMUNITY HOUSING CORPORATION: A PRODUCT OF CHURCH-SPONSORED LEADERSHIP[7]

Description

The DeSales Community Housing Corporation focuses its attention on renovating housing for moderate-income residents, the single most important problem facing the two neighborhoods served by DeSales. The Tower Grove East and Fox Park neighborhoods are located immediately southwest of Lafayette Square. Jefferson Avenue forms the eastern boundary, with Arsenal Street on the south, Grand Boulevard on the west, and Interstate 44 on the north. Part of this area also encompasses the Compton Heights historic neighborhood, but DeSales has had little direct involvement in the renovation of the many expansive turn-of-the-century homes in Compton Heights.

DeSales was established in 1975 as a nonprofit corporation and was originally sponsored and funded by the St. Francis DeSales Catholic Church. Although sponsorship has shifted primarily to a community base and funding is much more varied today, the DeSales corporation maintains its philosophy that the best way to invigorate its neighborhoods is to stimulate private reinvestment. Its decade-long success can be attributed directly to this continued focus on stimulating the private housing market. The corporation is presently governed as an independent, nonprofit orga-

nization. Its board of directors is made up of neighborhood residents who represent churches, schools, businesses, lenders, the elderly, and other neighborhood segments.

The housing corporation addresses its goal in a number of ways. Through its educational services, it compiles and maintains data on the DeSales housing market and provides this detailed information to lenders, appraisers, real estate brokers, developers, insurers, and city officials as well as to prospective homebuyers or renters. This service is essential to an aggressive marketing program for the community and to maintaining close relationships with lending institutions and city government.

The walk-in office provides information about contractors, insurance, and mortgage and home improvement loans. These referral services have become increasingly important as the corporation's visibility has grown.

Technical seminars provide assistance in rehabilitation. The sem-

inars focus on both homeowners doing their own work and on developers (particularly new companies), and help assure that they will comply with historic and architectural guidelines. The Housing Production Institute and the city of St. Louis selected DeSales to develop their combined curricula into an education program for small-scale developers.

Another critical activity has been to secure a close relationship with city officials. The decline of DeSales before 1975 was largely due to the fact that the city knew little about the neighborhood's needs and potentials. DeSales's 1978 inventory and plan for redevelopment, completed at the request of city officials, has today become a model for community studies in other areas of St. Louis and has

The neighborhood plan for the DeSales community.

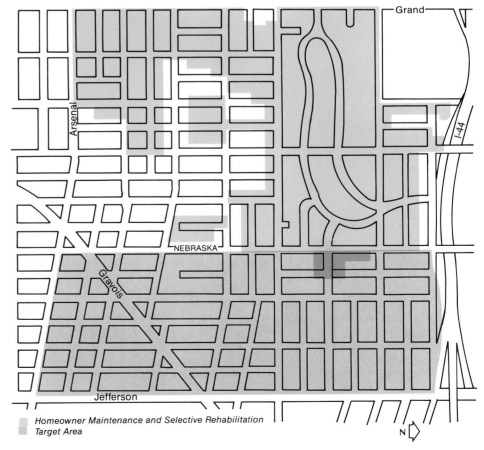

Homeowner Maintenance and Selective Rehabilitation
Target Area

[7] Prepared with information provided by Judy Carr, executive director, and Dennis Coleman, former executive director, DeSales Community Housing Corporation.

Source: DeSales Community Housing Corporation Report.

strengthened the relationship between the city and its communities.

Financing

Early financing for DeSales included $21,000—provided by the DeSales Church—for two years of operation. Local banks provided an additional $100,000 as a revolving fund to acquire and rehabilitate property. For the first two years, the church provided space for offices, which were staffed by part-time and volunteer help.

It was soon recognized, however, that greater commitments would be necessary if significant physical changes were to be made. In 1981, the revolving fund for property acquisition grew by $200,000 under a special program of the St. Louis Community Development Agency. The present budget has a $500,000 revolving fund and an operations budget of $100,000.

Operating income now comes from a variety of sources—CDBG funds, fees and commissions on real estate sales, property management fees, other government support, and contributions from individuals and businesses. Property acquisition monies come from CDBG funds, the Missouri Housing Development Commission, private bank loans from the Mercantile Bank and other local institutions, and, of course, from revolving funds from the resale of acquired property.

Development Process

The objective of the DeSales program was to assist existing homeowners in renovating their properties; these properties would then serve as an incentive to other homeowners. Rather than begin with the most run-down half of the area, the strategy was first to redevelop better parts of the neighborhoods, thereby minimizing risk and assuring maximum exposure and return on investment. Therefore, a section of the Tower Grove East and Fox Park neighborhoods was designated for "homeowner maintenance and selective rehabilitation" and became the focus of the first DeSales efforts. As it turned out, the corporation found that the most effective way to stimulate homeowner interest was to purchase vacant homes, renovate them, and resell them, usually at cost. This technique, applied to houses scattered about the neighborhoods, resulted in several "demonstration homes" that in turn triggered the interest of occupant homeowners.

The strategy of building on strength in the better parts of the neighborhoods proved its worth slowly but surely. The DeSales Community Housing Corporation gradually proved its credibility as the neighborhood improved. In part, the corporation achieved this by actually brokering sales when other real estate agents showed no interest in the area. Its data base and educational programs became stronger and its funding grew.

By 1981, the DeSales Community Housing Corporation was ready to attack the more troubled western half of the area—the primary target area. Forty percent of the residential buildings in the target area needed major rehabilitation. With expanded acquisition pool funds in hand, DeSales began ac-

The St. Francis DeSales Catholic Church has been actively involved in the revitalization of the surrounding neighborhood.

quiring and packaging larger numbers of properties for sale to private developers, now attracted to the area by city commitments, positive relationships with the neighborhoods, and the continuity of development and reduced risk of carrying costs made possible by the acquisition pool. As it gains a surer foothold, DeSales has been gradually working eastward, away from the better parts of the area and deeper into the areas most in need of revitalization.

Legal Issues

Legal issues have been few, partly because city government has not exercised directly its powers in the redevelopment area. Many property owners were delighted to have an entity step forth that was willing either to buy their property or to improve general market conditions. Most potential legal problems were avoided in two ways. First, DeSales decided early on not to press the city for concentrated code enforcement for the entire area, but instead to target absentee owners only. In the absence of a reasonable housing reinvestment market, it was better to encourage occupancy and focus on critical physical problems of housing rather than to encourage total abandonment of houses as strict neighborhoodwide code enforcement might have done. Second, DeSales did not press to have the area declared blighted, which would have opened the door for wide-scale condemnation of properties and neighborhood unrest. Instead, DeSales took a more gradual approach, relying on the normal market cycle of buying/rehabbing/selling to accomplish early objectives. Even today, Missouri's strong redevelopment law has been used only on selected cases in the DeSales area.

Status

To date, the DeSales Community Housing Corporation has, through its affiliate organizations, rehabilitated 30 single-family houses and facilitated the development of an-

other 225 multifamily units. Most of these latter units are in two- to four-unit buildings. New infill housing is now being constructed, and several old buildings have been adapted to new uses in a few highly visible locations. The 500-acre area in which DeSales has concentrated contains nearly 4,000 housing units.

Most of the 255 rehabilitated units were vacant when purchased. DeSales and its affiliates have invested over $11 million in these units, and the corporation estimates that private homeowners and small-scale developers have invested another $10 million.

Experience Gained

The key lesson learned from the DeSales program has been that neighborhood reinvestment requires time and patience. It takes time for market pressures to turn around a strong disinvestment trend. The gradual turnaround of the DeSales community, amply supported by local institutions, has grown into a community-based effort that relies on the commitment of many residents. Private developers have since targeted substantial redevelopment efforts to

A renovated house located within the DeSales Community Housing Corporation's boundaries.

DESALES COMMUNITY HOUSING CORPORATION

Land Use Plan	Rehab	New	
Residential			
Multifamily	225 units	6	
Single family	30 units	–	
Commercial	10,000 square feet	–	

Investment	DeSales	Other Private[1]	City[1]
Residential	$11,000,000	$10,000,000	–
Commercial	–	1,000,000	–
Public Improvements[2]	–	–	$4,000,000

[1] The city of St. Louis has committed Housing Implementation Program (HIP) and For Sale Incentive Program (FSIP) funds to help private developers lower housing rents and purchase prices.
[2] Street repairs, medians, trees, park improvements, and culs-de-sac.

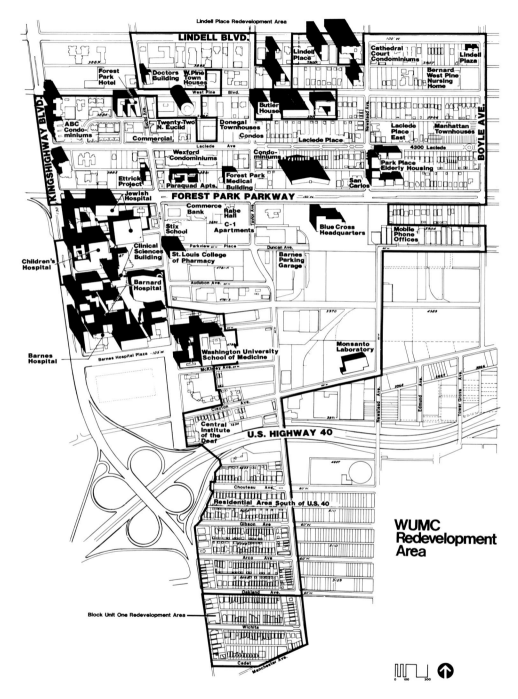

Lindell Place Redevelopment Area

LINDELL BLVD.

Forest Park Hotel

Doctors Building

W. Pine Town Houses

West Pine Blvd.

ABC Condominiums

Twenty-Two N. Euclid

Commercial

Donegal Townhouses

Condos

Wexford Condominiums

Laclede Ave.

Condominiums

Laclede Place

Ettrick Project

Forest Park Medical Building

Paraquad Apts.

Jewish Hospital

FOREST PARK PARKWAY

Lindell Place

Cathedral Court Condominiums

Butler House

Bernard West Pine Nursing Home

Laclede Place East

Lindell Plaza

Manhattan Townhouses

4300 Laclede

Park Place Elderly Housing

San Carlos

Commerce Bank

Rabe Hall

Stix School

C-1 Apartments

Parkview Place

Clinical Sciences Building

St. Louis College of Pharmacy

Duncan Ave.

Barnes Parking Garage

Blue Cross Headquarters

Mobile Phone Offices

Children's Hospital

Audubon Ave.

Barnard Hospital

Barnes Hospital

Washington University School of Medicine

Barnes Hospital Plaza -105 w.

McKinley Ave.

Monsanto Laboratory

Clayton Ave.

Central Institute of the Deaf

U.S. HIGHWAY 40

Chouteau Ave.

Residential Area South of U.S. 40

Gibson Ave.

Arco Ave.

Oakland Ave.

Block Unit One Redevelopment Area

Wichita

Cadet

Manchester Ave.

WUMC Redevelopment Area

0 100   300

weaker locations, which will help assure long-term viability of the overall neighborhood. Furthermore, the DeSales program is demonstrating to moderate-income neighborhoods throughout the nation that displacement is not always necessary in order for neighborhoods to become vibrant, growing communities. The success of this effort shows that a single major neighborhood institution—in this case a Catholic church—can revitalize its surrounding neighborhood by taking a leadership position in developing it.

WASHINGTON UNIVERSITY MEDICAL CENTER REDEVELOPMENT CORPORATION: A PRODUCT OF MAJOR INSTITUTIONAL LEADERSHIP[8]

Description

The Washington University Medical Center Redevelopment Corporation (WUMCRC) was formed in 1974 to upgrade the physical and social environment surrounding the Medical Center. The area was originally developed at the time of the 1904 St. Louis World's Fair as a residential area with large, single-family, upper-middle-class homes. After World War II, the neighborhood gradually declined as many homes were replaced or converted into apartment buildings, rooming houses, or nursing homes. As the neighborhood declined, however, the Medical Center expanded, becoming a major stabilizing force in the area as well as one of St. Louis's largest employers (with 13,000 employees as of July 1, 1986).

In 1970, the six medical institutions that make up the Medical Center began to prepare a redevelopment strategy. When the first plan was poorly received by the

[8] Prepared with information provided by Eugene Kilgen, executive director of the Washington University Medical Center Redevelopment Corporation.

public, the chancellor of Washington University, the president of the Medical Center, and two local developers affiliated with the Medical Center's board of directors hired a planning consultant in 1973 to devise an alternative strategy. Shortly before approval of the second plan, the six medical center institutions established a redevelopment corporation to implement it.

WUMCRC's redevelopment activities during its first decade were guided by a 10-year comprehensive master plan that identified 45 action areas and their specific uses. The plan has been altered several times over the years in response to evolving neighborhood-level market factors. With the initial plan nearly 90 percent implemented, WUMCRC received city approval for a second 10-year plan in 1984 to complete development of the area and monitor its accomplishments to ensure its continued viability.

Acting as a catalyst, coordinator, and facilitator in the redevelopment effort, WUMCRC fine-tunes and adapts the master plan to existing property uses and condi-

tions. It acquires properties that are dilapidated or underused, assembles and sells the properties to developers, provides developers with property tax abatements, manages property on an interim basis, plans the use of city funds for public improvements, and relocates displaced residents. WUMCRC has used the power of eminent domain, which was granted to it by the city under the Chapter 353 program as a leveraging device to negotiate property acquisitions.

The corporation is responsible for redeveloping a 38-block neighborhood surrounding Washington University Medical Center. This neighborhood has several strengths that made redevelopment possible. The expanding Medical Center serves as a major stabilizing force in the area; the architecture and ambience of the neighborhood are attractive; and the area is located halfway between downtown St. Louis and Clayton—the St. Louis County seat, which is second only to downtown as an office and commercial center.

A former police station was converted into office space.

The newly constructed St. Louis Children's Hospital and Washington University School of Medicine's Clinical Research Building are part of the ongoing expansion of the Washington University Medical Center.

Development Process

Five groups are directly involved in implementing the WUMCRC redevelopment plan: 1) the redevelopment corporation itself; 2) its parent organization, the Washington University Medical Center; 3) a steering committee; 4) Laclede Avenue Real Estate, Inc.; and 5) the Citizens Advisory Committee. The Medical Center's 15-member board includes representatives of the six medical institutions and local corporate leaders. WUMCRC, a subsidiary of WUMC, has a nine-member board that includes representatives of the medical institutions and chief executive officers of major corporations. The board is responsible for establishing policy to implement the redevelopment plan.

An informal, ad hoc 15-member steering committee, which met every other week during the first eight years and now meets monthly, makes management decisions and policy recommendations concerning the redevelopment plan and its day-to-day implementation. Its functions are similar to those of an executive committee. Most members are not on the WUMCRC board of directors, but are chosen by the WUMCRC president as key advisers on redevelopment issues.

The 22-member Citizens Advisory Committee, a group of area residents and employees, meets five to 10 times a year to review and comment on proposed development plans. The committee has one standing task force for design review. The local alderman and the WUMCRC executive director jointly select members of this committee.

The WUMCRC executive director and the Medical Center's president serve as the communication link between the various committees and boards affiliated with WUMCRC. The executive director reports to the WUMCRC board, sits on the steering committee and the Citizens Advisory Committee, and is secretary of Laclede Avenue Real Estate and vice president of Forest West Properties. (The latter two corporations are holding companies for property acquisition and sale.) The president of the Medical Center is actively involved with all of these groups except the Citizens Advisory Committee.

WUMCRC's operating budget—about $2 million from the Medical Center to support operating expenses during the life of the redevelopment effort (the first 10 years)—allowed for a staff with the expertise to carry out the corporation's catalytic role, while using professional consultation as needed. Care was taken to limit the staff and to avoid adding functions that would perpetuate it beyond the 10-year period.

The WUMCRC executive director, at the request of the local alderman, also helps oversee a state-designated enterprise zone that incorporates half of the redevelopment area. The zone will include a high-technology center and a business incubator program.

Financing

The corporation relies on the Medical Center as its major source of support. In addition to the $2 million grant for operations, the center has given it a $1 million interest-free loan for leveraging property acquisition. (The corporation's average annual operating budget of $200,000 covers the cost of staff, contract services, and rent.) Another $1.1 million to be used for acquiring property was loaned to WUMCRC by Civic Progress, a group composed of major metropolitan corporate and banking chief executive officers.

Had it had more funds to acquire property in the beginning, WUMCRC would have been able to

---

RELATIONSHIP TO CITY

WUMCRC relates to the city's Community Development Agency, the Board of Public Service, the Land Clearance for Redevelopment Authority (LCRA), and the Board of Aldermen. The Community Development Agency monitors implementation of the redevelopment plan; the Board of Public Service also performs a monitoring function and rules on disagreements over plan interpretations; LCRA supervises public improvements in the area; and the Board of Aldermen decides on revisions to redevelopment plans and on appropriations for public improvements.

Shifting city priorities have complicated WUMCRC's job. Although the city promised to make certain public improvements in the area, its priorities have changed with each of the three administrations it has had since 1975. Also, as the area and city have improved, the aldermen have become increasingly skeptical of any program using eminent domain and requiring relocation. Finally, CDBG funds originally designated to help marginal rental rehabilitation projects are being withheld from most of the area because the area's success has, in the city's eyes, made this assistance unnecessary.

St. Louis invests its resources to finance general public improvements and releases CDBG funds to finance public improvements in WUMCRC's redevelopment area. Also, the city administers a CDBG-capitalized housing assistance program for developers that has been helpful in financing low- and moderate-income housing projects in the area. WUMCRC has not participated in a UDAG-funded project because the corporation prefers not to tie up property waiting for approval to receive federal funds when that property can be sold more quickly on the market.

purchase property more quickly and cheaply when it was first established. As it is, the corporation has had to acquire property incrementally at increasingly higher prices, becoming to some extent a victim of its own success. It must then resell the property at its true cost, as no public money is available to subsidize this cost.

Legal Issues

In accordance with Missouri's Chapter 353 law, under which it was established, WUMCRC is a private, for-profit subsidiary corporation of the Washington University Medical Center. This law provides WUMCRC with the power of eminent domain and the benefit of passing on property tax abatement for up to 25 years. The law also requires that the city Board of Aldermen approve the WUMCRC itself, as well as its plan for redevelopment.

One advantage to being formed under the Chapter 353 law is that

the city is often willing to take responsibility for public infrastructure improvements specified in the redevelopment plan. To date, St. Louis has spent $1.7 million on public improvements in the area. A disadvantage of its for-profit status, however, is that WUMCRC cannot apply for federal or other public assistance to subsidize property acquisition or operating costs. Although the 353 statute requires a corporation to be for-profit, WUMCRC has never made or intended to make a profit.

Other subsidiary corporations of the Washington University Medical

A new convenience center located on Forest Park Boulevard near the Medical Center provided the area with its first new retail space.

The initial success of the redevelopment corporation in attracting new businesses to the area prompted Monsanto to build its Environmental Health Laboratory in the Washington University Medical Center area.

FIGURE 5-17
CHANGES WITHIN THE WASHINGTON UNIVERSITY MEDICAL CENTER REDEVELOPMENT AREA: 1975–1985

Private, Institutional, and Public Investment	
Private Investment Completed or Underway	$100,000,000
Institutional Investment Completed or Underway	330,000,000
Capital Improvements by City	2,000,000
Total Investment	$432,000,000
Floor Area of Commercial, Nonmedical Space	864,000 square feet
Housing Production	
Units Rehabilitated	685 units
Units Newly Constructed	641 units
Total Housing Developed	1,326 units
Estimated Net Growth (from 3,800 in 1975)	625 units
Increase in Households (from 8,900 in 1975)	600 households
Increase in Employment	
Blue Cross and Monsanto	1,350 employees
Medical Center Growth	3,540
Miscellaneous	400
Total Employment Growth (from 11,000 in 1975)	5,290 employees

Sources: Washington University Medical Center Redevelopment Corporation, "Progress Report," Fall 1984 with 1986 update; and records of the St. Louis Community Development Agency.

Center include Forest West Properties, a for-profit real estate holding company, and Laclede Avenue Real Estate, which oversees the $1.1 million loan from Civic Progress for property acquisition.

Status

WUMCRC's accomplishments include: 1) revitalizing a declining neighborhood without destroying the fabric of the area or alienating residents; 2) stimulating home-owner investment; and 3) improving the environment around the Medical Center so that it is both more attractive and more secure. Crucial to the success of the corporation was the financial and political support it received from the Medical Center, the timing of the redevelopment effort, and the use of the power of eminent domain and tax abatements. Figure 5-17 summarizes the investment and growth of the neighborhood.

LASALLE PARK REDEVELOPMENT CORPORATION: A PRODUCT OF MAJOR CORPORATE-SPONSORED LEADERSHIP[9]

Description

LaSalle Park is a 140-acre area located next to the corporate headquarters of the Ralston Purina Company, which has been associated with this area of St. Louis since the company's founding in 1894. The surrounding neighborhood was originally settled in the mid-1800s by French immigrants, and later by German, Czech, and

[9] Prepared with information provided by Fred H. Perabo, director of community affairs, Ralston Purina Company.

Lindell Place is a new condominium development located on Lindell Boulevard, site of many luxury high-rise developments. The project sold quickly and the developer is building similar units on an adjacent property.

Ralston Purina Company

Aerial view of the LaSalle Park redevelopment area.

Lebanese immigrants. But the character of LaSalle Park began to change in the late 1920s as the influx of immigrants ceased and descendants of the early settlers moved on. They were followed by rural white Americans who migrated to the city out of economic necessity. Gradually, the neighborhood declined in population and its buildings deteriorated from lack of care. By the 1960s, LaSalle Park was regarded as a slum. Of 875 dwelling units in the neighborhood, 800 were considered substandard.

LaSalle Park's redevelopment and revitalization began with a commitment from Ralston Purina to remain in the area and to expand its offices. This expansion began in the late 1960s and continues today.

Ralston turned to its real estate department to develop a program to help revitalize the company's surrounding neighborhood and to create a corporate "urban campus." A company task force, formed in 1968 to study the problem, worked with residents, outside experts, and the city and federal governments to develop an urban renewal plan that would be financed by a federal grant requiring local matching funds. Ralston pledged up to $2 million as the local match, and the plan was submitted in 1969.

The project was delayed almost two years because of changes occurring in both the federal and city governments concerning urban renewal philosophies, programs, and procedures. Out of this, however, came a new and better approach to LaSalle Park's redevelopment. The project would be done in three phases emphasizing rehabilitation, rather than in a single phase based largely on clearance and reconstruction. Early in 1971, the federal government contributed $4 million to help in the first 44-acre area.

A portion of the corporate headquarters campus of the Ralston Purina Company, sponsor of the redevelopment effort in LaSalle Park.

A typical renovated commercial building in LaSalle Park.

In 1971, Ralston formed (under Chapter 353) the LaSalle Park Redevelopment Corporation, a wholly owned subsidiary of Ralston Purina. This corporation became the official redevelopment entity, working with residents, businesses, and government officials to implement the plan that was adopted by the city under its Chapter 99 (urban renewal) regulations. Although Ralston continues to staff the corporation, the St. Louis Land Clearance for Redevelopment Authority (LCRA), the city's urban renewal agency, lends considerable assistance.

The first new housing developed in LaSalle Park in 1976 included 148 townhouse apartments—

LaSalle Park Village—designed for low- and moderate-income families. The redevelopment corporation built this turnkey project and then sold it to the St. Louis Housing Authority, which, in turn, contracted with Ralston to manage it.

Also included in the first phase were more than eight acres of new commercial buildings, as well as a Kinder-Care Learning Center that was set up to serve the needs of working parents at Ralston and other businesses in the vicinity. Several existing industrial facilities remained and rehabilitated their buildings within the guidelines established for the area.

The next phase involved a massive restoration program in which existing structurally sound buildings were rehabilitated. Ralston helped launch this phase by rehabilitating a storefront building and opening a marketing office, which was staffed by the LCRA. It purchased 12 homes for rehabilitation and sale and restored the exteriors of several of these houses while the new occupants to whom the houses were sold completed the interior work. Ralston also rehabilitated completely a row of four townhouses, all of which were sold in 1979. The company uses a fifth house in the same row for offices.

By the early 1980s, the area was attracting private developers. Gaps had developed in many blocks as unsound structures were razed while more stable houses were left standing. The situation invited infill housing and LaSalle Park led the city in the building and selling of such housing. While contemporary on the inside, the new houses are practically indistinguishable on the outside from the surrounding 19th century construction. Enhanced with new sidewalks, streets, and streetlights throughout the neighborhood, the infill units— nearly 50 of them—have proved very popular in the market. The principal developer of these for-sale homes has since applied his successful style to several other historic neighborhoods in St. Louis.

Also active in the redevelopment of the neighborhood has been St. Raymond's Maronite Catholic Church, which was responsible for the construction of a new church, rectory, and parish hall. St. Raymond's also sponsored the development of 150 apartments for the elderly and handicapped in LaSalle Park.

Financing

In 1971, the LaSalle Park Redevelopment Corporation was first financed with a $2 million commitment for operations from Ralston Purina. In addition, the St. Louis Land Clearance for Redevelopment Authority authorized expenditures of up to $3 million to acquire and improve property. As of 1986, most of this amount had been repaid to LCRA through the resale of property to individual owners. Ralston has not recovered, nor does it expect to recover, its $2 million for operations.

The redevelopment corporation has currently budgeted about $25,000 a year for operating expenses and $100,000 a year for property acquisition. Ralston Purina will provide funds for operations from the original $2 million and funds for acquisition from the company's overall capital budget.

Development Process

A principal goal of the redevelopment effort was to acquire as much property as possible in order to assure control of the neighborhood for the critical startup period. No rehabilitation or development can occur in LaSalle Park without compliance with the plan. Authority to enforce the plan and to approve individual projects rests jointly with Ralston Purina and LCRA.

Early in the redevelopment program, Ralston itself, through the redevelopment corporation, functioned as the developer—buying, renovating, and reselling properties. These projects were kept to a minimum to preserve funds, but were necessary to create a climate in which existing businesses and residents might begin renovating their own properties. Ralston's commitment to the area gave new residents the confidence to invest thousands of dollars and years of work in LaSalle Park homes.

Most of the development process is now in place, with private market forces providing most of the energy. While public programs still help finance construction or the purchase of property, virtually all redevelopment is now done by private developers or individual property owners. Ralston continues to enforce compliance with the plan and assists in seeking buyers and sellers and in securing financing.

Legal Issues

When redevelopment began, the neighborhood around LaSalle Park was largely abandoned. Therefore, legal problems with existing residents were minimized. Nevertheless, problems of displacement were important considerations in the official redevelopment plan, and mitigating measures had to be taken. Ralston Purina, through the redevelopment corporation, assumed this responsibility, although the federal government provided relocation funds, which were then administered by LCRA.

With LaSalle Park, St. Louis made the transition from a traditional urban renewal policy involving land clearance to a policy involving the preservation and rehabilitation of structures, and from directly managing the redevelopment process to placing it under private guidance. With this transition, the leading city agency became the Community Development Agency, which administers St. Louis's 353 law, as well as the CDBG funds that provide the major support of the various 353 areas in the city. LCRA remained the principal provider of property acquisition funds.

No other example of this mix of plans and responsible entities exists in St. Louis. Today's major redevelopment programs throughout St. Louis are all run by 353 corporations under 353 plans. LaSalle Park tested these legal relationships and helped institute the private redevelopment approach in the city's neighborhoods.

Status

The LaSalle Park Redevelopment Corporation will continue to function until the work called for by the redevelopment plan is completed. To date, the following has been accomplished:
- One hundred fifty single-family homes have been rehabilitated at a cost of $9 million.
- Buildings used for other purposes have been converted into 35 single-family homes at a cost of $1.4 million.
- For a total cost of $11 million, 50 single-family homes and 300 multifamily homes have been constructed; because 50 housing units were demolished, the net gain in housing is 335 units plus the 150 single-family units that were rehabilitated.
- Office space totaling 70,000 square feet has been rehabilitated.
- New office space totaling 100,000 square feet has been built at a cost of $9 million.
- At a cost of $1.3 million, 79,000 square feet of industrial space has been rehabilitated.
- As a result of redevelopment, 200 jobs have been created and 200 jobs have been retained, outside of those at Ralston Purina.
- Ralston itself has retained 1,500 employees in the neighborhood and has added 1,000 from its corporate headquarters expansion.
- In 1983, 130 homes and about half of LaSalle Park were placed on the National Register of Historic Places.

Historic St. Vincent's Church in LaSalle Park.

Experience Gained

The principal lesson of the LaSalle Park redevelopment experience has been that a major private corporation can, and should, be a vital force behind the redevelopment of its own surroundings. LaSalle Park resulted in new housing and employment opportunities, a safer and cleaner environment in which to live and work, and the retention of a major source of jobs and taxes in the city of St. Louis.

Ralston Purina showed that, given the right tools and incentives, its corporate goodwill and enlightened self-interest could be readily extended to the redevelopment process. Its management skills and long-term stability as a business committed to the St. Louis area were transferred to a public arena to expedite redevelopment, and its financial strength provided the backing so critical to initiating the project. A close working relationship between the private and public sectors has dramatically transformed a historic neighborhood.

PERSHING-WATERMAN REDEVELOPMENT CORPORATION: A PRODUCT OF PRIVATE DEVELOPER LEADERSHIP[10]

Description

The Pershing-Waterman Redevelopment Corporation was the first redevelopment corporation in St. Louis formed by a private real estate development company, the Pantheon Corporation. Having started out as a general contractor for individual rehabilitation projects, by 1976 Pantheon had begun redeveloping one of the most rundown and largely abandoned neighborhoods in the city's central corridor—the DeBaliviere area.

When originally developed in the early 1900s, DeBaliviere Place was one of the finest low- to mid-rise apartment neighborhoods in St.

---

[10] Prepared with information provided by John Roach, executive vice president of the Pantheon Corporation.

Louis. Most of the area consisted of three- to four-story apartment buildings with a few higher structures and a limited amount of commercial space. It provided an elegant adjunct to the city's West End with its magnificent homes and its high-fashion shopping environment.

DeBaliviere Place extends from the 1,200-acre Forest Park on the south, to Delmar Boulevard on the north, to Union Boulevard on the east, and to DeBaliviere Avenue on the west. It covers 107 acres and, in 1976, contained about 70 buildings and nearly 900 dwelling units.

Until the early 1960s, the area remained a middle-class, multi-family residential neighborhood, but in the mid-1960s, physical decline began. Apartments were subdivided, overcrowding occurred, and the mobile middle-class population vacated the area.

Land use map of DeBaliviere Place.

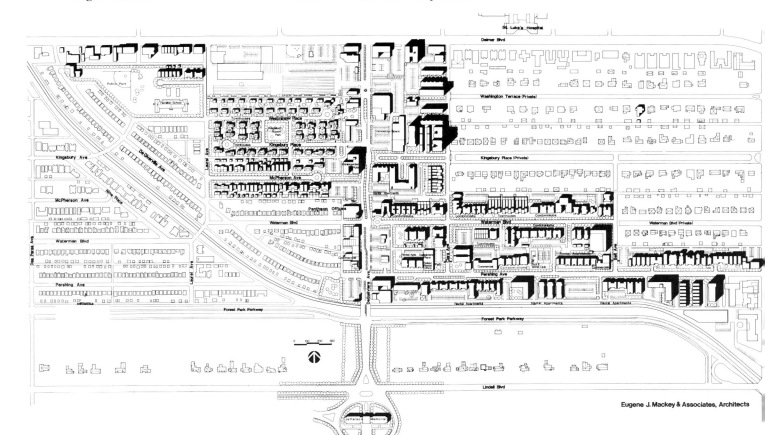

Eugene J. Mackey & Associates, Architects

Physical deterioration, disinvestment, and an increasingly unstable population continued to reinforce each other until, by 1976, most of the dwelling units were vacated and less than 15 percent of the buildings were judged in sound condition. About 50 percent of the buildings needed extensive rehabilitation.

Pantheon's solution was to bring back a strong mix of households—particularly middle-class families—to the apartments. To attract homeowners, condominium owners, and tenants who would take an active interest in the neighborhood's welfare, Pantheon had to win their confidence by showing that it exercised total control over all planned redevelopment, thus assuring the continued rehabilitation and revitalization of DeBaliviere Place. Under the name of the Pershing-Waterman Redevelopment Corporation (named after the two principal east/west streets), Pantheon has served as the general contractor on almost every project in the area, although other developers have redeveloped specific buildings.

The project has consisted primarily of converting the many multifamily buildings into condominiums, which are then either rented or sold. A few buildings that were beyond reasonable repair were razed to make room for critically needed parking areas. A small amount of new construction occurred, notably the owner-occupied townhouses known as Kingsbury Square.

Financing

Securing initial financing for DeBaliviere Place posed the most difficult problem. The project's sheer size, exceeding that of any project before attempted in St. Louis, as well as the neighborhood's poor reputation, did not sit well with lenders. Nevertheless, Mercantile Bank in St. Louis decided to commit $3 million to the project, and Pantheon's owner, Leon Strauss, committed $500,000 raised from

Renovated apartment units cover a major part of the Pershing-Waterman area. These apartments are located on Clara Avenue.

family resources and contributions from friends and business acquaintances.

Over the long term, these investments paid off, spearheading a redevelopment effort that created over $76 million of housing and commercial space in 10 years. DeBaliviere Place has been eminently successful. The project also catapulted Mercantile Bank into the front ranks of the St. Louis financial community—primarily because of the foresight it showed in supporting local redevelopment efforts. In addition to its acquisition loan, Mercantile provided construction financing and part of the long-term debt for DeBaliviere Place.

Because DeBaliviere Place is a Chapter 353 redevelopment area, the city granted the developer up to 25 years of property tax abatement on redeveloped property—10 years with taxes frozen at predevelopment levels and 15 years at 50 percent abatement. Further-

The Kingsburys offer an excellent example of the rehabilitated historic apartments found in DeBaliviere Place.

more, the developer can exercise eminent domain powers to secure property at fair market value. These factors have resulted in lower development and operations costs, the savings from which are passed on to owners and tenants; thus, Chapter 353 has been instrumental in the overall financing and marketing of the rehabilitated buildings.

FIGURE 5-18
SUMMARY OF DEBALIVIERE PLACE REDEVELOPMENT:
1976–1986

	RESIDENTIAL	
	Number of Units	Development Cost
PANTHEON CORPORATION		
Rental Housing		
DeBaliviere Place I	146	$ 3,291,000
DeBaliviere Place II	242	7,914,000
DeBaliviere Place III	132	4,545,000
DeBaliviere Place IV	219	11,869,000
DeBaliviere Place V (Low- and Moderate-Income)	309	17,925,000
Winter Garden Apartments (Elderly)	112	3,197,000
Savoy Court Apartments	53	2,911,000
Delmar Parkway	129	8,000,000
Subtotal	1,342	$59,652,000
For Sale Housing	161	$ 8,065,000
Subtotal	1,503 units	$67,717,000
OTHER DEVELOPERS		
Rental Housing	233	$11,650,000
For-Sale Housing	122	10,980,000
Subtotal	355	$22,630,000
Total	1,858	$90,347,000
	COMMERCIAL	
	Square Feet	Development Cost
PANTHEON CORPORATION		
	77,230	$3,260,500

Source: Pantheon Corporation.

Because DeBaliviere Place is within the Central West End Historic District, Pantheon has also taken full advantage of federal tax credits for the rehabilitation of older and historic property. Again, the cost savings are passed on to the tenants and buyers.

DeBaliviere Place received Community Development Block Grant funds from the city for public area improvements and was to have received the proceeds of a UDAG loan for DeBaliviere Arcade, a major retail and office rehabilitation project. Due to the impact of the 1986 Tax Reform Act, however, the arcade is being reconfigured into a less ambitious, new construction format. Some apartments, particularly those units designated for senior citizens, received Section 8 housing subsidies.

Development Process

Pantheon's early development strategy focused on creating a "safe" enclave for development by ridding the area of undesirable commercial and other influences, closing some streets and reshaping the circulation system, and relocating about 300 residents.

These actions emptied an already largely abandoned neighborhood of all but a few businesses and residents. Pantheon then began systematically rehabilitating buildings as opportunities arose, serving as general contractor as well as developer. To date, it has completed 21 separate projects, most of which involved groups of buildings developed in phases. As the area stabilized, other developers undertook infill projects under the guidance of the Pershing-Waterman Redevelopment Corporation.

Renovated and new commercial structures supply the neighborhood with restaurants, specialty shops, services, and office space. Shown above is the Pershing Arcade building.

Status

To date, Pantheon has been responsible for the rehabilitation and construction of 1,503 housing units in DeBaliviere Place at a total cost of over $67 million. (See Figure 5-18.) Eighty-nine percent of the units are rental—of which one-third are set aside for Section 8–eligible households—and 11 percent are owner-occupied. Pantheon has developed or redeveloped 81 percent of all the units in De-Baliviere Place, while other developers have rehabilitated or built 19 percent. Occupancy currently averages 95 percent throughout the neighborhood.

Now that virtually all housing construction is completed, Pantheon is focusing on completing the planned commercial development. In addition, it has renovated or created 77,320 square feet of retail and office space in DeBaliviere Place at a cost of $3.2 million.

Experience Gained

The key lesson learned from the DeBaliviere Place redevelopment program has been that large-scale redevelopment of a largely abandoned neighborhood can be successful if it is well managed and if the redeveloper is given sufficient development control over all the properties in the area. Such control is critical when an area is badly deteriorated and has numerous owners.

Before Pantheon's redevelopment of DeBaliviere Place, the only large-scale redevelopment projects were under the control of major institutions (e.g., Washington University Medical Center, St. Louis University), major corporations (e.g., Ralston Purina Company), or associations of public corporations (e.g., the Civic Center Redevelopment Corporation, which developed Busch Stadium). The De-Baliviere project demonstrated that a single private developer is just as able to manage a large redevelopment project as a major corporation or institution. The typical suburban development process involves a single developer; this same principle can readily be applied in a redevelopment area if the developer has adequate experience in urban construction and is provided with the tools to gain development, management, and marketing control of an area.

A view of Old Courthouse and Gateway Arch from Kiener Plaza.

DOWNTOWN ST. LOUIS[11] AND PROFILES OF SELECTED CHAPTER 353 REDEVELOPMENT PROJECTS

Description

Downtown St. Louis is clearly the central focus of the city's overall revitalization efforts. The Gateway Arch and Busch Stadium, two downtown projects built in the mid-1960s, ushered in a fertile period of revitalization that St. Louis has enjoyed for more than 20 years. Economic activity for the city and the region is concentrated in the downtown; also, the downtown is the principal destination of visitors from outside the city. Thus, the central business district has played an extremely important role as the focal area for revitalization.

---

[11] Prepared with information provided by Edward A. Ruesing, president of Downtown St. Louis, Inc.; the St. Louis Community Development Agency; Thomas Purcell, president of Laclede's Landing Redevelopment Corporation; Larry Troyer, general manager of St. Louis Centre, Inc.; Donna Laidlaw of St. Louis Union Station; and Christine Vincent, former executive director of the Washington Avenue Redevelopment Corporation.

FIGURE 5-19
CHAPTER 353 REDEVELOPMENT AREAS IN DOWNTOWN ST. LOUIS: 1986

353 Area	Number of Projects	Constant 1985 Dollars	Project Type
1. 21st Street	1	$ 116,000	Industrial Renovation
2. 500 Broadway	1	30,189,000	New Office Building
3. 714 Locust	1	796,000	Rehabbed Office Building
4. 707 HBE	1	105,000,000	Adam's Mark Hotel
5. Boatmen's Tower	1	49,566,000	New Office Building
6. Broadway/Olive	1	110,000,000	New Office Building
7. Century Venture	1	21,000,000	Rehabbed Office Building
8. Civic Center	14	544,230,000	Stadium/Garages/Office Buildings
9. Convention Plaza	–	–	Project Pending
10. Frates	2	46,254,000	New Office Building
11. Gateway Mall	1	70,000,000	New Office Building
12. Laclede's Landing	24	56,880,000	Rehabbed Office/Retail
13. Landmark City Block 191	–	–	Project Pending
14. Lucas Park	1	5,000,000	Housing: Loft Apartments
15. Missouri Athletic Club	1	3,000,000	Parking Garage
16. Mansion House	2	84,902,000	Apartments/Hotel
17. Marquette	1	4,750,000	Rehabbed Office Building
18. Mayco/Mercantile	8	298,117,000	Offices/St. Louis Centre Retail
19. S.W. Bell Garage	1	7,000,000	S.W. Bell Garage
20. S.W. Bell Headquarters	1	125,000,000	S.W. Bell Headquarters
21. Union Station	1	140,000,000	Retail/Hotel
22. Washington Avenue	4	44,400,000	Rehabbed Apartments/Office
Total	68	$1,746,200,000	

Source: St. Louis Community Development Agency.

Like other CBDs, St. Louis's downtown is highly complex and diverse, making it virtually impossible to assign redevelopment responsibilities to any single entity, be it a private developer or a public agency. Therefore, a redevelopment strategy was put in place that encouraged the creation and implementation of diverse redevelopment mechanisms (like the Chapter 353 law).

After successful experience with "spot blighting" for individual projects in the 1960s, the city's Board of Aldermen declared the entire downtown core blighted in 1971, making it eligible for redevelopment under the Chapter 353 law. This action informed the development community that downtown was ready for revitalization and that a major step had already been taken for anyone desiring to build or rebuild.

Downtown St. Louis, as defined by the city and by Downtown St. Louis, Inc. (a business and civic group), is an area of approximately 1.7 square miles, bounded by the Mississippi River on the east, 21st Street on the west, Chouteau Avenue on the south, and Cole Street on the north. The Board of Aldermen designated as blighted only the core of this area east of Tucker Boulevard. Other parts of the larger area, however, were declared blighted under different ordinances and different state-enabled programs (primarily urban renewal and planned industrial expansion programs).

These actions have resulted in the formation downtown of 22 Chapter 353 redevelopment corporations whose activities range from redeveloping a single building to redeveloping a large number of city blocks. Also located in the down-town area is the DeSoto-Carr Urban Renewal Area (blighted under Chapter 99 of the Missouri statutes). This area includes several new office buildings and most of the new housing in the downtown area, as well as the 240,000-square-foot Cervantes Convention Center, which was built in the mid-1970s.

Figure 5-19 indicates the names and types of uses in the 22 separate Chapter 353 areas, the number of individual projects contained in each, and the development costs associated with each area as of early 1986 (stated in constant 1985 dollars) as a portion of the overall redevelopment of the central business district.

In 1958, Downtown St. Louis, Inc., was formed to promote and enhance the downtown environment. Since then, development in downtown St. Louis has totaled

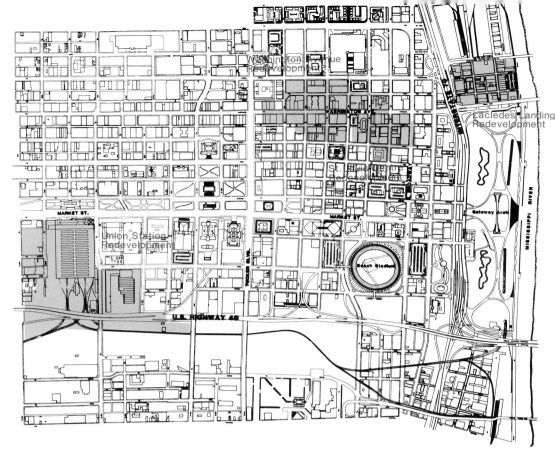

Downtown Redevelopment Projects

FIGURE 5-20
DEVELOPMENT IN DOWNTOWN ST. LOUIS[1]

Type of Development	1958–1969	1970–1979	1980–1986	Total
Gateway Arch and Grounds	$105,751,000	$7,178,000	$7,810,000	$120,379,000
Office Buildings	$228,694,000	$380,376,000	$823,457,000	$1,432,527,000
Square Feet:	3,358,800	4,873,000	10,739,700	18,971,500
Retail Space	$16,339,000	$3,222,000	$331,948,000	$351,509,000
Square Feet:	1,384,900	490,900	2,688,000	4,563,800
Churches	$5,260,000	$517,000	$3,208,000	$8,985,000
Cultural, Recreational, and Riverboats	$90,927,000	$64,003,000	$60,894,000	$215,824,000
Hotels and Motels	$59,102,000	$98,075,000	$238,327,000	$395,504,000
Rooms:	929	2,304	2,966	6,199
Industrial Buildings	$0	$0	$8,870,000	$8,870,000
Square Feet:	0	0	199,800	199,800
Transportation Terminals	$7,207,000	$1,576,000	$0	$8,783,000
Highways and Streets	$111,606,000	$10,897,000	$42,106,000	$164,609,000
Other Public Improvements	$3,395,000	$1,126,000	$1,200,000	$5,721,000
Parking Structures	$86,765,000	$12,158,000	$40,231,000	$139,154,000
Parking Spaces:	11,850	2,600	7,285	21,735
Residential Units	$231,616,000	$15,929,000	$124,460,000	$372,005,000
Dwelling Units:	2,185	700	1,215	4,100
Total	$946,662,000 (29%)	$595,057,000 (19%)	$1,682,511,000 (52%)	$3,224,230,000 (100%)

[1] All dollar amounts stated in constant 1985 values.
Source: Downtown St. Louis, Inc.

over $3.2 billion (in constant 1985 dollars). Development ranged from the Gateway Arch, to the many new and rehabilitated office buildings, to improvements made to churches, streets, highways, and bridges.

As shown in Figure 5-20, over half of this development is occurring in the 1980s, while about one-fifth occurred in the 1970s and nearly one-third was completed between 1958 and 1969, when the Gateway Arch and Busch Stadium were constructed.

More than half of the $3.2 billion invested in downtown since 1958 has been in the 22 Chapter 353 redevelopment areas. This total of over $1.7 billion (constant 1985 dollars) has been invested in tax-paying private development projects and, therefore, excludes projects such as the Gateway Arch, public improvements, and churches.

The first of the downtown 353 corporations was formed in 1965 to construct Busch Stadium and related buildings. If all downtown development shown in Figure 5-20 before 1965, along with all nonprivate projects, is excluded, the 353 areas represent two-thirds of the approximately $2.6 billion of private downtown development since 1965. The remaining one-third consists primarily of development within the DeSoto-Carr and Mill Creek urban renewal areas, on the northern and western edges of downtown, respectively. The urban renewal areas have been the focus of most of the housing and industrial development downtown, although they also include office buildings and related structures. The following four profiles of 353 projects in the downtown area are intended to demonstrate the variety of approaches taken in redeveloping downtown St. Louis.

Located on the riverfront, LaClede's Landing is an entertainment, retail, and office section of the downtown.

Laclede's Landing

Background. Founded in 1764 by Pierre Laclede and Auguste Chouteau, Laclede's Landing was the last French settlement in North America and marked the beginning of St. Louis. Its location, history, urban form, and architecture offered the chance to build a truly distinctive and exciting environment. The Landing rapidly became a hub of commerce and warehousing vital to the river trade. By the late 19th century, its current shape had been largely formed in a nine-block area now bounded on the north and south by bridges. But by the 1960s, the Landing had deteriorated into an underused group of historic warehouse buildings next to the grounds of the Gateway Arch. It had been abandoned for more efficient and accessible facilities in other parts of the St. Louis region. Like other waterfront warehouse districts, it had been made obsolete by the greater transportation flexibility offered first by railroads and later by highways.

The challenge in revitalizing the Landing was to formulate a development framework that would stimulate reinvestment in the area for different uses. In the mid-1960s, the City Planning Commission evaluated conditions in the Landing and found that it would

190

qualify for designation under the Chapter 353 redevelopment law in Missouri. The Board of Aldermen approved this designation in 1966.

The development program formulated in 1968 for the Landing envisioned a single redeveloper, who was to rehabilitate selectively some of the buildings while incorporating new construction where appropriate and occasionally removing existing structures. This program, however, for many reasons never got underway and, in 1972, the city terminated the redevelopment contract.

In late 1974, when the Landing was 95 percent vacant, a group of businessmen, property owners, and government officials met to discuss how it could be redeveloped. They preferred corporate ownership to single ownership. The corporation was to be formed under the Chapter 353 law and would obtain from the city the right to administer the law by submitting a redevelopment plan for the area. Property owners now own half the stock of the Laclede's Landing Redevelopment Corporation, while members of the business, financial, and institutional communities own the other half.

After agreeing that this "umbrella corporation" concept was the realistic alternative to the traditional single-ownership concept, the corporation prepared a redevelopment plan and submitted it to the city's Community Development Agency in July 1975. By the end of 1975, the plan had become the official guideline for revitalizing Laclede's Landing.

The development plan continues to be the guiding force on which all the reinvestment in Laclede's Landing is based. In addition to emphasizing the ability of the corporation to grant property tax relief to individual property owners and clearly stating the intention to mix rehabilitation with new construction, the plan has other important elements. It establishes categories for the existing buildings in the Landing, indicating whether each building should remain, should

A typical streetscape in LaClede's Landing. Buildings have varying heights and vintages.

possibly be removed, or should definitely be removed. The plan also outlines strategies for pedestrian and vehicular movement, parking, and public improvements.

Soon after the redevelopment corporation was designated as the official developer of Laclede's Landing, it created two other vitally important documents that are still instrumental in its development activities. The first is the Parcel Development Agreement between the property owner and the Laclede's Landing Redevelopment Corporation setting the terms and conditions under which the property owner can develop Landing property. The property owners must submit development plans, architectural specifications, and financial strategies for their parcels to the corporation for review and approval. When the corporation approves the plans, a contract is signed permitting the property owners to receive a tax abatement for 25 years. Thus, the Parcel Development Agreement provides the stability that permanent lenders and investors are looking for, while maintaining the flexibility that developers need to accommodate

changes dictated by various development factors.

The Parcel Development Agreement also requires owners and tenants to join the Laclede's Landing Merchants' Association. This has proved to be a vital requirement in that the principal responsibility of the merchants' association is to promote the collective interests of Laclede's Landing. Without this support, promotion of the area would be, at best, piecemeal and would not create the desired public image of a unified and special area.

The second important document adopted by the corporation is the Urban Design Guidelines, which expands upon and refines the development plan. The guidelines were formulated to: 1) assist the redevelopment corporation in determining policy for a wide range of environmental design issues; 2) provide developers and architects with preliminary design criteria to avoid duplication and lower front-end costs; and 3) help the corporation and agencies of the city to develop standards for the design and maintenance of capital improvements.

Armed with all of the appropriate management instruments, the redevelopment corporation is now in the 11th year of its program. The plan calls for the rehabilitation of 45 buildings containing 1 million square feet and for the new construction of another 1 million square feet. The project is composed of a mix of office, residential, entertainment, retail, and hotel uses.

In August 1976, Laclede's Landing was placed on the National Register of Historic Places, making federal grants available to the developers. Under the Economic Recovery Tax Act of 1981, developers have obtained accelerated depreciation for projects that include the rehabilitation of significant historic buildings. As of the end of 1985, total investment in 24 separate development projects in the Landing had reached $56.9 million (in constant 1985 dollars).

Experience Gained. A project of the scale and complexity of Laclede's Landing offers several important and valuable lessons. One of the most important aspects contributing to the success of the Landing was, and continues to be, the multiple ownership and participatory element of the redevelopment corporation. Many of the usual obstacles to the redevelopment process are avoided or removed by the institutional and organizational framework that identifies and deals with issues.

Another key to the project's success has been the strategy of making improvements incrementally as the redevelopment corporation and property owners are able to manage them; this allows each effort to stimulate the next. Incremental improvements are also carefully timed so that public sector improvements immediately precede private sector development, which assures that development goals are met.

But perhaps central to the success of the Laclede's Landing experience is that the redevelopment corporation can encourage incremental growth while never losing sight of the overall redevelopment plan for the Landing. Thus, while individuals may come and go, the corporation holds to its goals and assures that the last project developed bears a strong relationship to the first.

Because the redevelopment corporation has been able to envision the finished product before it is implemented in the marketplace, the Landing has never incurred debts or operational costs that exceeded what the market could support. Individual owners and developers, not the redevelopment corporation, undertake individual projects. Therefore, projects do not come on line before the owners/developers are comfortable with economic and market conditions. Although this may result in a slower redevelopment process, it keeps Laclede's Landing financially in the black. Meanwhile, the redevelopment corporation and other associated groups retain control of overall goals, promotion, and public relations.

The redevelopment program was built upon a strong foundation composed of:
- a comprehensive development plan responsive to change,
- a redevelopment corporation making a sincere effort to interrelate with all facets of the community, and
- the legal instruments needed to implement and maintain the plans and concepts of the projects.

These three elements working together provided the basic framework for orchestrating a redevelopment effort of the magnitude of Laclede's Landing.

It is important to note that the adjacent property owners financed many of the public streetscape improvements. For instance, they provided sidewalks, planters, sandwich boards, awnings, and other streetside improvements to supplement the benches and waste recep-

LACLEDE'S LANDING

Land Use Plan

	Square Feet		Percent	
	Rehab	*New*	*Rehab*	*New*
Residential	50,000	100,000	2.5%	5.0%
Commercial	250,000	–	12.5	–
Office	700,000	–	35.0	–
Hotels	–	900,000	–	45.0
Total	1,000,000	1,000,000	50.0%	50.0%

Site Development Costs

	Rehab	*New*	*Total*
Public	$ 1,200,000	$ 400,000	$ 1,600,000
Private	59,000,000	141,000,000	200,000,000
Total	$60,200,000	$141,400,000	$201,600,000

Gross Buildable Area: 2,000,000 square feet
Dwelling Units: 52
Parking Spaces
  Residential: 6
  Commercial: 4,000
Hotels (2): 875 rooms
Restaurants: 16

Raeder Place, a renovated ironfront building with a restaurant on the lower floor and office space above.

St. Louis Union Station

Among the grandest of train stations when opened in 1894, Union Station maintained its lofty position through World War II. The 17-acre property included the main headhouse (the main terminal), the midway, a train shed covering 11.5 acres, 42 tracks, signal towers, and various express agency buildings. The headhouse contained restaurants, passenger services, and a hotel. As many as 100,000 passengers per day arrived at and departed from Union Station.

Following the war, Union Station quickly lost status as train travel declined. Amtrak finally moved out in 1978, leaving the building vacant.

Today, however, St. Louis Union Station ranks among the most outstanding examples nationwide of adaptive use of a registered historic property. Oppenheimer Properties of New York, as director of the Union Station Redevelopment Corporation (a Chapter 353 corporation), spearheaded the station's complete renovation, which included the headhouse and the space within the train shed. The Rouse Company of St. Louis, Inc., an affiliate of the Rouse Company of Columbia, Maryland, created an enclosed two-level specialty shopping and dining mall, a one-acre lake, a private rail car facility, a beer garden, and a parking lot under the shed. The project also includes a 550-room Omni International Hotel. A new structure built underneath the shed contains 480 of the hotel rooms, while the remainder are in the historic headhouse, fronting on Market Street on the edge of downtown.

In a private letter ruling by the Internal Revenue Service, the

tacles installed by the city. The city's investment thus far amounts to about $1.2 million, compared to nearly $57 million in private investment.

Parking was a critical issue from the outset. To provide adequate parking for each stage of development in the Landing, the redevelopment corporation not only works closely with developers, but it also leases, for the life of the project, space adjacent to the Landing for any additional parking needed.

Laclede's Landing was the first major redevelopment on the St. Louis riverfront to follow the Gateway Arch (1965). It has spawned a number of related redevelopment organizations that deal with other aspects of the riverfront's improve-

ments, extending from Chouteau Avenue south of the Arch to Biddle Street north of Laclede's Landing. A special organization now oversees ongoing physical improvements of the public areas of the riverfront and its promenade. Redevelopment corporations have formed to improve, and add to, the commercial riverboats. North of the Landing, the Riverside Redevelopment Corporation has assured future riverfront development within its boundaries. With the completion of these programs, total private reinvestment since the Arch was built is projected at $500 million. All of this was the outgrowth of the 1960s' development of the Arch and its grounds at a public cost of approximately $50 million.

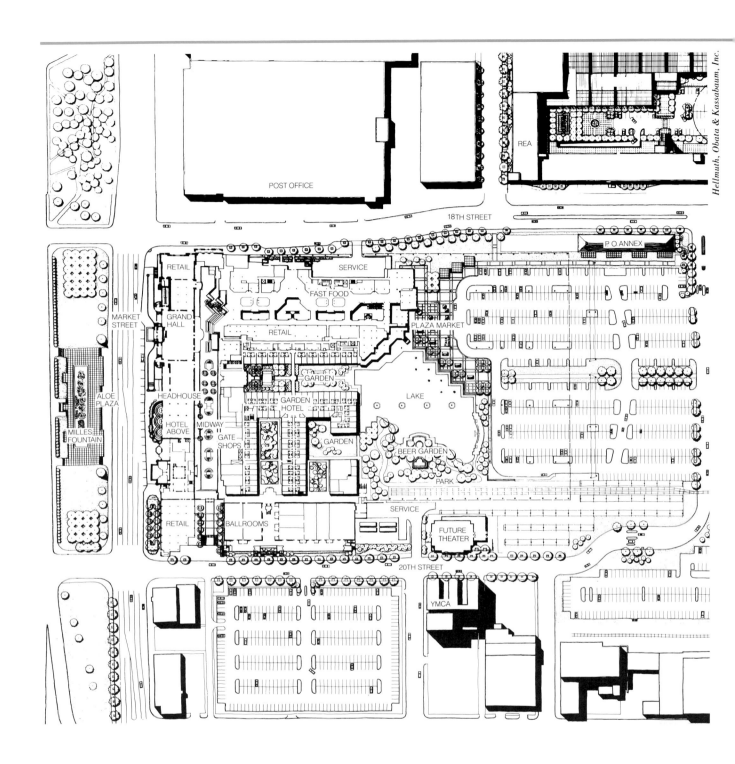

POST OFFICE

REA

18TH STREET

P. O. ANNEX

RETAIL

SERVICE

FAST FOOD

MARKET STREET

GRAND HALL

RETAIL

PLAZA MARKET

GARDEN

ALOE PLAZA

HEADHOUSE

GARDEN HOTEL

LAKE

HOTEL

MIDWAY ABOVE

MIDWAY GATE SHOPS

GARDEN

MILLES FOUNTAIN

BEER GARDEN

PARK

SERVICE

RETAIL

BALLROOMS

FUTURE THEATER

20TH STREET

YMCA

Site plan of St. Louis Union Station.

headhouse, train shed, and midway were designated as a single historic building. Therefore, under the federal incentives for the rehabilitation of historic structures, anything built within the shed's space qualified for a 25 percent tax credit, which enabled the 480 hotel rooms and 160,000 square feet of retail facilities to be built. The tax incentives thus made the whole project feasible.

Financing. Planning for the redevelopment began in 1979. The Rouse Company became involved in 1980. When the completed station opened in August 1985, total investment was approximately $155 million. The project was financed with $35 million in equity; a $10 million Urban Development Action Grant loan with payments at a below-market interest rate deferred for five years; a $65 million mortgage from the Bank of Montreal and the Bank of America; and a $25 million loan from the Globe Investment Pension Fund.

The success of the project and a more favorable financing climate enabled Oppenheimer to refinance the project in mid-1986, replacing all the debt with a $125 million loan from Teachers Insurance Annuity Association and allowing for additional capital improvements. The city also contributed $1 million in public improvements. Furthermore, the project benefits from property tax abatement and powers of eminent domain gained through Missouri's Chapter 353 redevelopment law.

Status. One year after Union Station opened, even the developers were happily surprised by its performance. The average retail/restaurant tenant achieved sales of $450 per square foot (although this figure was expected to decrease as the novelty of the station wears

View of St. Louis Union Station and the refurbished train shed, part of which is enclosed and contains a festival market developed by the Rouse Company and Omni International Hotel.

South entrance to the festival market-place in the train shed of St. Louis Union Station.

Interior view of shops and restaurants in Union Station.

ST. LOUIS UNION STATION

Land Use Plan

	Square Feet
Retail (specialty)	160,000
Hotel (550 rooms: 70 rehab, 480 new)	385,000
Other (park areas and parking)	500,000

Site Development Costs

Public: $1,000,000
Private: $156,000,000

Financing

Equity: $35,000,000
Private Loans: $110,000,000
UDAG: $10,000,000
City: $1,000,000

off). The hotel achieved an average of 70 percent occupancy—compared to a projected 68 percent—in a downtown market in which nearly 2,000 new hotel rooms were built between January 1985 and July 1986. Although the 1,900 parking spaces provided for the project (many of which are under the train shed) were well above the number projected to be needed, they have proved too few for actual peak activity in the hotel, restaurant, and retail areas.

The Union Station Redevelopment Corporation controls in and around the station more than 50 acres of land on which it is now concentrating. Little needs to be done to market these areas because the station's success alone attracts developers who are looking for opportunities. Planned projects include office space, more parking, another hotel, a 10-screen movie complex, and a special large-screen movie theater.

St. Louis Centre[12]

Background. St. Louis Centre is the latest project in the nine-project Mayco redevelopment area in downtown St. Louis; when it opened in August 1985 it became the nation's largest enclosed downtown shopping mall. On four levels, the mall contains 350,000 square feet of retail space connecting to a 900,000-square-foot Famous-Barr department store, a 200,000-square-foot Dillard's department store, and a 60,000-square-foot retail area in the new parking garage building.

The mall itself covers two city blocks, while the two department stores and the parking garage (accommodating 1,450 cars) each cover a city block, totaling five city blocks. All of these structures were built or renovated as part of the St. Louis Centre project, which also includes a 412,000-square-foot office building atop the shopping mall.

The total cost of developing the Centre—including the renovation of the two department stores—was $120 million. The garage and related retail space cost $14 million, and the office building—which opened in 1986—cost $41 million. It is estimated that the shopping mall alone generated 1,200 jobs, while it was responsible for another 500 jobs' being retained or relocated from elsewhere downtown.

The entire Mayco redevelopment project is largely the result of the patience and perseverance of Mercantile Bank, which has its headquarters in the Mayco area. In 1971, Mercantile was operating out of five separate and highly inefficient buildings located in the downtown area, between Dillard's and Famous-Barr.

Even though the department stores were doing reasonably well, the two retail blocks between them were deteriorating rapidly, and the quality of many of the smaller retailers was declining. Mercantile decided it needed a new building both for its own use and to stabilize the declining areas around it. Because banks are prohibited by law from being in the development business, Mercantile jointly developed the building with Trammell Crow.

In October 1972, Mercantile announced a redevelopment plan for six blocks in the retail area of downtown St. Louis. The plan included a 36-story Mercantile Bank tower, a three-level atrium retail mall, two other office buildings, and a major hotel. Construction began on the bank tower in 1973 and was completed at the end of 1975. Mercantile bought out Trammell Crow's interest. When the country fell into a sharp economic recession, the remaining components of the redevelopment plan were temporarily shelved.

△

East entrance to St. Louis Centre, a new mixed-use development in St. Louis.

▷

Edison Brothers Corporate Headquarters Building, developed in association with St. Louis Centre shopping mall.

---

[12] Prepared with information provided by Melvin Simon & Associates, Inc., May Department Stores Company, and Mercantile Bancorporation.

ST. LOUIS CENTRE[1]

Land Use Plan

Retail Space: 1,400,000 square feet
Office Space: 412,000 square feet
Parking: 1,467 parking spaces

Site Development Costs

Shopping Mall and Department Store Renovation	$118,925,000
Parking Garage and Retail Space	14,500,000
Office Tower (One City Centre)	41,000,000
Public Improvements	1,075,000
Total	$175,500,000

Financing

Equity	$ 17,550,000
Private Loans	138,606,800
UDAG	18,000,000
Other Public Loans	268,200
Public Improvements	1,075,000
Total	$175,500,000

[1] Includes the St. Louis Centre shopping mall, renovation of two department stores, office building atop the mall, and the parking garage/retail space.

Interior of the St. Louis Centre atrium during the Christmas season.

By 1981, Mercantile had revised its construction and financing plans to reflect new economic realities and had found a developer for the shopping mall. Melvin Simon & Associates of Indianapolis joined with the May Company—owner of the Famous-Barr department store—to codevelop the mall. The project began with the construction of the parking garage, which contains 60,000 square feet of retail space and helped to accommodate the merchants who were located in the two blocks where the mall was to be built. Development of the mall then began with major renovations of both the Dillard's and Famous-Barr stores.

Financing. Financing for the entire St. Louis Centre project involved equity from the Melvin Simon & Associates/May Company partnership, purchase of the land by the St. Louis Land Clearance for Redevelopment Authority, an $18 million Urban Development Action Grant, a $35 million permanent loan from an insurance company, $3 million in public improvements by the city, and $31 million in 34-year bonds purchased by the city's two largest banks (Mercantile and Boatmen's).

Melvin Simon & Associates was instrumental in attracting Cabot, Cabot & Forbes of Boston to build the office building atop St. Louis Centre. One St. Louis Centre is a 21-story, 412,000-square-foot building that opened in the summer of 1986.

The third—and final—office building in the Mayco redevelopment area was constructed adjacent to the parking garage as the new headquarters of the Edison Brothers Stores, Inc. Completed in 1985, this building contains 500,000 square feet on 12 floors.

The last component of the Mayco project is a hotel that is currently planned to be built on top of the Dillard's department store building. As Dillard's (formerly Stix, Baer & Fuller) no longer occupies the entire building, the vacant floors above the department store's four levels are available for rehabilitation. The hotel market in downtown St. Louis, however, has recently seen a spurt of growth in the supply of rooms. The hotel has therefore been put on hold until the market is more clearly defined or until other opportunities arise.

Washington Avenue

Located on the north side of downtown St. Louis, Washington Avenue functioned as the city's principal corridor of commerce before the early 1950s and as the Midwest's largest garment district. Most of the buildings along the six blocks of the Washington Avenue Redevelopment Area (which extends into a 14-block district) were constructed between 1890 and 1929. After World War II, the area quickly deteriorated as businesses departed.

Washington Avenue is the last key redevelopment area in the core of downtown St. Louis. As such, the Washington Avenue Redevelopment Corporation (WARC) is the newest of the major redevelopment corporations in the downtown area. Formed in 1984, it is managed by the Pantheon Corporation. WARC is an umbrella group that oversees development but does not necessarily develop projects itself.

The redevelopment area covers 14 blocks extending one to four blocks north and south of Washington Avenue from Seventh Street west to Tucker Boulevard. The plan proposes that the area's vacant or underused warehouses be converted to office use and that new structures be built on the numerous empty lots. WARC's plan will also introduce residential buildings into the center of downtown St. Louis. Other nonoffice uses will be multipurpose support facilities for the Cervantes Convention Center (which abuts the redevelopment area), parking structures, convenience shopping facilities for residents, entertainment facilities, including the revival of the American Theatre, and specialized retail shops on the street-level floors of most buildings.

The redevelopment plan is to be carried out in three phases, the first of which is already well underway. Phase I includes redevelopment of most of the property currently held by the principals of the Washington Avenue Redevelopment Corporation and other affiliated developers. In this way, the project can show substantial and rapid progress. Phase I involves converting the Lammert Building into a luxury office complex, developing a performing arts center, converting a warehouse building into loft residential condominiums, renovating the Merchandise Mart and turning it into office and retail space, converting the Lennox Hotel into a luxury rental apartment tower and two additional historic buildings into office and retail space, renovating the Mayfair Hotel, and building a new plaza for the hotel.

Washington Avenue Redevelopment Plan, 1983.

WASHINGTON AVENUE REDEVELOPMENT CORPORATION

Land Use Plan/Phase I Only

	Square Feet
Residential (conversion—109 rental units)	85,000
Office Space (conversion and rehab)	539,000
Retail Space (conversion and rehab)	33,000

Site Development Costs

Private: $45,600,000
Public: $4,400,000

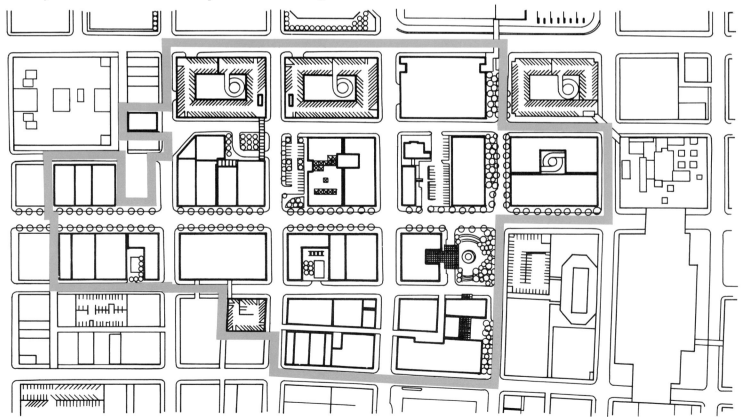

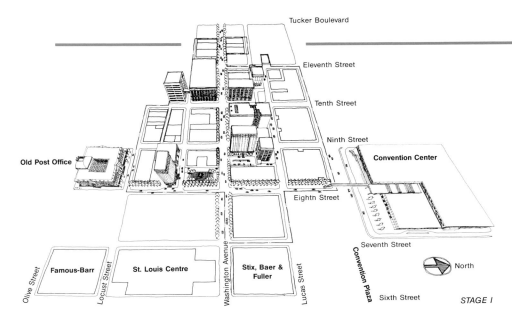

STAGE I

Phase II will include new construction and a continuation of restoration and conversion of existing structures, and Phase III will involve additional renovation and in-fill construction.

The first completed installment of WARC's plan—the Lennox Apartment Building—opened in April 1986. Formerly the Lennox Hotel (built in 1929), the $12.2 million rehabilitation and adaptive use project resulted in a 109-unit building. Many successful lower-density projects have been developed on the fringes of downtown, but the Lennox is the first high-density project in many decades to be developed in the heart of St. Louis.

Aerial perspective of the three phases of development planned for the Washington Avenue redevelopment area.

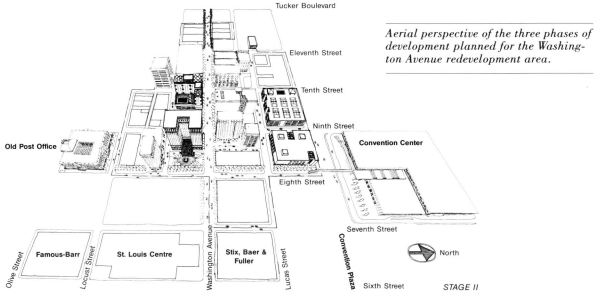

STAGE II

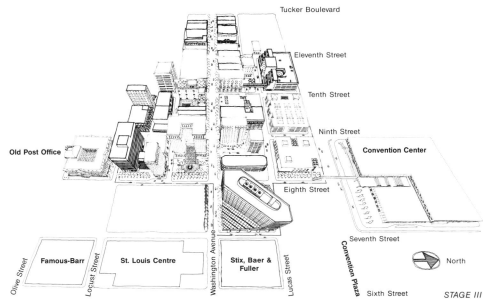

STAGE III

The building features on its east facade a 25-story mural that duplicates the original facade on the west side. The east wall originally backed up to an adjacent building that was removed for structural reasons and to provide parking.

Also opening in April 1986 was the rehabilitated Lammert Building, which was originally built as a furniture showcase in the late 19th century. Costing approximately $8 million to renovate, it is today an elegantly appointed, 100,000-square-foot office building with a central atrium extending the full seven stories of the building.

In addition, the Mayfair Hotel is undergoing renovation and the hotel's courtyard is now in place. Construction is underway on the 300,000-square-foot Merchandise Mart, which is to be completed in 1987 and will be renamed Renaissance Square.

WARC plans on an investment of $225 million by 1995 to complete the plan. New structures are also planned, mainly on vacant lots or parking areas.

Experience Gained

Even though critics have been displeased by the fact that downtown receives more attention than the neighborhoods, this attention is probably warranted. Downtown employment alone grew from 102,000 in 1985 to 110,000 in 1986—the first real growth in the downtown workforce since the 1920s. Both the city and region continue to regard the downtown as the focus of the metropolitan area's activities, thus encouraging its leadership role in the revitalization of the city.

Innovative solutions to special circumstances in the downtown environment have served as models to create redevelopment mechanisms elsewhere in the city. The market itself has been the strongest indicator of the most efficient patterns of land use and the most efficient order of priorities in revitalizing the downtown. Although this approach has not been without

controversy, the downtown has proved a good laboratory for testing ideas and for encouraging diversity, a characteristic of the downtown that makes it the exciting place it should be. The city is currently revising its plans to encompass an overall view of downtown development over the next decade.

The arched entrance to the Lammert Building, which was recently rehabilitated to provide office space.

Interior view of the Lammert Building's lobby.

The newly renovated Lennox Building offers luxury apartments in the heart of downtown St. Louis. The ornate facade is actually painted on the brick building.

LESSONS LEARNED

Even with a market-driven re-development strategy and an array of tools and incentives to stimulate public/private cooperation, the private market cannot respond overnight. Rehabilitation in an existing urban environment depends on many actors—developers, investors, lenders, builders, skilled craftsmen, suppliers of specialized building materials, architects, consultants, realtors, and public officials, among others. Most critical to this industry are, of course, the buyers and renters of the spaces created.

But to begin the rehabilitation process, there must be people with the vision to recognize inner-city opportunities. These "urban pioneers," political leaders, and developers must possess a dedication to city life to risk rehabilitating a 75-year-old, 250,000-square-foot office building, or recycling turn-of-the-century apartments into modern day residences (and finding tenants for them), or returning an early 19th century mansion from a

decaying rooming house in an abandoned neighborhood to its former splendor. They must also be able to convince lenders and equity partners of the economic sense of such undertakings. They must find architects and other professionals who are skilled in analyzing, designing, marketing, and managing old properties and recycled neighborhoods. They must be willing and able to rehabilitate old structures as well as to build new structures on small urban lots rather than on large tracts of land. Finally, builders and homeowners need a strong cadre of craftsmen skilled in renovation, particularly when historic preservation or restoration is required. All of these requirements make for a hard bill to fill in revitalizing an old and deteriorating city like St. Louis.

The rebirth of the city of St. Louis is notable to both its visitors and its residents. After wearing the label of a "dying" city for so many years, St. Louis has made a dramatic turnaround.

Two basic facts place the city's progress in proper perspective. First, the changes leading to this success did not emerge overnight or without effort. Second, the job of physical and economic revitalization is far from complete.

Successive city administrations have carefully cultivated the seeds of St. Louis's revitalization. In the process, the city's leaders have become increasingly skilled at leveraging available local and federal resources to attract private investment not only in downtown but also in the neighborhoods and secondary employment centers.

The opening of St. Louis Centre and the St. Louis Union Station in 1985 and the completion of almost 10,000 new and rehabilitated housing units between 1978 and 1986 present compelling testimony to the success of the long-term commitment of both the public and private sectors. This redevelopment

The historic 555 Washington Building is being converted to first-class office and retail space.

experience contains lessons that other cities may find helpful:

- City incentives must be designed to encourage and enable the private sector to lead in taking advantage of development opportunities, fashioning appropriate development vehicles, and selecting locations where new investment can build upon economic strengths. Such private sector investment will, over time, result in improving adjacent areas and, eventually, the entire city.

- The public sector must become a development partner with the private sector. It must make it feasible to develop projects that are desirable, but economically risky, by establishing an acceptable financial environment through the investment of its own resources.

- Long-term public development strategies must be adopted that encourage private development initiatives to build upon and reinforce one another. Without clear public strategies, which can be used to convert individual private redevelopment successes into new ventures, widespread city revitalization cannot occur.

- The public development incentives that are established must continually be refined and modified to respond to ever-changing physical and fiscal considerations. No one set of public tools or incentives should become a fixed or inflexible public program for urban redevelopment.

- To attract its fair share of regional investment, a declining central city must be willing to risk its own resources and to use inventive and sometimes costly incentives to compete effectively with adjacent suburban communities. Long-term economic and social gains in deteriorated areas can be won only through aggressive, innovative public sharing of some of the private economic risk.

Although the achievements have been great, much remains to be done in the city of St. Louis. Re-vitalization must be extended farther to the north and south of the major urban reinvestment corridor, which stretches from downtown westward to the suburban office center of Clayton. To rest on the accomplishments of the past 15 years or, because of these accomplishments, to forget the public sector incentives and leadership that have been crucial in catalyzing the rebuilding of St. Louis would be a grievous and dangerous error.

St. Louis is still in a critical period. The level of housing production must be sustained to prevent the city from slipping back into a pattern of neighborhood disinvestment. The revitalization of downtown—which is the regional center of service jobs and entertainment and convention facilities—also cannot lose momentum. In addition, while retaining those manufacturing jobs that can be saved, the city must be more aggressive in addressing issues such as its transition from a manufacturing center to a competitive location for a growing service economy.

These tasks will be difficult. Federal resources are shrinking while the challenges of redevelopment continue, and the state probably will not be able or willing to replace these federal programs and resources. Thus, the city must work even harder in the future to continue its successful record.

St. Louis has developed a significant ability to attract investment for revitalization over the last 15 years. Today, city leaders are revising the city's economic development strategies to respond to current economic realities and to the reduction in intergovernmental programs. One emerging resource is the millions of dollars that have been and will be repaid from UDAG, CDBG, and HIP loans, among others. Also, as Chapter 353 tax-abated projects mature, they will be added to the real estate tax rolls. If the city can make creative use of resources such as these, it can leverage the returns of previously successful redevelopment projects to minimize the negative effect of reduced federal programs.

St. Louis would not have the bright future it has today if it had not fully exploited past opportunities. The challenge is to continue to adapt and use available resources for future progress. Although St. Louis clearly has come a long way, maintaining this momentum will demand the continued commitment of civic leaders and long-term public/private cooperation.